the inner Game
of SOCCER

the inner Game of SOCCER

by eric sellin

WORLD PUBLICATIONS
P.O. Box 366, Mountain View, CA 94042

© 1976 by
WORLD PUBLICATIONS
P.O. Box 366, Mountain View, CA 94040

Second Printing, January 1977

*No information in this book may be reprinted in
any form without permission from the publisher.*

Library of Congress Catalog Card Number 75-21407
ISBN 0-89037-107-5 (Hb.)

Some paragraphs in this book first appeared in unrevised form in brief essays in *Soccer America, Soccer World,* and *Can-So-Ref!*

Our special thanks go to the Federation Internationale de Football Association (FIFA) for granting permission to reproduce the *Laws of the Game.*

Contents

THE REFEREE'S CREDO

S teadfast impartiality
O bjectivity in viewing and reporting incidents
C onstructive use of criticism
C orrect positioning
E ven-tempered administration of cautions and ejections
R espect for the rights of others

R eview of the laws and rules changes at frequent intervals
E xcellence in knowledge and interpretation of the laws
F itness as a means to better performance
E nforcement of the laws with accuracy and consistency
R eliable use of the advantage clause
E quanimity in the face of turmoil or adversity
E ndless study and practice toward self-improvement
S elf-sacrifice and modesty coupled with self-respect and dignity

C ommon sense or the unwritten "Law 18"
R ational handling of the unexpected
E asily understood and timely signaling
D edication to one's task and thereby to the game in general
O rganizational loyalty to one's Association and fellow referees
at large

—E.S.

Introduction

I certainly hope that this initial part of my book is to some extent extraneous. I am writing briefly of the referee's calling and the factors that make refereeing an attractive pastime, but presumably most persons who are reading these lines have felt and are responding to the vocation, either as a registered referee who is wont to read anything about soccer refereeing that he can get his hands on, or else as a referee in training who is on the threshold of a career but has already made that first all-important emotional decision to become an official.

For those readers who have no special interest in refereeing but are confirmed "soccer nuts" who will devour any literature dealing with any aspect of the game: I welcome them to these pages with the hope that they will not be bored by the sometimes highly technical details which referees thrive on but may well seem pedantic or trivial to the uninitiated.

As a player who played school, college, and sandlot soccer in the United States, Europe, and Africa for some thirty years (from spontaneous recess games at the age of seven, when I and another kid named Hendrick Drake regularly challenged the rest of the class and usually won, till an injury sidelined me at age thirty-seven), I was practically unaware of referees as individuals. There was always an official or else we could not have a "real" game, so his presence was crucial; but I can remember the faces of no referees from school or college and only four or five from my amateur-soccer days.

Three or four stand out in my memory as having poise,

authority, and complete sound knowledge of the laws and refereeing technique. When these qualities were combined with an almost palpable sense that the man was out there to referee because he wanted to be there and loved the game, the referee had charisma and was able to relate to the players and coaches. After I abandoned the game as a player and donned referee's garb, it was these men who served as my retrospective mentors, as referees to emulate.

Alas, *one* of the referees out of the hundreds who took the field to officiate games in which I participated served as a negative inspiration. In the two of our games which he officiated, this man turned benign games in a benevolent league into ugly unsportsmanlike confrontations. He had to work hard at it, but by dint of incompetence and persistence, he even put the calmest player on either side out of sorts.

The case of this man—rightfully dropped slowly down and out of the registers — serves me as a reminder that the poor referee is as much a liability to the game as a superior one is a benison to it. Even as I hoped fervently that I might develop the charisma I respected in several outstanding referees, I prayed that I would have the wisdom and vision to give up the whistle if I were, to the contrary, like the referee I have just discussed. Fortunately, his was a rare case and most referees do a journeyman's job.

Now, what makes one go on refereeing? Why would one go out week after week to pursue this anonymous calling, walking off the fields unthanked when he has done a good job, being abused vociferously when he has had the gall to preside over a defeat? Ignorance of the laws is pandemic among players, coaches, and spectators, and even an outstanding job is often met with criticism and disapproval. Who would willingly go out every weekend, rain or shine, in heat wave or cold snap, to be heckled and even sometimes assaulted? Well, the men and women—for more and more women are playing and officiating soccer every year*—who tolerate this nonsense as a part of their

---

*I have used the terms "men," "his," and so forth throughout this book as a rhetorical convention—everything applies as well to women players and referees.

job of refereeing are people from all walks of life, steam-fitters, realtors, barbers, teachers, salesmen, meat-packers, doctors, preachers, drill-press operators, construction workers, and students. They can only be stereotyped by the avocation they share; and their common calling does, indeed, shed light on them as human beings.

Many people would assume that a referee must be a masochist. I despair of communicating to those not already aware of it the referee's calling which goes far beyond any generalization and is a psychologically complex phenomenon; however, my only personal regret about taking up soccer refereeing is that I did not do so ten years earlier, although the fact of having played on until "over the hill" has stood me in good stead when dealing with older players whose very special frustrations I can readily comprehend.

I shall try to outline some of the qualities required of a good referee, no doubt in any sport, although I am concerned here solely with soccer officiating. In this context, I should add that it has been my experience that the best soccer referees are not those who are just interested in refereeing—that is, who also officiate basketball, wrestling, baseball, and so forth as the seasons rotate—but those who are exclusively *Soccer* referees. I am often asked if I referee other sports, to which I must reply that I do not like refereeing *per se* but do love refereeing soccer. When officiating, you are at the nucleus of the game, and it is the inner game of soccer that interests me. Love is indivisible at the absolute level! One cannot referee two sports equally well but will tend to neglect one or both.

I have let slip the word "love," and that is perhaps the most important ingredient in the making of a good official. I am not speaking of some "corny" notion of love for mankind, the players, or the great outdoors, but of a love for the game, something like the irresistible appeal for the actor of the smell of the grease paint and the roar of the crowd. It is only a genuine love of the game—combined with a deep respect for the majority of those other participants who, like himself, love the game—that will permit the referee to hear but pay no heed to the unjustified abuse from the thoughtless, unapprised, or over-excited spectator, to remain calm in the face of player dissent, and to learn from his mistakes as well as from his triumphs as he strives to become a better official.

Ted Copeland, a coach who appears to have some understanding of what makes referees tick has written as follows:

> Knowledge of the rules and good physical condition are important elements in the make-up of a referee, but there is a third factor that is somewhat more intangible, but nonetheless desirable. I refer to the official's love of the game. Psychologically, the difference between the referee who is officiating only to earn a few extra dollars and the referee who in addition, feels deeply that soccer is the greatest sport in the world, is obvious to most observers.[1]

I could not agree more with this successful high school coach. As an indication of the extent of my belief in what he says, I will lay odds that no one who falls only in the dollar-earning category (and there are a few, some of them fairly good referees) will read these words, for such an official seldom feels motivated to go beyond the minimal requirements to fulfill his function, seldom attends meetings, usually lags behind in rules interpretations, and does little "skull practice" or professional study. I am, in this book, addressing myself primarily to those who love the game although I hope anyone might derive some little benefit from my ideas. As coach Copeland goes on to say:

> There is something about the latter [official who loves the game] which psychologically 'communicates' itself to those present, and which is lacking in the former type of official. Knowledge of the rules and good physical condition can be acquired by effort, but this love of the game is something which an official either has or he doesn't. Hopefully it could have been the primary reason for his becoming an official.[2]

Love of the game *should* be the primary reason for becoming an official, not only because that is a laudable motivation from a humanistic viewpoint, but because any other reason is either countereffective or pernicious. For example, if you go into refereeing on the assumption that you will earn a great deal of money, you are bound to be disappointed. All but a few referees will actually do little more than break even after they pay their taxes, buy their equipment, and absorb the cost of travel and of time lost from other employment. In the past year I have refereed sixty games and made less than $900. Almost any other work would have paid more per hour, and my family would, I am sure, gladly have paid that amount to have me with them on week-ends.

There are, probably, a few referees in officiating for the extra money, but it seems to me they would have to be rather obtuse to remain in it for very long if that is their only motive. Similarly, if the referee has chosen his calling with the expectation that it will shed some widespread glory on him, he should be quickly set to rights: he will not be noticed by most people if he does a good job, and few people will be qualified to recognize the brilliance of his best performances. He will, if he is dedicated and achieves a high level of performance and consistency, receive the esteem of his referee colleagues and the importance of this esteem should not be underestimated. There is great satisfaction in hearing feedback from a coach, another referee, or a player to the effect that one had done "one hell of a fine job" the previous week, and there is also great personal private satisfaction in coming up with the right call or the right procedure under enormous pressure. Just as the "love" of the game is communicated to others, the referee knows in his heart when he has done a good job, and there is a subtle pleasure upon returning home and, when asked by one's wife how the game went, replying simply: "Another routine one under the belt."

The extremely subtle pleasures of refereeing make it a fact of life of this calling that only another soccer referee or a confirmed "soccer nut" can fully appreciate your enthusiasm. Recently I met Leo Weinstein — a soccer journalist, coach, announcer, and general factotum — at the Modern Language Association convention in New York where our "real-life" jobs had brought us together. We escaped from the monotony of scholarly seminars and sought refuge in a quiet lounge and then over lunch at a nearby delicatessen. We discussed soccer for several hours, indefatigably recounting anecdotes from our separate backgrounds which nevertheless met more urgently on the note of soccer than they could have on the basis of the apparent common denominator of our mutual profession.

What, then, are the pleasures and rewards of refereeing if it provides only a limited opportunity for glory and no chance to receive a significant income? The answer is that it provides the opportunity for a real, professional, applied outlet for one's passion for the game, a passion of the sort that makes hobbyists sacrifice their time and money to build model trains, play golf in a blizzard, sew Mummers' costumes all year for one glittering New Year's Day on Broad Street, or spend hours tuning a ham radio transmitter in quest of the new or the remote interlocutor.

Norman Burtenshaw tells how, upon finding that his employer would not permit him to take time off to go abroad to referee games, he quit his job rather than sacrifice his career advancement in refereeing. He became self-employed and opened a candy store, fitting his job to his avocation!

Referees gladly sit up into the wee hours of the morning talking about their experiences, laughing about their awkward moments, relating unusual game conditions and challenging situations, dragging up case histories involving burst soccer balls, capricious winds, and the like, to illustrate the finer points of the rules. Aside from the immediate pleasure of involvement in a hard-fought, well-played match, there is the secondary pleasure of meeting or officiating with one's colleagues who share the same curious passion. There are certain rewards, then, in being part of the game and in keeping the company of one's colleagues.

Not everyone in the world should referee soccer—or any sport— for refereeing demands certain traits not held by all. Some of these character qualities will be discussed throughout this book, but let it suffice for me to say at this juncture that, in order to be a good official, one must be dedicated almost to the degree of absurdity and be prepared to make sacrifices quite disporportionate to the small tangible rewards involved. Dedication and sacrifice? Yes, and with a smile! It helps if one possesses certain virtues like patience, dignity, respect for others, humility, impartiality, a sense of humor, and a general liking for people. If one is dedicated and willing to endure sacrifice in the pursuit of excellence and self-fulfillment as a referee, some of these qualities will be brought out through the demands made of the person who officiates.

Conversely, the *hubris*, the tragic human failing or flaw will not be able to remain hidden for long under game pressure and has been the undoing of some referees. As in the ancient Greek tragedies, the flaw that most commonly undermines one's performance is arrogance. If love of the game can, indeed, communicate itself to players and coaches, so can arrogance; and arrogance contains a corollary of self-destruction, for it will make one choose or obstinately pursue paths which it is wiser to avoid. The Canadian referees' bulletin, *Can-So-Ref!*, recently printed the tenets of "Murphy's Law of Random Perversity" which are clever and apt:

a) Left to themselves, things go from bad to worse.
b) Anything that can go wrong, will go wrong.
c) If there is a possibility of several things going wrong, the one that will go wrong is the one that will do the most damage.
d) If you play with a thing long enough, you will surely break it.
e) Nature always sides with the hidden flaw.
f) If everything appears to be going well, you have obviously overlooked something! [3]

Most of these dicta are appropriate to refereeing and in order to avoid falling victim to any or all of these laws of random perversity during a game, the referee must not grow complacent or think too highly of himself. When I once told one of my revered colleagues (one of those with the aforementioned charisma) of having consecutively refereed an unpleasant game from an unexpected quarter and a good game where I had feared it would be a bad game on the basis of the reputation of the two teams meeting, he replied with conviction: "The bad games are never the bad games."

This is true and not as simplistic as it might appear at first glance! Human nature, siding with the hidden flaw, can turn the smoothly running game into a nightmare in a trice; and one can wait in vain for the tough game to fall apart at the seams. Perhaps, when things are going smoothly, one tends to lose his concentration and does not function at peak performance level as he will when riding herd on a potentially explosive game. Thus, every game presents its challenge. The easy game taxes the referee's concentration, the difficult game challenges his ability to remain unflustered and fair in the face of adversity, and any game at any level can present him with a myriad of small tests of his technical competence and physical conditioning.

There are, aside from the obvious satisfaction of doing a job well under variable conditions, other rewards to be derived from refereeing. One travels to different places in his immediate area, meets interesting people from all walks of life, and has an unequaled opportunity to observe the ethnic patchwork that makes America such a variegated and energetic country. The oft-maligned ethnic soccer of the German, Irish, Greek, Italian, Polish, Ukrainian, Latin-American, Armenian, and other minority communities provides fascinating clashes in temperament and in soccer style which provoke not only the occasional violence one reads about in the newspapers, but also yield, for the most part, interesting soccer matches, with no two alike. As a player, I saw the same teams in one league over and over again for several months of the year; as a referee and linesman I see hundreds of different teams of different ages in different leagues and in cup competition all year round.

Although the referee is not supposed to become emotionally involved in the game he is officiating, he is obviously present on the field during the entire game and once it is over he knows whether the game he has refereed was a stimulating one or a poor and ineptly played one and he will naturally enjoy more having participated in the good game. In fact, I have been involved in games of a far higher level of competence of play as a referee than I could have been involved in as a player since my skills in the latter department only brought me as high as the amateur First Division and only once as part of a championship team, and that at the tail-end of my career when I was only playing irregularly as a disgruntled reserve.

A referee has the opportunity to see and be involved in soccer which is varied and often interesting. Whether the game is an under-ten league game or a senior National Cup match, the soccer official plays an important and usually unsung role; but the wisdom, self-control, and impartiality he displays on the field during the game will, in fact, permit the players to pursue their inspired vein of play, develop their strategy, and display their abilities without unfair interference from chronic infringers or the occasional bully who can tax the good will of his most mild-mannered opponent.

The good referee does not orchestrate the game, he allows it to flow freely within the specific confines of the laws and according to common sense and the spirit of sportsmanlike play. It is for this reason that his function is vital at all levels, from Mini games to the World Cup, at the lower levels because those fledgling players are just trying out their soccer legs and must be handled with patience and understanding as they strive to learn the basic moves, and at the top level because of the effect the big game can have on spectators, especially on the young impressionable player-spectators. There is a never-ending cycle, and referees are needed at all levels of this cycle, all levels being equally important to the game, albeit not equally satisfying to the referee's ego.

In this context, we should add that there are limits to the heights of recognition most officials can reach. There are only seven international FIFA referees per country, and the selection is based on many variables, including the individual's age, his geographical situation within his own country, his performance when assessed, his physical fitness, and so forth. However, as a matter of policy, every official should set his sights as high as he can and approach each and every game as though he were being assessed for the FIFA list. The Peter Principle obtains here, as elsewhere. Some officials are able to referee games up to a certain age level but have difficulty controlling senior players. Recently an official in my local association requested that the assignor no longer use him on senior games, limiting him to games between players up through eighteen years of age. This referee at least had the sense to recognize his limitations; some do not.

I have found that the best referees, even with 25 years of experience, have never lost the ability to practice self-criticism and are always looking for new ways to improve their performance. We shall speak at greater length about this matter in another part of this book, but let me simply pass on Weinstein's comment that he has never seen a group of college students with the ability to accept constructive criticism or to learn from their errors with the same *elan* or readiness as referees taken as a group. Perhaps the official knows that by correcting his mistakes and improving his performance he will not be striving for paper kudos but will be achieving greater competence before a peer group of players and coaches and spectators on the following and ensuing week ends. To adapt ever so slightly the adage John F. Kennedy liked to quote: "If you get away with a foul or misconduct once, shame on you; if you get away with it twice, shame on me!"

The American and Canadian referee can take some satisfaction in the role he is playing in the development of soccer in North America. The joy of witnessing the phenomenal growth of the game he so loves carries with it certain responsibility, however. The growth must not be solely one of numbers. It must also entail improvements in safety standards, in coaching, in officiating — in short, in all phases of the game.

As the game moves out from behind factories and into municipal stadiums, as it abandons solid old-fashioned "hotspur" tactics for new and exciting strategies, as it seeks to impose a new image on the professional and amateur level alike (and these two are intimately related although each has its special dynamics), so must refereeing become standardized, more consistent in its excellence insofar as technique and understanding of the laws are concerned, and polished even down to such details as tidiness of attire and uniformity of hand signals. Perhaps, in a very small way, the following pages can contribute to that ongoing growth and refinement of soccer in this country.

I certainly hope so. That is, at least, one of the main reasons for my having undertaken the writing of this book. Of course, to write a book-length study was a natural extension of my having written a number of short essays on soccer for various journals over the past several years, that activity having been born, in turn, out of my wish to think through for myself a number of game situations and controversial clauses in the laws of the game. My desire was to improve my own personal performance on the field and I find that I articulate things more concisely via the written word than in the abstract area of random thought. Once these writings were committed to paper, I thought others in the fraternity might be interested in my ideas, even if only to disagree with them.

The following pages, then, reflect my own thoughts on a number of matters, sometimes at variance with Association-sanctioned interpretations. I do not claim to be spokesman for anything or anyone save logic and objectivity. I have tried to write without pretensions, but had no choice but to speak firmly when logic guided my pen. I have tried to point out the various sides of approaches whenever high-level disagreement prevails, as in the interpretation of the several sentences governing the taking of a throw-in, and then demonstrated my own sense of the law. There are a number of good books on the laws of the game, many of which are listed in the bibliography at the end of this book and some of which I quote from in these pages. I do not claim to have superseded these books, but I hope that readers will find here some new thoughts, insights, or glimmers—if not beacons—of knowledge.

One of our referees is wont to say, at rules interpretation meetings, that a referee should consider such a meeting worthwhile if he has come away with just one new technical or theoretical insight on, say, how to administer a drop ball or how to determine noninvolvement by a player in an offside position. We might go so far as to say that the meeting itself has been worthwhile having if only one of the referees in attendance comes away with one improvement or insight which can help his performance on the field. I would like to think that every reader will learn something—one little thing at least—from this book which will contribute to his understanding of the inner game of soccer; surely one reader somewhere can learn one practical thing from it; and, regardless of how much will have been learned by how many, I hope the reader will find the book enjoyable. To that end I have, wherever possible, avoided a heavy style and have inserted personal or anecdotal material. Perhaps I have been a bit too personal, but I make no apology for that. Those who are into the same thing will understand and forgive. We are brothers.

To conclude this introduction, I should like to discuss the overall structure that I have adopted. Soccer refereeing subdivides neatly into three categories: (1) refereeing and the laws of the game, (2) the technique of refereeing, and (3) the referee and game control. I have dealt with the first category in Part One and the other two in Part Two. As the earlier quotation by Ted Copeland suggested, knowledge of the laws, technique, and conditioning can be achieved through effort. Game control will have something to do with that intangible x-factor of "love of the game" and entail a good bit of psychology, but there is a certain amount of relative game control which results—positively with the felicitous flow of the game or negatively with a loss of game control—from full or inadequate knowledge of the laws and proper or improper technique. I shall also discuss physical fitness, which cannot be stressed enough although it alone will never make for a competent referee.

Each of the three major sections is inextricably intertwined with the other two. Mastery of the laws, physical presence, competent technique, and an understanding of the psychology of those involved in the event at hand, must all be present to assure successful coverage of the game by the referee. To the smallest detail, one realm sustains another, such as fitness sustaining knowledge of the laws. There is a saying about refereeing handed down by Eddie Pearson: "Presence lends conviction"; and there also is its converse: "You can't call 'em all."

In the larger sense, refereeing performance is not unlike the demanding job of being a parent. One must constantly be on his toes to do the best thing in order to raise his children properly and wisely. If then something goes wrong, he can at least say: "It may have been my fault, but I could not have done better than I did as I constantly tried to do my best." The referee who says he has never made mistakes or claims he has never found himself struggling to maintain game control, suffering unbearable moments of abuse from players, coaches or spectators, either is lying, has refereed very few games, or is inordinately dense.

When suffering one of those periodical games in which—due to a slight illness, psychological distractions, or extraordinarily poor behavior on the part of players, coaches, or spectators—things seem on the brink of disaster, the referee will be better off for having had greater training, given the problems more thought in advance, and having developed a certain humility-authority behavioral quotient. If he is prepared technically, mentally, physically, and psychologically to the best of his potential at any given time, he has a better chance of avoiding difficulty; and, should there be problems despite a capable performance, he can at least know in his heart that he did his very best. Hopefully, however, he will not depart with a serene brow, but rather will ponder how to improve the edge of his performance in one category or another with an eye to coping better with the problem should it arise at another time.

I owe a great deal to a number of people, to individuals whose teaching and communications have helped me to specify my thoughts, to fellow referees with whom I have officiated in the diagonal and dual systems who have given me valuable tips, and to authors whose interesting books have been an inspiration to me in this undertaking: the fact that they dared to write books on such an esoteric subject — and I am delighted they did — has encouraged me to feel that there might be interest enough for yet another such book.

I cannot possibly list all the people who have helped me with constructive criticism, but I wish to thank several people who have been especially important in my own development: Al Heery, an inspiration over the years; Jim Ross, who was my first instructor and who showed faith; Roger Schott, to whom I have turned repeatedly when desperate for advice and who always had the technical and psychological answers needed; Paul Harris, Ken Mullen, Harry Rodgers, Larry Harris, Diego De Leo, Edwin Fair, William Hoyle, Paul Avis, Henry Georgi, Ian Jackson, Bob Anderson, Don Byron, Rene Courte, and others for their communications; Tom Mertens and Clay Berling of *SOCCER America* who were there with support and kind words for my first attempts at soccer writing; and my family—Birgitta, Fred, and Chris—who every Sunday afternoon are only too aware of what I mean when I speak of sacrifice as an adjunct to self-improvement.

I would be remiss, too, if I did not, in conclusion, give my far-flung thanks to the players and coaches without whom we would have no games at all and who, for the most part, realize that referees are not just a necessary evil but are interested in fostering good soccer games. Finally, any credit for good aspects of this book must be shared by many, whereas I assume sole responsibility for its shortcomings.

Part One

When association football, or soccer, was first developed, the rules governing it were few and their administration was left to the players. It was assumed that the players would not be so unsporting as to attempt to eschew the rules or to wittingly break them. Alas, as the game developed and the matches became a sport—amendments and refinements were important. The first "referees" were little more than judges who were called to arbitrate disagreements between players as to fouls or misconduct, but slowly they were to become endowed with more and more responsibility, and with it more and more authority.[4]

The referee's accorded powers are so sweeping that he is a virtual master of the proceedings on the field and in its immediate environs. It only takes a few games, however, for the new referee to realize that few players and coaches are aware of the sweeping powers with which he is vested. By the time the referee finds it necessary to remind them of his full authority, it is likely that it is too late and that they are in no frame of mind to listen to reason. In short, although the laws officially give him great power, the referee must basically impose his authority by unofficial means on the field of play, his officially sanctioned authority being primarily of use to him in filing postgame reports regarding events on the field of play and points of fact during disputes.

The referee's authority during the game will hinge on a number of factors, some of which we shall discuss under the rubric of psychology, but the principal bastion of authority is self-confidence. This trait, which should not be confused with arrogance, will be sensed by the players and coaches. Some referees can approach the playing field where the players are warming up and the latter will declare, "Hey, we have a good ref today!" although the official is a hundred yards away and they are seeing him for the first time. Something in the walk, the bearing, and the attire can attest to the fact that this man cares! Self-confidence, like arrogance, can be transmitted at a great distance.

Self-confidence cannot be counterfeited. Sham self-confidence will crumble under pressure. How, in that case, does one achieve self-confidence? There are many ingredients in the recipe of self-confidence, from physical fitness (so that one knows he will not wilt during a tough game) to experience (having overcome difficulties before will inspire one's faith in his ability to cope with the same or a similar situation again). But the initial stage in the development of self-confidence is a complete knowledge of the laws of the game and a deep understanding of the spirit behind their creation. This step is a *sine qua non* of effective officiating. If the official has only partial or vague command of the rule book, he is subject to unlawful but understandable dissent and will be vulnerable in his dealings with those occasional players and coaches who sensibly make a point of knowing the rules. Furthermore, blunders based on inadequate knowledge of the laws lead to appeals by coaches — with attendant forfeitures or rematches — and not only embarrass the referee as an individual but also embarrass the local referees' association of which he is a member.

Despite rigorous training programs, astonishing decisions are sometimes made by officials who have either not kept up with the annual changes of the laws or have gotten rusty in their overall rules competence. It is important to reread the laws at frequent intervals. I usually try to peruse the laws before each game, especially with regard to seldom-invoked situations which might very well occur, such as impingement during the taking of a penalty kick. Recently I had neglected to do this and officiated after several weeks of rain-outs. The fact that I am a serious student of the laws of the game came to my rescue. I signaled for the taking of a penalty kick. As a kicker was approaching the ball, I noticed that a teammate of the kicker was standing on the eighteen-yard line inside the restraining arc. I had somehow not noticed him as we prepared for the taking of the kick. I blew my whistle again and shouted "Hold It!" so that I might conform to International Board Decision 1 in Law 14 which states: "When the Referee has awarded a penalty-kick, he shall not signal for it to be taken, until the players have taken up position in accordance with the Law."

The player taking the penalty kick did not have time to prevent his kick before my signal and the goalkeeper blocked the shot. As soon as I whistled to halt play, I realized that, having signaled for the kick to be taken, I should have let the kick proceed, called for an indirect free kick after the ball was deflected, and cautioned the infringer, for such is the policy specifically laid out in Board Decision 4. Even as I sensed my blunder, I realized that as the kick was about to be taken, the goalkeeper had moved about a foot in front of the goal line, and I invoked the further Board Decision (5,a) that if the goalkeeper moves his feet and a colleague of the kicker impinges after the signal but before the ball is in play, "the kick, *if taken*, shall be retaken." The players were not aware of what went on in my mind, nor did they complain, nor did I offer an explanation other than to point at the two guilty parties. The kick was properly taken and once again saved by the goalkeeper.

The lesson for me was to remember to reread the rule book, the referee's "Bible", before a game after a layoff of several weeks or more. To know the rules thoroughly instills confidence in the official. As one of my charismatic colleagues once told me, "if you know the rules very, very well, you will find that this knowledge, coupled with common sense, will permit you to come up promptly and consistently with correct decisions when confronted with the unexpected."

So every referee should be a student of the laws. He should know the self-evident rules (such as field dimensions) thoroughly, and he should not only know the specifics of the more subtle laws like Law 11 (Offside) but should also have thought through their ambiguities and ramifications to a coherent conclusion so that he possesses, in fact, a *working* knowledge of those laws. He will have to study and analyze certain clauses of the laws and it is those portions of the laws which require analysis which most interest me. In this section I shall dwell, on the one hand, on the equivocal or controversial laws and, on the other, on reviewing helpful hints for the better enforcement of both the clear-cut and the subtle laws.

Again, I cannot stress enough the importance of a total and thorough understanding of the laws. I spoke earlier of some astonishing decisions. I have seen or heard tell of referees who have made calls the likes of which make one's eyeballs spin. My immediate reaction to horrendous blunders is one of compassion and protectiveness, but most of the cases I am now alluding to could have been avoided through the most cursory knowledge of the laws. And in almost every case the referee was adamant when challenged by the coach. Here are a few samples of real decisions which did lead or could well have led to the granting of a rematch:

1. the referee whistles for "obstruction" in the penalty area and awards a game-winning penalty kick;

2. the referee declares "hands" in the penalty area and then, feeling the prescribed punishment would be too severe, awards an indirect free kick;

3. a player is ejected in a game played under international rules and the referee allows him to be replaced and his replacement subsequently scores the only goal of the game;

4. a ball strikes the referee and bounds into the goal but he disallows the goal and calls for a drop ball where the ball had hit him*;

5. An indirect free kick sails directly into the opponent's goal untouched by another player and the referee awards a goal.

---

*This man is guilty of two things: insufficient knowledge of the laws and very careless positioning!

There are many more such cases that one hears about when referees gather to discuss the game. Some are not likely to affect the outcome of the game but surely would lead one to suspect that the official has such a fuzzy knowledge of the laws that he is bound one day to encounter difficulties. An example of these strange calls is the penalizing of players for such exotic infringements as "spiking the ball" or kicking the goalkick out of the penalty area to the side instead of over the front line of the box (so help me, I'm not kidding!).

Every referee will miss some infractions. He cannot see them all as he will occasionally be screened from the action or a foul may occur behind his back, and even the swiftest and fittest referee will sometimes be left behind on a booming kick and be in a poor position to judge offside. These "errors" are unavoidable and must be handled by the official as best he knows how, but there is no excuse for errors in the laws involving explicit stipulations as to infraction and pursuant punishment. One simply *must not*, for example, award an indirect free kick for tripping or "caution" a player for violent conduct.*

Before proceeding further in this book, the reader should review the international Laws of the Game provided in *Appendix I* (See page 307); he should, in addition, be prepared to refer to this Appendix from time to time as he proceeds through the following discussion.

Let us turn then, to the laws themselves. There are basically three sets of rules widely used in the United States. Amateur and professional teams under the aegis of FIFA (Federation Internationale de Football Association) and its American national affiliate USSF (United States Soccer Federation) play the game according to the international rules promulgated by the International Board of FIFA in Zurich, Switzerland. It is these rules which govern the game throughout the world and upon which our discussions shall center.

---

*These charges call for a direct free kick or penalty kick and for ejection, respectively.

It is appropriate, however, to make some reference to the other sets of rules, for many referees officiate school and college games as well as amateur matches. The collegiate, or NCAA rules, published in the annual *Soccer Guide,* are used by colleges and many high schools, most of the remaining high schools using the **Soccer Rule Book** of the National Federation of State High School Associations. These books vary one from the other and both of them differ radically from the FIFA **Laws of the Game.**

The various sets of rules introduce changes every year. The most obvious differences between officiating in school and college games and those played under FIFA's laws are the different uniforms usually worn by the school and college referees (A black-and-white striped shirt rather than the international black shirt with white collar and cuffs) and the fact that they generally work with a dual-referee system as opposed to the customary system of either one referee or a referee assisted by two "neutral" or official linesmen. We shall deal with these factors elsewhere, especially under technique.

It is best if the referee knows the FIFA rules as his point of departure and then learns the other variations as needed. For the most important laws he can generally abide by the international rules, toward which the other rule books are slowly moving and with which they will perhaps one day coincide.

I shall, for my part, deal essentially with the FIFA laws and only occasionally mention departures from them in the other rule books. I have appended the important variances in a special section at the end of the book (Appendix II) and it is important that those officials refereeing school and college games keep in mind the pertinent differences, as failure to know the variances could give rise to a game-losing blunder. If, for example, I speak of the location of the drop ball as inside the goal area, one must remember that in the scholastic and collegiate rules drop balls must take place outside the penalty area. If a drop ball were administered on the goal line in a college game and a game-deciding goal resulted immediately therefrom, the losing coach would clearly be justified in lodging a protest on the grounds of a technical error by the official and it might very well be that the game would have to be replayed.

The laws of the game consist of seventeen sections or laws accompanied by official International Board Decisions (IBD or Decision hereafter) or clarifications as well as advice to referees. The British Football Association version (Chart) also contains advice to referees, players, and team officials. These seventeen laws and their IBDs must be mastered by every would-be referee before he dons a uniform and should be reviewed frequently thereafter so that he has control of the material therein whenever he takes to the field.

In the following pages we shall discuss and analyze portions of these laws which present problems or frequently meet with misunderstanding. The application of the laws might technically belong elsewhere under "Technique and Game Control," but we shall have to deal with some aspects of their application here, too, as it is only when applied that some of them become meaningful.

One could conceivably know the laws verbatim and not make the right calls on the field. For example, the referee might know that a violent charge calls for a direct free kick or penalty kick but whistle for obstruction when a classic case of charging actually occurs before him. Or he might "freeze" and let it go by altogether.

It is a good idea when learning or reviewing the laws to picture the rules in action, visualizing game situations. It is also an excellent idea to study films of world-class games to see how topflight officials interpret match action. In fact, the dedicated soccer referee cannot attend a soccer match—or even another type of sporting event—without observing the positioning, attire, signals, and general comportment of the officials.

To some extent, then, refereeing changes one's optics and prevents him from ever enjoying the game in the same way as before; he will now always be interested in seeing how the referee does his job and hopefully will be picking up some pointers or taking note of some mannerisms or defects to be avoided.

During the 1974 NASL championship game shown on national television, referee John Davies became incapacitated and was unable to continue. He turned the game over to his standby and it seemed to me that the cameras spent an eternity focusing on Davies' prostrate form being attended to on the sideline. All my fellow referees later commented on this unfortunate event, but when I asked five or six people who were players, not referees, what they had thought of the Davies incident, they stared back in bewilderment. Not one had even noticed the referee or that he had had to leave the game, and one even growled that when watching a game he doesn't have time to "look at those clowns." We might conclude that Davies had done a good job in turning the game over to his stand-by without much fanfare and without drawing undue attention to himself, getting on with the game at hand through a smooth transfer of authority.

The seventeen rules cover or allow for sensible decisions with regard to most contingencies, but a number of referees like to cite "Law 18" as being of the utmost importance. This is the unwritten law of common sense which should be invoked in conjunction with all the other laws. "Law 18" will receive considerable attention later in this book when we deal with psychology and game control, but it is appropriate to mention it briefly here. A slavish adherence to the letter of the law will strip any game of imaginative development and annoy the players and spectators for whose pleasure the game was invented and developed in the first place. If one were to follow religiously the laws in administering cautions, for instance, the average game would occasion a welter of yellow cards. We are reminded at several points in the laws that they shall under certain circumstances yield to more urgent considerations such as the spirit of fair play or the enjoyment of all involved.

It is important, however, that one not simply fail to apply the laws through timidity or ignorance but rather that he know them letter-perfect and with thorough understanding so that he can know in an instant whether they should be tempered with patience, wisdom, or common sense or enforced rigidly in the interest of game control.

The laws of the game are broken down into the following categories:

Law 1—The Field of Play
Law 2—The Ball
Law 3—Number of Players
Law 4—Players' Equipment
Law 5—Referees
Law 6—Linesmen
Law 7—Duration of the Game
Law 8—The Start of Play
Law 9—Ball in and out of Play
Law 10—Method of Scoring
Law 11—Offside
Law 12—Fouls and Misconduct
Law 13—Free Kick (Direct and Indirect)
Law 14—Penalty Kick
Law 15—Throw-in
Law 16—Goal Kick
Law 17—Corner Kick.

In dealing with the laws I shall not reiterate them in every detail, referring the reader rather to Appendix I. I shall limit my remarks to a cursory prose resume of the essentials of the laws, only quoting fragments under examination or several laws, such as law 11, which are brief but the basis for much discussion. I shall dwell on certain ambiguities and oft-misunderstood aspects of the laws and provide helpful hints with regard to application of the laws.

Law 1
The Field of Play

This law is seldom adhered to in every detail. Law 1 stipulates the dimensions of the field of play and its various parts. It is an important law, for a professional-looking field will foster a better brand of soccer, and the latitude permissible regarding width and length can become a factor in the playing of the game, just as a short right field line can be a factor in a baseball park. For this reason, full-scale international games are played on more uniform fields (110-120 yards by 70-80 yards) than other matches for which a field may be as small as 50 x 100 yds. or as large as 100 x 130 yds. and may be nearly square (it *must* be longer than it is wide) or very long and narrow, that is 100 x 101 yds. or 50 x 130 yds., respectively. The size and shape of the field will have an effect on play as it affects the referee. A large field will make demands on him physically if he is to stay close to the play whereas a small field may prove easy to cover but provoke a higher incidence of side-line and end-line calls to tax his mental alertness.

The outermost dimensions will usually be dictated by the amount and disposition of available ground. Once the basic rectangle is laid out, the remaining dimensions must not vary no matter the size of the field. All lines should be clearly marked and of an appropriate width not greater than five inches. The areas themselves are to be marked out as illustrated on page 30.

The markings of the field are considered part of the area they circumscribe or delimit. It is important to stress this concept as the notion of the thickness of the line being included

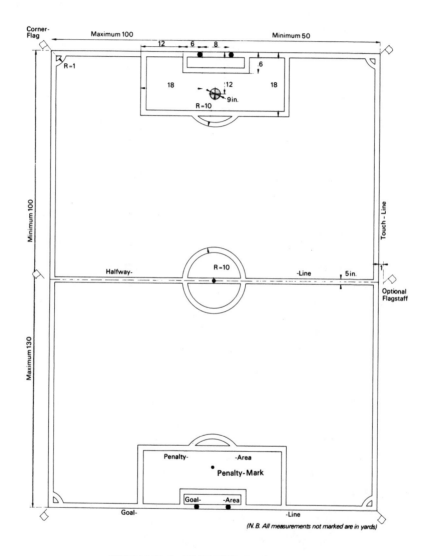

FIGURE 1: THE FIELD OF PLAY

in the area it outlines is not consistent with some other sports, such as American football, in which it is sufficient to step on the line to be out-of-bounds.

This judgment is spelled out in Decision 6 of this law: "The space within the inside areas of the field of play includes the width of the lines marking the areas." This will become very important in applying some of the other laws, such as those governing goal kicks and corner kicks, and it provides a logical if relative basis for judging if a man standing on the midfield stripe is in "his own half" of the field or not. It is vital in regard to determining consequences due to the location of infractions. For example, the referee should *never* place the ball on the line outlining the penalty area and declare a direct free kick for the attacking team. If the infraction did, indeed, occur at that spot, a penalty kick should be awarded. This contradiction forms at least half the basis for Denis Howell's derision in an anecdote he provides of an incident in a New York soccer tournament (the other half of the derision would involve the hedging on the penalty call):

> Midway through the second-half Cliss was going through when he was fetched down in front of the American linesman. Because of the scorching sun the grass was kept quite long and it was very difficult to see the markings. I was aware that my U.S. colleagues had little lining experience, so I fixed my eye on the spot where the foul had taken place and advanced towards it. As I did the linesman advanced towards me. Before we met I was able to satisfy myself that the offence was about a yard or so inside the area. 'Another penalty, it seems,' I said to my colleague as we met, only to receive, in the broadest American accent, 'Sure, I guess it was. But if you want to put the ball on the line, it's all right by me!'[5]

There is only one law in which the line is referred to in a way incompatible with Law 1, IBD 6; that is Law 15 on the throw-in. This inconsistency has been the basis for some differences in interpretations of what constitutes a foot fault. We shall discuss that at length in the appropriate place; let us merely point out that other than Law 15 which refers to a position "on or behind the line", the lines themselves are to be considered part of the area they mark. We shall see in a later section of this study that some simple words like "within" are actually potential semantic traps or can, in their context, have important implications; however, with the exception of the positioning of the feet during throw-ins, all situations covered by the laws and deriving from the general logic therein may be judged on the premise that the given area's dividing point is the outer edge of the line, whether we are talking of a goal scored (wholly over all the line) or an infraction occurring on the penalty-area line. For example, the goal area is that outlined by the bold line in our illustration:

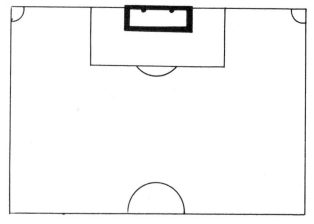

Figure 2: GOAL AREA
boundaries are indicated by bold line

The measurements of the goal mouth, the goal area, and the penalty area along the goal line are all measured from the inner edge of the goal post, and the goal line shall, between the goal posts, conform in width to the depth of the posts themselves. This proviso obviously appears in order to allow the referee to make a definitive goal judgment from a side view using the post as a gauge. The dimensions of the goal posts, whose uprights shall be eight yards apart and equidistant from the closest corner flag, are as follows:

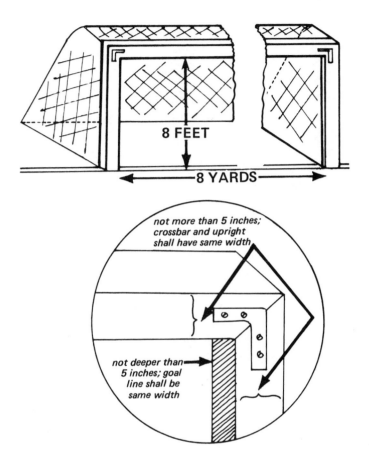

not more than 5 inches;
crossbar and upright
shall have same width

not deeper than
5 inches; goal
line shall be
same width

Figure 3: THE GOAL

There are some further refinements in the laws, such as the authorized materials, shapes, and colors of the goal posts, and one should check Law 1 carefully for these stipulations before laying out a field.

As I said at the beginning of this section, the law is seldom conformed to in every detail. I have seldom come to referee on a field in which I could not find one shortcoming as to the measurements or some other requirement of Law 1. Some of the more frequent violations are listed on the following page:

Corner flagstaffs under five feet in height and/or of dangerously thin doweling. *Remedy:* Clubs can buy six-foot lengths of "full-round" at a lumberyard. While at it, they might as well make six flags and use the optional midfield flags. These will assist the referee in judging whether a player is offside or in his own half of the field. In addition the coach should have a mallet to drive these flags into hard ground.

Corner flagstaffs standing on a flat or tripod base. Encountered on artificial turf, these can, if knocked over, become very dangerous to the players.

Goal posts with crossbars and uprights of different widths.

V-shaped ruts instead of or at the locations of field markings.

No goal line between uprights.

No corner quadrants.

No penalty kick restraining arcs, or ones that are improperly traced. Frequently those marking the field erroneously begin the arc at a point straight out from the corner of the goal area; this will, of course, not give a true radius from the penalty spot.

Incorrectly marked goal or penalty areas. Frequently the goal area is lacking altogether.

The important thing is to get on with the game. The players are not interested in the referee's encyclopedic recitation of Law 1. He should, however, point out certain violations to the home coach and captain (dangerous corner flagstaffs, incorrect penalty spot, incorrect penalty-area dimension) and, if appropriate, mention them in his game report. The referee should not, short of an absence of goal posts or something like that, refuse to referee the game for violations of Law 1, but when and where they can be rectified prior to the start of play, he should see to it that they are.

It often will occur that there are no lines — such as late in the season after league play has ended and "make-ups" and exhibitions are being played — or that they have been rained out before game time. Sometimes the coach or players are marking the field and have only a small amount of chalk left. In such instances, the referee should oversee the operation and see to it that certain lines are laid out first. Some lines are more critical to the referee than others. For example, the restraining arc at the eighteen-yard line (or the goal area in college and school games) is only used in connection with a restart of play from a dead ball and is not as essential to the referee as is the delineation of the penalty area.

Below is an illustration with the most critical lines in bold marking:

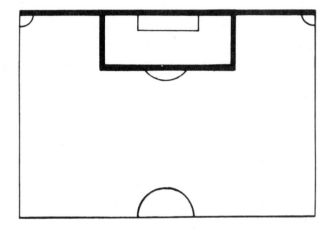

Figure 4: THE MOST CRITICAL MARKINGS (Bold Line)

The referee should not take lightly Law 1, for it is a general principle that the better the lining and the better the weather, the better are the referee's chances of having a good day. In this context, the most important items besides the field markings, are two whose absence might cause a referee to make an unfair call in no way directly related to his relative skill or experience level: corner flags and properly affixed goal nets.

Officiating with no corner flags will possibly create problems since from twenty yards away the referee may innocently award a throw-in whereas the attacker near the ball, having seen that the slow roller has gone out for a corner kick, will thereafter mistrust the referee's judgment. If no flags are available the referee should note that fact in his postgame report and see to it that some object — like a bright training jacket — is placed at each corner before calling for play to commence.

I personally feel that staunch nets are one of the most important allies a referee can have. They are not required by international rules ("Nets may be attached. . .") but fortunately most leagues require them. On a dark day, with gray pipe goal posts, no nets, and no neutral linesmen, it is extremely difficult for a referee to tell from a side view if a hard shot has gone inside or outside the goal post. If there are nets, but these are full of holes, he may have the same problem.

I always see to it that coaches fasten nets securely and I have not hesitated to assist them in retying them or in patching holes so that I know that no spot has been missed. To this end, it is a good idea to have strong tape, twine, and a small knife in one's kit. Approximately once in every 20 or 30 games the referee will, despite good positioning, have his view of play partially obscured during a shot on goal. If the nets are secure and one knows that the ball nestled inside the goal could not have gone in through the side net, he will have less difficulty arriving at the correct decision regarding the validity of the goal.

When arriving at the field, the referee should make an "eye-check" of its dimensions and appurtenances: are there corner flags, restraining arcs and center circle; is the side of the penalty area at least three yards from the touchline indicating that the field width is at least fifty yards? He should then proceed to pace out the critical penalty area, goal area, goal line between the posts, penalty spot, and so forth.

As I have said, violations of Law 1 are almost predictable. If the critical areas are out of whack or incorrect, but not outrageously so — as they would be if the penalty area were, say eight yards by twenty-four yards, the referee should mention the fact to the coach and captains, inform the players that they will play the markings "as is" (both teams will have equal time at each end), and then proceed to play, being certain to file the pertinent information in his game report.

Prelude to a top level soccer match — Dynamo Dresden stands to attention. (Horst Müller)

When lines are far too incorrect and cannot be corrected, the referee should inform the players that he will deal with the penalty area, the goal area, and so forth as he would had they been rained out, that is, according to his good estimation of where the correct lines would be. He might point out to them that he will desist from calling for a penalty kick unless absolutely certain the infraction occurred within the hypothetical area.

It is, in any case, wise to make a full check of the field and its appurtenances, for one never knows when the resulting knowledge will prove vital. Two men in my referees' association told of going to officiate a professional game in another city. They had arrived at the stadium ninety minutes before game time as they are supposed to and had gone out to make a field dimension check. They discovered that one penalty area was a bit too narrow and found several other discrepancies. Just prior to game time, the visiting coach stormed out onto the field and said belligerently to the officials: "Hey, have you checked out that penalty area over there?" The referee pulled out a small card and said: "Yes, it is two yards too narrow; would you like to have the other dimensions?" The coach asked how they had made the check and one linesman pulled out a thirty-yard tapeline. The coach appeared nonplussed but satisfied, for it was obvious that the officials had made a thorough check and would presumably make sensible allowances during play and file a report to the league. In short, if they had discovered the idiosyncrasies of the markings, they would know what to do with them.

A preliminary field check can also provide information useful to the referee or linesman during play. For example, if he paces off the distance from the corner to the penalty area and finds that it is ten yards — or even some other distance, like seven or twelve yards — he can exploit this knowledge when enforcing the ten-yard distance opponents must keep when a corner kick is being taken.

The violation of Law 1 may not be vital to play itself, but it is not by chance that it is the initial law, for it is, indeed, the law of the game whose violations chronologically come first to the attention of the referee. The outcome or the flow of the game will perhaps not usually be radically affected by those violations, but the way in which the officials deal with them may be of great importance. The way they handle the violations will serve notice to players and coaches as to how they will handle the game.

In this matter, then, the referee should be fair, rational,

courteous, and helpful, and he should be firm if the violations are serious or are taken lightly by the home club. He should, in addition, already invoke the unwritten law of common sense and avoid making too great an issue of minor matters. Confronted with a field whose forty-nine-yard width could not be rectified without major relandscaping at a cost of thousands of dollars, the referee should point out to the coach that he is aware of the problem (the coach is no doubt painfully aware of it), perhaps make a soothing joke about the "postage stamp" field, and get on with the game. Excellent games are sometimes played on small fields and poor games are sometimes played on large ones. Just because the laws state that fields hosting international games shall be a maximum of 80 x 120 yds. and a minimum of 70 x 110 yds. does not mean that a game played on a field of these dimensions will be of international class.

Law 2 - The Ball

The ball must be spherical and of leather or other approved materials (a special synthetic ball was approved and used in Germany at the 1974 World Cup). Its circumference shall be not more than 28 inches and not less than 27 inches and pressure shall be equal to "0.6-0.7 atmosphere, which equals 9.0-10.15 lb./sq. in. (600-700 gr./sq. cm.) at sea level." The ball, which should weigh between 14 and 16 ounces at the outset of play, shall not be changed during the game without the referee's approval.

The ball is an important item, obviously, and yet some matches are played with old "clunkers," frayed "potatoes," or oblong "balloons." Too light a ball will sail or curve, too heavy a ball will slip through the goalkeeper's hands or knock a player unconscious, and a misshapen ball will flutter or fail to bounce true. And yet often the home team has but one ball which is, as likely as not, underinflated. The referee shall select the best ball available, even using the visitor's soccer ball if necessary and if they are willing.

One might think that both teams derive the same benefit or disadvantage from the type of ball used, but the use of a light, underinflated ball which "takes off" will produce an additional advantage for the team with the best goalkeeper should the players start shooting from far out.

How does one check the complicated legality of a ball? There are professional pressure and weight gauges available, but they are costly and cumbersome and normally the referee will

Swiss referee Jean Dubach presides over the greeting by team captains from Bulgaria and Germany. (Horst Müller)

judge a ball by its looks and its "heft", spinning it, squeezing it, and bouncing it. It is easy enough to see if it is true and spherical and the size can be checked with a tape measure if there is some question as to the legality of its circumference. Weight and pressure cannot really be judged accurately by feel or with the old "thumb-pressure" test, but one generally makes do with these homely methods. You can usually tell a really good ball and such primitive gauges will suffice to eliminate the patently unacceptable balls.

Having selected a ball*, the referee should see that it alone is used throughout the game unless it becomes defective or dangerous or goes into a ravine or over a fence and to wait for its return would entail undue delay. If a new ball is brought in, the official should check it before authorizing its use.

It is not the responsibility of the referee to see to it that there is a proper ball for the game, but if he referees a great many sand-lot games, he might keep a tire pump and gauge in his car as often the only available ball is woefully underinflated with no pump available!

Recently I was assigned to a Second Division game. The field was changed at the last minute and the nominal home team, having suffered a last-minute managerial change, had no nets, flags, or ball (the former manager having taken them with him). The visiting coach, rather than protesting for an inevitable forfeit, stated that he and his men had come to play and would rather play and lose than win by forfeit. He then opened the trunk of his car, pumped up a ball, and brought out nets and flags. Thanks to his attitude there was a good game played that afternoon.

The referee should not feel above giving a helping hand by supplying a pump or the like if he has them. Despite the "bad press" referees often get, they are an integral part of the game of soccer and as interested as anyone in promoting the sport. I know several referees who even keep a ball in their car for the eventual game where the ball is altogether lacking. One need not do this, and teams should certainly not be led to expect to be bailed out in this manner when they infringe on Law 2, but such foresight could mean that a soccer game is *played* instead of twenty-two boys sent home to watch football on television.

---

*And Law 5 forestalls a cantankerous insistance that the ball is illegal and that it be checked scientifically, for Law 5(j) declares not that a legal ball shall be used, but that it shall be the referee's decision as to whether or not the "ball provided meets with the requirements."

3

Law 3
Number of Players

The law states that a "match shall be played by two teams, each consisting of not more than eleven players, one of whom shall be the goalkeeper." International rules state that there shall be no more than two substitutions per game and that a player may not return to action after leaving for a substitute. This is generally adapted, however, in local league requirements which range from unlimited substitutions to the absolute two. In all games played under international rules, however, a player ejected by the referee may not be replaced. It is recommended that a game not be allowed when there are not a minimum of seven players on one of the sides and this policy is quite universally observed.

The referee should always keep a notebook containing the substitution rules of the various leagues in which he officiates. Information will include such items as how many players may suit up for a competition, how many names may appear on a line-up, how many substitutions per half or per game, whether players may be re-used or not, and when — with the approval of the referee — teams may make their player changes.

Some leagues do not allow substitutions on corner kicks, during the opponent's throw-in, and so forth, and variations are considerable, but the referee should make a point of being familiar with a league's or cup competition's given variations when he reports to the field.

There are several matters which remain in the hands of the official, however, and which are not at the discretion of league

officials. Any substitutions may only be made with the referee's approval which must be secured *before* the change is made. Usually there will be no problem, for when there are only two substitutions per game, for example, the tactical advantage of making a substitution on any given free kick is minimal. The referee will, therefore, usually accept the substitution at any given stoppage, assuming he has seen the awaiting substitute before the restart of play.

When there are free substitutions, however, a winning coach will sometimes stall for time by incessantly moving players on and off the field. The referee must not let this occur. There are several ways of handling such a situation. The referee can conspicuously call "time out" during these excessive tactical substitutions and, if the coach fails to get the message, the referee can inform the coach that if he continues to use what are in the referee's opinion delaying tactics which bring the game into disrepute, he will have no choice but to caution him for ungentlemanly conduct. Usually the "time out" policy and, if necessary, a few courteous but unequivocal words to the offending coach will put a stop to these delaying tactics.

One must be careful not to interfere with a team's rights to certain tactical manoeuvres, however. A player may sometimes legally obstruct a player if he is, himself, shielding a ball which he is playing; similarly, a degree of slowing down the game is tolerable and even good strategy when a team is trying to eke out a victory. Such tactics are part of the defensive game. It is a matter of judgment – in this case in the eyes of the referee – when the substitution activity becomes unsportsmanlike "gamesmanship" requiring the referee to take some action.

It is technically a cautionary offense for any player to enter the field without the referee's approval and the punishment for infringement is an indirect free kick. In 1972 a rules change made it mandatory for the departing player to leave the field before the incoming player comes on, and the latter should do so at midfield. It is this rule that led to the use of the large numbered "pit" cards – as means of communication – so conspicuous during television coverage of the World Cup in Munich.

The referee will find it difficult to enforce rigorously this rule in any competition with unlimited substitution. He will restart play after a goal and notice, after a few minutes that a player has come in unacknowledged during the break. It is not in his own interest to be too "uptight" about this if the game is moving well and it has not been a trend on the part of the coach but rather an isolated oversight. During an appropriate stoppage – a throw-in near that bench, say – the referee might remind the coach to have his incoming men report to him.

It is virtually impossible to enforce the rule that outgoing players leave before the new ones report in when many substitutes are authorized. Coaches usually have the ingoing ones inform their teammates that they are being replaced. The only alternative would be a bullhorn and this would be disagreeable and could even be construed as coaching from the sidelines, which is disallowed under FIFA rules. The referee must, in these situations, liberally invoke that unwritten law of common sense we referred to as "Law 18."

There is one other item in Law 3 which has, for several years now, been the center of a thorny debate at the highest official levels. An authoritative statement in the matter is sorely needed or perhaps a rewording of the law.

A major change of Law 3 was made in 1972 in order to remedy a longstanding conflict between two of its clauses. The change was so mysteriously made, however, that many referees continued — and some still continue — to operate under the pre-1972 policy while others who knew of the change began to try to think through the consequences of the change in wording. I am speaking of the illegal substitution of a goalkeeper and the illegal exchange on the field between a goalkeeper and a teammate.

For many years Law 3 stipulated that a substitute goalkeeper who fails to report to the referee shall, upon subsequently handling the ball in the penalty area, be charged with an infraction and a penalty kick awarded to the opposition. This punishment was quietly dropped from the 1972-73 rule book. Despite some publicity in bulletins and clinics, the implications of this omission were not immediately fully understood by many.

The emendation entailed not so much a rule change as the eradication of a previously unnoticed inconsistency within Law 3 itself, for the longstanding practice of awarding a penalty kick for handling by a nonreporting goalkeeper was realized to be, in most cases, contradictory to the overall logic of the laws and spirit of the game as well as in direct contravention of the specifics laid down in Law 3 which have long maintained that a match shall be played by two teams of no more than eleven players, "one of whom shall be the goalkeeper." To deny an

The free-flowing and ballet-like movement of world class soccer, as well as the less practiced play of juniors, is kept intact by strict adherence to the Laws of the Game. (M. Julius Baum)

incoming substitute goalkeeper the functional right to touch the ball would be to deny the side a goalkeeper, contrary to the clause just quoted. The nonreporting goalkeeper is, however, guilty of an illegal substitution and is to be cautioned and play restarted, if necessary, by an indirect free kick to the opposition.

The area of controversy centers on the illegal exchange of a goalkeeper and a teammate on the field of play. Feedback from FIFA clinics at first seemed to indicate one interpretation but recent feedback has been quite different. The matter is so important — the punishment being in the one interpretation a penalty kick for handling and in the other an indirect free kick for ungentlemanly conduct or even just a caution after the ball has gone out of play — that a *ruling* from FIFA, not just a referee instructor's opinion, is needed in writing. Dozens of games every year are no doubt being won and lost according to how the referee reads this law regarding such keeper-player exchanges.

Since, at this date, no authoritative public written decision has settled the debate, I shall report the two views. Logic favors the first one, but I happily adopt the second one since Mr. Rene Courte of FIFA has endorsed it. In the meantime, I shall personally do my utmost to see to it that I pre-empt the problem by catching the exchange before it reaches the culminating offense of handling although one of the clauses instructs the referee not to stop play for the infringement of a keeper-player switch but to wait until the ball has gone out of play to caution them, meaning that he may not be able to avoid the occurrence of handling without himself violating that clause!

Two sections of the law are involved in the debate. Law 3, paragraph 4, states that "Any of the other players may change places with the goalkeeper, provided that the Referee is informed before the change is made, and provided also, that the change is made during a stoppage in the game." Later, under *punishment (a),* the law states that "Play shall not be stopped for an infringement of paragraph 4. The players concerned shall be cautioned immediately the ball goes out of play." Like the old optical illusion which seems to protrude from the page or burrow down into it depending on how you look at it, these two clauses can be made to embroider quite disparate interpretations.

I, personally, see a great difference between a substitution and a player exchange. One involves a twelfth man, the other the original eleven players of record. In short, if the goalkeeper and another player exchange jerseys during the flow of play they have not met the requirements of notifying the referee and making the exchange in a stoppage.

With a side-line substitution of the goalkeeper you could not refuse to recognize the new keeper without denying the side its stated rights, but you can refuse to recognize a switched goalkeeper because the original one is still on the field. It seems to me that the punishment bears this idea out since it tells the official not to stop play for an infringement of paragraph 4 (which does not deal with handling but with exchanging!) but to wait until the ball goes out of play to caution the offending parties for ungentlemanly conduct, in this instance for not giving him prior notification or waiting for a stoppage. He does not stop play because he is not recognizing the switch. For those who endorse this viewpoint, handling by the "new" goalkeeper would be quite apart from the idea of letting the ball go out of play before cautioning and they would grant a penalty kick, just as you would if the goalkeeper or any other player tripped someone before the ball went out of play. This, at least, was the basic view that came out of FIFA's Mexico City clinic in December, 1972.

Many excellent officials disagree with this approach to these two clauses in the law and they can build a good case by approaching the problem from another angle. They view that when the "new" keeper dons the goalkeeper's jersey he is guilty only of not waiting for a stoppage and possibly of not giving prior notification — although some contend that donning the jersey is a form of body-language notification of the change. Illegal substitutions call for cautionary discipline, but there is no specific offense to cover "deluding the referee by jersey change" or "not waiting for a stoppage to make a jersey change," so we must turn our full attention to the only pertinent punishment clause.

If we agree that the illegal exchange is only a cautionary offense, then *punishment (a)* takes on an absolutely new meaning. When the "new" exchange keeper handles the ball, he is not guilty of any infraction by virtue of that particular deed and the referee, therefore, does nothing at that point but lets him proceed to clearing the ball and cautions the two players when the ball eventually goes out of play or there is some other stoppage. This then, is the other viewpoint which would never allow for a penalty kick for handling by the jersey-bearing goalkeeper of record despite any irregularities preceding the donning of that jersey.

This latter policy is the one referees should adopt as it is the one officially espoused by FIFA. In reply to a query as to what action the referee should take if the player and goalkeeper switch jerseys during the flow of play or during a stoppage or between periods without proper notification, Rene Courte — Senior Assistant Secretary of FIFA — has informed me that "Play should not be stopped. The players concerned should be cautioned immediately the ball goes out of play — see Law III, para. 4 and punishment (a)..." Should the original goalkeeper after such a switch run back and handle the ball in his penalty area it will be a penal offense as there can only be one goalkeeper, he who is wearing the legitimate colors. (Letter from R. Courte, dated August 15, 1975.)

Hopefully this proper approach will be indicated by FIFA to its thousands of referees around the world, and at an early date. At the moment the two areas where all would agree, I think, are that you never give a penalty kick for handling by *substitute* goalkeepers and that the only time a jersey-bearing goalkeeper would be subject to a penalty kick would be if a named reserve goalkeeper were to run on the field and handle the ball in the penalty area while the original goalkeeper was still in the game; in this latter instance there would be two goalkeepers and not the authorized one goalkeeper and since the player is guilty of two offenses (illegal substitution procedure and handling), the more severe punishment would apply. If the incoming goalkeeper were not a named substitute he would simply be an outside agent and a drop ball would be executed where he had handled the ball. The intelligent and sensible referee will try to avoid these hassles through preventive action, but there is little he can do if two players at one end of the field exchange jerseys while he is busy refereeing down at the other end. The need for an unequivocal clarification in the wording of the laws is heightened by the fact that, unlike trivial controversies such as over throw-in flaws, this one culminates in action by the referee which can turn a ball game right around.

Law 4
Players' Equipment

The critical nucleus of this law is the opening line stating that "A player shall not wear anything which is dangerous to another player." It is logical that teams wear distinct colors and that goalkeepers' colors be different from those of other players. Recently the much-favored black attire of goalkeepers was dealt a mortal blow with the insertion of a clause to the effect that the goalkeeper shall not wear the same color as the referee.

The law does not require footgear, and with good reason, for there are some countries affiliated with FIFA where the average per capita annual income is less than the cost of a good pair of soccer shoes! An Indian player once told me that in local competition in his country they play barefoot, winding a band of material repeatedly around the middle of the foot. This inexpensive device gives some arch support at the same time that it affords protection at the point of impact where the instep meets the ball on a power kick.

The law does not allow some players to be with shoes and others without, however, for this would be dangerous to those without shoes and in contravention of Law 4, Decision 2.

Glasses are allowed, but the referee shall not allow the wearing of dangerous casts, rings, watches, and whatnot. This rule was invoked — with dire consequences — in 1973 in the African World Cup preliminaries. Two West African countries were meeting. One team had placed on their jerseys some amulets which had been charmed by the tribal priest. When the other team noticed the amulets and complained, the referee tried to make the players remove these objects which he deemed "dangerous" to the opponent. The irate fans rioted and the match was abandoned. Such way-out cases are uncommon, but one never can be sure what will occur.

The object most likely to elicit protest is a cast on the arm. The referee should only allow a player with a cast to participate if it has been safely bound in foam rubber or similar material and, in the referee's opinion, no longer constitutes a danger to other players.

The greatest part of Law 4 deals with lawful and unlawful footgear. Nowadays, most players wear shoes with moulded soles and these are generally safe and law-abiding. The referee should know this part of the law well, however, for a surprising number of shoes are manufactured which do *not* meet the requirements of any of the rule books. The most common violations are cleats which are too long (exceeding ¾") and cleats which have a threaded hole in the bottom and screw onto a metal bolt attached to the shoe sole:

Figure 5: CLEATS

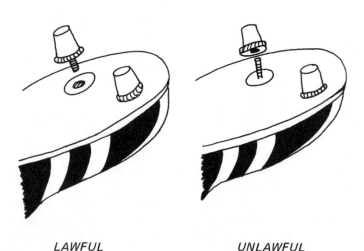

LAWFUL   UNLAWFUL

These are especially dangerous as the cleats have a tendency to come loose, exposing an extremely hazardous metal point.

Metal cleats *per se* are not illegal and one finds legal cleats of aluminum, plastic, and half plastic and half metal. In the case of these, they should be smooth and not have scoring or spurs which can cause injury to others, opponents and teammates alike. Norman Burtenshaw, in his book **Whose Side Are You On, Ref?**, speaks of having to watch carefully to see to it that cunning players not, subsequent to the pregame shoe inspection in the locker room, deliberately scuff up their cleats on the cement floor on their way out to the field.

The referee should always be prepared to inspect shoes — some coaches will demand that the referee inspect the opponents' shoes in an effort to psychologically upstage, intimidate, or dictate to the official — and to this end he should have a short ruler or gauge in his kit. I always have a penny in my pocket as the diameter of the penny is three-quarters of an inch.

5

Law 5 - Referees

Obviously Law 5 is of special importance and interest to referees. A full knowledge and intimate understanding of this law and Law 12 (Fouls and Misconduct) are indispensible to good refereeing. Referee training courses, review clinics, rules interpretation lectures to coaches and players rightly devote considerable time to these two laws. They contain important data and shall, each in its turn, detain us for a good many pages.

Serious students of the laws keep coming back to Law 5, for it has — to the degree possible in a bare, concise set of regulations — all the potential material for a classical drama. The referee is decreed by Law 5 to have near-absolute authority and sweeping discretionary powers lacked even by most modern monarchs and presidents; but, as I have already mentioned, he shall have to vouchsafe this authority by various means, calling on his own store of knowledge, experience, strength, intellect, and psychology to establish and to maintain it.

The law lists the referee's powers and responsibilities, not separately but intermingled as, for example, when it states that he shall have the discretionary *power* to terminate play for a number of reasons and, so doing, has the concomitant *responsibilities* to send a full report of the events to the proper authorities within a prescribed time.

Another example of a clause entailing both a power and a responsibility is the so-called "advantage clause" which instructs the referee to refrain from penalizing when "he is satisfied that, by doing so, he would be giving an advantage to the offending team." This all-important clause — which we shall discuss in some detail in a moment — is couched in terms of responsibility ("He shall refrain"), but its implementation is dependent on whether or not the referee is satisfied that he is doing the right thing for the game; in other words, its implementation is left to his discretion.

The referee's responsibilities, according to Law 5, encompass three distinct areas: (1) *application of the laws* (enforcement), (2) *technique* (keeping a record of the game, filing a report, etc.), and (3) *game control* (the responsibilities inherent in his discretionary powers to caution and eject, and the control element of calling stoppages to enforce the laws). His powers are elucidated piecemeal throughout Law 5.

Law 5 opens with an indication of the uncompromising scope of authority to be granted the referee: "A Referee shall be appointed to officiate in each game. His authority and the exercise of the powers granted him by the Laws of the Game commence as soon as he enters the field of play." It goes on to point out that the referee's power to penalize is not limited to the running time of the game but "shall extend to offences committed when play has been temporarily suspended, or when the ball is out of play." Furthermore, under "Advice to Players", the wording of the F.A. **Chart** maintains that "Any misconduct towards a Referee away from the field of play will be dealt with as if the offence had been committed on the field."

Several times, I have heard players or coaches claim that the referee has no authority or power over them at half time or when the game is over. In one instance, I overheard a junior player discussing the previous day's game with a friend. He was complaining that a teammate had been "ejected" and his player's pass lifted by the referee when the player had threatened after the game to throw a rock at the referee. I told this fellow that the referee had done the right thing, but he simply would not believe that the referee's authority to penalize, caution, and eject extends in place and time until he has left the area and ceased to be considered in the context of a

referee associated with a given game. If a disgruntled player met a referee on the street a week after a pertinent game and assaulted him, he would be subject to suspension and, of course, a civil suit for assault and battery.

It may seem irrelevant to discuss assaults, but there has been an increasing amount of physical abuse of officials by players who take themselves too seriously and, in so doing, make light of the sport. He who takes soccer seriously has no time for behavior detrimental to the game. Furthermore, violence on the field is counter-effective. The player who is dissatisfied with the standard of officiating will not improve it by misconduct or violence. He will only distract the referee from his immediate task and, through violent behavior, lead the most dedicated referee to throw in the towel. Referees do not expect praise, but they do not expect, nor should they be expected to tolerate abuse.

The initial paragraph of Law 5 concludes with a condition which some coaches lament but which obviously is essential if games are not to be prolonged with incessant bickering, match outcomes and league titles tied up in long arbitration, and traditional "post-mortems" translated into litigation. The sentence in question establishes that the referee's "decision on points of fact connected with the play shall be final, so far as the result of the game is concerned."

Since 90% of the decisions made by the official are judgmental as to a player's intent, the degree of danger or violence involved, and so forth, this little phrase grants great power to the referee. But it also places on his shoulders a burden, for he must be sure of his decisions if he hopes to be fair; and, in the 10% area which is not judgmental but technical, he must not commit errors. He must not, for example, raise his arm to indicate an indirect free kick and then allow a shot going directly into the net to count as a goal, nor penalize "hands" with an indirect free kick. These are not "points of fact connected with the play" but unalterable technical procedures.

I co-refereed a college game in which a skirmish developed in the goal mouth. The other official, at whose end the incident occurred, concerned himself with the action at the near post where an attacking player was apparently kicking viciously at the goalkeeper who lay on the ground with the ball in his arms. I concentrated on two players to my side of the penalty area who had grappled and shoved one another momentarily. I had cautioned one of these two players earlier, so he would have been sent off even for a cautionary offense, but I sent his opponent off as well, even though he had only rather harmlessly pushed the other player. I informed both that I was ejecting them for violent conduct and they left quietly.

My colleague, however, in throwing out his man, whose misconduct had been much more serious, informed him that he was being ejected for "playing dangerously." The player and his coach, who knew the rules thoroughly, were fit to be tied and made a big fuss over the matter during the remainder of the game and after the game. The referee was quite correct in his interpretation and subsequent action, but his explanation was mechanically faulty, for "dangerous play" is a cautionary offense according to the laws. He put himself out on thin ice needlessly.

They could have rationally argued as vociferously that what I had considered violent conduct in ejecting my players was really no more than ungentlemanly conduct, but to do so would have been to question my decision on a point of fact, not my knowledge of the laws. I was correct in my procedures and therefore unassailable technically. In this instance, I tried to prompt my colleague by intervening and suggesting pointedly that he meant that the player had been "dangerous in a violent manner," but before he caught on, much damage was done and when he finally realized what I was trying to tell him, he said, "Yes, he was violent," at which the coach said facetiously, "Now you are changing your decision." He had, in fact, not changed his decision, only the wording.

Referees are, then, not infallible, but they are for expediency endowed with infallibility regarding points of fact. The referee should know this and make sure he does not jump to conclusions. If he does not see something occur, and has no linesman to assist him, he cannot attest to the occurrence. He is, in a sense, "under oath" during the game and must proceed accordingly. He is answerable to his own conscience and to his official assessors. Dedicated referees are neither consoled nor their egos inflated as a result of this "infallibility"; they are rather troubled by it, for whereas no referee has ever officiated a flawless game,* every good official strives to be perfectly fair.

Before going on, I should mention that Law 5 states that "A Referee shall be appointed to officiate in each game." In some areas of the United States, games supposedly played under FIFA rules are covered by the dual system using two officials on the field of play. This is a departure from the laws. It may not seem of grave consequence, but by thus eschewing the laws, the referees are in a sense in turn inviting the players to eschew laws governing their conduct.

---

*Remember the law of perversity: "If everything appears to be going well, you obviously overlooked something."

This proviso for a single authority extends to the procedure for replacing an incapacitated referee who is being assisted by neutral linesmen. Harris & Harris suggest that, should the "man in the middle" be unable to continue, the two linesmen shall continue the job using the dual-referee system. This would be a very efficient and equitable solution to the problem, but it simply is contrary to the intent, spirit, and letter of the law. The designated senior linesman shall rather take over — unless there is a designated reserve referee — and a club linesman shall be selected to assist the referee in calling balls out-of-touch along one side. If there are no neutral linesmen and the referee cannot continue, the game shall be abandoned as he alone was "appointed" to officiate.

Having thus laid down the general guidelines for the referee as well as, by inference, some of the desiderata of good officiating, Law 5 goes on to sketch out the scope of the referee's duties and powers in ten paragraphs. For obvious reasons, a question commonly asked on referees' examinations is: "List the ten areas of authority and responsibility of the referee." (Turn to Appendix I and read Law 5 [(a) through (j)] carefully.)

As I said earlier, the referee's responsibilities fall, with some overlapping in areas covered, into the three areas of (1) application of the laws (clauses a, b, d, e, h, j), (2) techniques of officiating (clauses c, d, e, g, i, j), and (3) game control (a, b, e, f, g, h). Of course, all the laws are related to game control; for example, "adding . . . time lost through accident or other cause" (clause c) could be construed as an item which when appropriately applied can assist in game control, as in the above-mentioned case of taking "time out" to discourage a team's making use of substitutions to delay the game.

Assuming that the reader has now read this section of Law 5, let us analyze these clauses in depth one at a time.

Enforce the Laws! These three simple words ring out with unambiguous clarity, and yet this brief phrase contains all the pitfalls that can beset a referee. His success, assuming for the moment that he knows the laws correctly, will hinge on *how* he

Despite being marked closely, a striker makes his deft inside of foot pass to a teammate. As in top level chess, each player movement is countered by a corresponding movement from the opponents. (M. Julius Baum)

enforces the laws of the game. If he either enforces them blindly or disregards them altogether, he is bound to provoke problems for himself within a very short span of game time. The enforcement must be tempered with the recollection that one is not stacking cinder blocks but dealing with people, and that they deserve the same respect that the referee would want to receive from them.

It is wise, in sum, to remember why everyone has gathered on the field at this preappointed time, whether it is, on the one hand, for the purpose of entertaining an audience and in order to earn one's living as in the case of the professional player, or on the other hand, a children's game primarily scheduled for fun and for the instruction of the players in the fundamental skills and sportsmanship.

It is significant that the very next clause (Law 5, b) to some extent codifies the notion that one shall not slavishly enforce the laws, but rather view their application in terms of the given data and circumstances at the particular moment that a violation of the laws occurs. This next clause is the much-quoted and all-too-often-neglected or abused "advantage clause" which instructs the official to "Refrain from penalizing in cases where he is satisfied that, by doing so, he would be giving an advantage to the offending team."

Hardly has the referee been instructed to enforce the laws when he is told not to enforce them! But this clause is a crucial reminder that the referee is not present as a visual computer meting out punishment but as a highly refined arbiter: to enforce the laws blindly would soon lead to situations in which the slyest culprit inevitably wins out. Therefore the referee will not stop play to award a free kick if he considers that to do so would actually be detrimental to the sporting chances of the party fouled. I shall take an example from a real situation.

A player dribbles the ball past the last defender other than the goalkeeper at a point some thirty yards from the goal line. The player who has been beaten tries in vain to overtake the attacker and shoves him in the back just outside the penalty area. The player staggers but regains his balance and goes on to get off a clear shot on goal, missing by several feet.

The referee has had several things to decide in that instant. First, to allow play to continue since the attacking player, even slightly off balance, has a better opportunity to make a goal with play flowing on than his team would have of scoring from a direct free kick outside the penalty area against a defense which has regrouped. If the infraction had occurred inside the penalty area, the referee would in all probability have stopped play and imposed a penalty kick.

It is even conceivable under the original conditions stated

above that the referee will decide to blow the whistle immediately if friction has been developing between the teams or players and there appears to be a possibility that a delay in cautioning or ejecting the offending player may turn the game into a riot.

Of course, if the referee makes up his mind to allow play to continue, even if he hasn't waved or called out, he should not change his mind, even if the shot has missed the goal or if the fouled player has finally fallen down after all. The rule book is explicit in this matter. International Board Decision 7 states: "If the Referee has decided to apply the advantage clause and to let the game proceed, he cannot revoke his decision if the presumed advantage has not been realized, even though he has not, by any gesture, indicated this decision."

The advantage clause cannot be perfectly applied in all instances, for the referee can never know how the free kick would have turned out had he not decided to let play continue, nor can the referee wait indefinitely to determine advantage but after a certain delay must either stop play or call "Play on!" A referee might call a foul just as the ball pops up over the bunch of players and falls at the feet of a member of the offended team who has an inviting unobstructed area between him and the goal. If the referee could not have foreseen this outcome of the play, however, he should feel serene about his decision. He was, as it were, satisfied at the time of the infraction that it was to the advantage of the offended team to award the free kick.

There is, of course, a side-effect that sometimes accompanies the use of the advantage clause, especially among less sophisticated players: namely, anger and frustration at not seeing immediate and obvious punishment for infractions. If it takes a subtle mind on the part of the referee to make good use of the advantage clause, it is also true that it takes a subtle mind on the part of the player to appreciate its less obvious interpretations.

The referee may find it expedient to curtail his use of the advantage clause partially or altogether if he senses that its use will erode his authority and game control. The referee must be

Following a high clear from the goalkeeper, the ball descends near midfield and the referee must make a quick decision. Contact was made between the two players. Was it dangerous play? (M. Julius Baum)

certain that players understand that he has seen infractions and is opting for the advantage and, to this end, he must use clear signals, waving his arms (or, in college games, raising his fist over his head) and calling "Play on" so all can hear.

The skilled use of advantage is a beautiful thing for connoisseurs of officiating to behold. There is, in particular, one instance when its application requires intelligence, wisdom, experience, and quick thinking, namely within the penalty area.

The application of the advantage clause within the penalty area has been the subject of several essays and interpretations. I have noticed, however, that those who discuss this aspect of officiating sometimes tend to overlook the complexity of the problem, limiting their thoughts rather to the decision between permitting play to continue and the awarding of a penalty kick. This decision, however, only involves the nine major offenses and most people would agree that a goal must virtually be assured before one would opt for the advantage. Al Heery, a brilliant referee who has for years been an inspiration to younger officials, summed it up, I think, when he said that the referee must go on the "basic theoretical and practical assumption that there can be no greater advantage than a penalty kick."

What some people overlook is the fact that the infraction may be a lesser one calling for an indirect free kick in the penalty area and relative circumstances may dictate allowing play to flow on rather than enforcing the laws. For instance, in an otherwise fine essay on "Soccer's Advantage Clause", D. C. Emerson Mathurin writes:

> Many referees argue that the penalty box is the only area on the pitch where real advantage can take place. I doubt if the majority of the players share this argument. I have even greater doubts about the acceptance of this argument by coaches, the majority of whom operate on the premise that 99.99 percent of all penalty shots should end up at the back of the nets. This is one reason why I hardly ever play the advantage in the penalty box. Unless there is absolutely no doubt in my mind that the non-guilty player has a very excellent chance of scoring in spite of the offense against him, I always opt for the award of a penalty shot.[7]

The attitude reflected in the above remarks also is that held by Denis Howell and reiterated in the 1974 NISOA **Official Manual**. Although Patrick J. Smith, who borrows his answer from Howell, does not specifically refer to penalty kicks in his NISOA "Casebook", he seems to be operating on the notion of the high percentage of goals resulting from the prescribed punishment, which is only true, in fact, of the penalty kick. From their remarks, we should retain one valuable concept, however: "If a foul has been committed but the goal is scored before the infraction has been awarded, the goal must stand." They go on to state, as does Mathurin, that they would only invoke advantage in the penalty area if it was inevitable that a goal would be scored.[8]

This is an excellent stance with regard to major direct free kick offenses, but the referee's task is compounded by the fact that an indirect free kick may very well be less of an advantage than a continuation of the play situation.

One of the finest applications of the advantage clause that I have witnessed occurred when a defender made a high dangerous kick near the head of an attacking player receiving a center out by the juncture of the goal line and the goal area line. Here was a clear case of dangerous play, punishable by an indirect free kick awarded to the attacking team, but the referee indicated "play on" and the attacker, who had maintained possession of the ball, dribbled into the center and scored. The quick-thinking referee (who else but Al Heery), who would have been giving at least an equal advantage with a penalty kick had it been a major offense, had the presence of mind to realize that an indirect free kick for dangerous play could not, in this case, equal the advantage immediately at hand.

This critical decision in the penalty area is perhaps one of the hardest to make, but it is beautiful to behold when properly made. The proper application of this clause in the penalty area bespeaks an alert, intelligent, and poised official since the decision must be made rapidly and irreversibly — one will recall that he is not supposed to reverse his decision even if he has made no outward indication of the decision — and yet it requires that the referee make, in effect, two vital decisions rather than one: first whether it is a direct or indirect offense and then whether to allow the advantage or to stop play, noting also in that split second whether the infraction has occurred in the penalty area or outside it in the case of action in a marginal location.

Law 5 (c) pertains to the referee's clerical duties. He must act as timekeeper, bookkeeper, scorekeeper, and general factotum — aside from officiating! I shall discuss the physical aspect of these duties (things like what kind of watch to wear and how best to keep a concise record of the game) in another part of this book, but I should mention here that the referee's proper and conscientious acquittal of his functions in this matter can be quite important. The referee should have all pertinent information in writing when the game ends so that he has a permanent record of the game just ended. This information, jotted down in a booklet or on a scorecard, will be vital when he files a game report and can also be used to refresh the official's memory should he later be required to testify regarding some detail of the game.

What constitutes a "record of the game"? Well, anything that he might say in writing about it would become part of the referee's record, but there are certain things which are generally considered to be indispensable or valued in a game report and should therefore automatically be recorded by the referee. He shall make a note of every goal and the player who scored it by name, jersey number, and team affiliation. He might also add the time at which the goal was scored.

The referee shall also keep a record of the times of the start and finish of the match, of weather and field conditions, and the visibility and correctness of the field markings. He must be sure to make clear and accurate notations concerning the circumstances involved in all cautions, ejections, and in the event of noteworthy misconduct by players, coaches, or fans. When cautioning or ejecting a player, the referee should make a note of the offense (ungentlemanly conduct), the nature of the offense (leaping up to handle the ball in order to thwart an attack), and the time; and he must be certain to take the player's name and jersey number.

We shall discuss the mechanics of administering cautions

elsewhere, but it is imperative that the record be clear in such cases or else the subsequent game report may be vague. Make a note of any unseemly incidents, extraordinary behavior, and the like. In the event the referee has spectator problems or loses game control and must abandon the contest, it is most important that his records be precise and impartial as he may well be required ultimately to live up to the faith placed in him by that clause stating that his decision is final in points of fact connected with the play insofar as the result of the game is concerned. In this instance the "result" is early termination!

Finally, the referee should note down the circumstances of any injury which might conceivably prove serious. The information may prove useful to the player or the league in the collection of health or accident insurance.

As timekeeper, the referee must determine what things, if any, warrant the taking out of time. I have, as a spectator, timed many matches in various countries, and often running time turns out to be full time, meaning that the referee has not deemed it appropriate to add on time for "time lost through accident or other cause."

Time is usually added for delays due to injury, a ball lost in the bushes, stalling tactics by players, and incidents involving spectator encroachment and the like. Once I refereed a game in a forty-mile-an-hour wind. Every time a shot at one end of the field went over the crossbar, it carried into the school's vacant parking lot (it was Sunday) and rolled a full quarter-mile so that a parent had to stand by with his car and fetch the ball each time. Despite the low chill index of -5 degrees, I took time out for these delays.

There are two schools of thought regarding the technique of adding time. Most referees have a stopwatch and stop the clock when they decide to invoke this clause. Others literally "add" time lost, letting time run out and, if appropriate, adding

A player is called for dangerous play and a short exchange of words results. The interruption in play lasts only momentarily. (Horst Müller)

estimated time. This seems to be the method espoused by Norman Burtenshaw in his book mentioned above. In this case, he will add one minute, two minutes, three minutes, or whatever, according to his impartial assessment, not bothering with split minutes.

Some referees do not take time out for an injury until a minute has passed at which time they assess a minute's delay. If the player gets up after forty seconds, no time is taken out. Others wait thirty seconds or some other amount of time during an injury and then stop the watch for the remainder of the delay on the field. Yet others practice a combination of the two methods, taking time out on the stopwatch for clear-cut delays due to injuries or problems with crowd control, and then perhaps adding some estimated time at the end of the game to compensate for additional niggling little time losses through delay of game by players and the like. One would clearly risk forgetting to restart his watch if he kept stopping it every half-minute, as those who kept time in school games when time used to be stopped on every substitution will plainly testify.

Of course, the time can be viewed to some extent in terms of a reverse advantage clause. If a losing team prefers to dally in getting a ball which has gone out of touch, the referee might well decide to let time continue, especially if by stopping the clock the falling darkness would abbreviate the contest and annul it or require that its remainder be played out another day. If the home team is losing and the crowd will not stay off the field, the referee should not take time out until absolutely necessary, but if they are winning, he should take time out right away so that rowdy behavior will not be rewarded in any manner. Rather than stopping the clock, he might do well to tell the captain of the appropriate team that he has one minute or some other designated span of time to get the fans and/or nonparticipating players off the field or the match will be terminated altogether.

Each referee must, I think, find the method of keeping time and compensating for time lost which best suits him. The referee is the sole judge of what constitutes time "lost" and what shall come under the labels of "accident" and "other cause".

Lest one think that I am urging the referee to overstep the power accorded him under the laws by suggesting he threaten to terminate a match before it has run full time, let us hasten on to Law 5 (d) which clearly authorizes the official to stop the game for any infringement and to terminate it altogether when, "by reason of the elements, interference by spectators, or other cause, he deems such stoppage necessary." Again, it can be for any "cause" and effective as of the moment the official *deems* appropriate. As in so many other passages in the seventeen laws, the decision to act is left at the discretion of the referee.

When I was beginning to officiate, I asked an experienced colleague at what point you abandon a game for any reason: rain, darkness, spectator interference. He replied that when it was the right time, I would know it. There is, in fact, no one else who can tell the referee when to stop play due to bad weather nor what constitutes a point of no return in crowd interference. That will be the official's decision based on a myriad of contributing factors. The input may even be heavily weighted psychologically from his viewpoint. He may be in no frame of mind to tolerate disreputable behavior for even the shortest amount of time, or he may wish to see that a game is played out.

I remember that for two weeks running the first senior-game assignment of my career was rained out. On the third Sunday it was raining again, but my game was not called off by the league. As I drove out to the assignment, I prayed that both teams would be there. It was a Third Division game, but it might have been the World Cup final as far as I was concerned. I arrived to find that the field was in fairly good shape but that in one of the goal mouths there was a puddle about three inches deep which covered the goal line and most of the goal area. The coach of the home team arrived.

"Well, do you want to play?" I asked him.

"That's your decision," he replied. "Do you think it's playable?"

There was no way in which I was *not* going to get that first senior game under my belt, and the players looked like they wanted to play.

"You'll each have to cope with that lake for half the game," I said, pointing at the puddle. "I've played on worse fields. We'll have the game!"

The game ended in a lopsided score but there were some good moments of play and I returned home soaking wet but happy.

There is no set rule regarding termination for cause of the elements. Rain and mud are not the worst things to play in and games are canceled by the leagues under these conditions mainly to protect the turf for future matches.

I played as a schoolboy in Switzerland and we played one game in a foot of snow with lines marked in coal dust from the school's boiler room. It was a good game. The following week we played on the field which was a quagmire and then it froze that night. The following week we played our final game, an exhibition against the University of Geneva which ended in a 4-4 tie, and we were cut and sore afterwards because of the sharp frozen mud-licks and as a result of tripping in our old footprints. The field had been playable but not very conducive to good soccer.

The worst field I ever saw was when I played briefly for the Scandinavian Athletic Club of Worcester, Massachusetts, a First Division team in the Greater Boston District League. In late November or early December, I reported to our field for a home game. It was a beautiful cold day and all the snow that had accumulated earlier in the week had been melted by several days of rain before the cold snap. We found that the entire field between the penalty areas was a frozen lake. One could take a running start and slide thirty or forty yards. Although there was not much snow that winter, that field remained frozen and dangerous to play on until March.

Some rules of thumb have been proposed. If rain is not particularly dangerous, lightning certainly is. The referee should temporarily suspend and, if necessary, terminate a match in the event of a thunder storm. It would be tragic if a player were electrocuted while playing and, a bit closer to home, the referee might suddenly find that he raised his arm aloft to indicate one indirect free kick too many.

Diego De Leo submits two rules of thumb as to when a field is unplayable and when there is insufficient daylight to continue play. If a ball dropped from waist height will not bounce, the field is too wet for play (in my above-mentioned game I would have avoided testing the ball in the watery goal area!), and if the referee cannot see the goal posts from the opposite end of the field, he should deem it too dark to play. The referee is advised in the **Chart** only to "suspend or terminate a match on account of the weather after very careful consideration."

Clauses (e) and (h) are mandates to the referee and entail both his powers and his duties. They instruct him and grant him thereby the power to caution any player guilty of ungentlemanly conduct and, should he persist, to suspend him from further participation in the match; and to eject any player whom he considers "guilty of violent conduct, serious foul play, or the use of foul or abusive language." These matters shall be covered more fully in our discussions of technique and game control. Let it suffice to mention, at this point, that the referee's power to caution and eject — when fully backed by the leagues and the regional arbitration boards — constitutes the only tangible "teeth" in the authority he is supposed to have according to the laws.

Cautions and ejections and circumstances which, under clause (d)'s contingencies, lead a referee to delay or terminate a game for what he deems to be due cause must be documented in some detail. In these instances there will normally be a disciplinary follow-up and the only disinterested testimony is likely to be the referee's presumably impartial report. Many grievance and arbitration boards have a sliding scale of penalties in order than the "punishment fit the crime," and they have to know if "violent conduct" was, descriptively, a shoving match or a brutal beating and whether it involved another player or a referee. The suspension resulting from violent conduct could vary from one game to life!

Both clause (d) and clause (e) stipulate that the referee shall file a report. Most leagues and associations require that an official game report be submitted within a prescribed time, such as forty-eight hours after the game. These reports, whether homemade or on a form furnished by one's association, should be filled out clearly, concisely, and fully; and they should be sent in immediately so that scores can be recorded and discipline cases dealt with promptly. In my own local referees' association, we are supplied triplicate forms. If a game has been routine with no noteworthy problems, the original is sent in to the league commissioner, the two other copies are not sent in, but I use one of them to make a personal copy and retain the other for future use should I run out of forms.

If there have been cautions, ejections, spectator problems, termination due to the elements, or anything like that, the second copy goes to the state arbitration board and the third copy goes to the co-ordinator of referees, our General Secretary. In this eventuality, I make an extra carbon copy so that I can retain a copy. There is also a supplementary form on which one can give a full resume if his problems require some elaboration; otherwise one can simply attach a plain sheet. This form is reproduced on page 79. Although it is from the Eastern Pennsylvania Soccer Association, the form is typical of those in use throughout the United States.

It is of the utmost importance that the referee, when filling out his report, weigh his words carefully and be certain to conform to the criteria laid down by the laws of the game. If he is vague, full justice may not be done one way or another, and if he finalizes in print such a blunder as we mentioned earlier — that is, listing the grounds for ejection as "dangerous play" on the part of a player without prior caution — his report will more than likely be thrown out on mechanical grounds, the player will go unpunished, and the referee's competence will be questioned by league and association authorities. Furthermore, it is possible that subsequent legitimate and correctly phrased

EASTERN PENNSYLVANIA SOCCER ASSOCIATION

Affiliated With The United States Soccer Football Association

COPY TO LEAGUE

REFEREE REPORT

This report must be mailed within 48 hours after completion of game to proper authorities.

GAME _____ [SCORE] VS. _____ [SCORE]
       Home Team   Visiting Team

Association _____   Cup

League _____   Division _____

Date of Game _____ 19 ___   Exhibition

Scheduled time _____ AM/PM

Field and Address _____   Actual kick off _____ AM/PM

_____   End of game _____ AM/PM

_____   Score at half time _____ — _____

REFEREE _____   Linesman #1 _____

Linesman #2 _____

Conditions of field _____ Weather _____

Was the home team on the field on time?   Yes / No   If not, how late? _____   No. of Spectators: _____ approx.

Was the visiting team on the field on time?   Yes / No   If not, how late? _____   Markings of field: Good/Fair/Poor

Players Passes of home team were/were not received and checked.

Players Passes of visiting team were/were not received and checked.

	of Officials:	Excellent/Good/Fair/Poor
Conduct:	of Players:	Excellent/Good/Fair/Poor
	of Spectators:	Excellent/Good/Fair/Poor

Line-up of home team is/is not enclosed, not available.

Line-up of visiting team is/is not enclosed, not available.

Dressing room for: Referee: satisfactory/unsatisfactory   Players: satisfactory/unsatisfactory

SCORING

Home Team   Away Team

Injuries during the game

Name	Pass No.	Team	Nature of Injury
Name	Pass No.	Team	Nature of Injury
Name	Pass No.	Team	Nature of Injury

Players cautioned during the game

Name	Pass No.	Team	Type of Misconduct
Name	Pass No.	Team	Type of Misconduct
Name	Pass No.	Team	Type of Misconduct

Players ordered off the field — Player passes must be retained after the game and returned to proper authority with this report.

Name	Pass No.	Team	Type of Misconduct
Name	Pass No.	Team	Type of Misconduct
Name	Pass No.	Team	Type of Misconduct

I received
I did not receive   the referee fee of $ _____ Referee Signature: _____

For additional remarks use supplementary sheet.   Date _____ 19 ___

reports by the same referee will be met with skepticism or even derision.

Law 5 (f) states that the referee shall not allow anyone other than the players and his linesmen to enter the field without his permission. This law is often marginally violated without malice by substitutes coming on to report, by coaches coming to attend to an injured player, and so forth. Technically these and other people should wait for a signal from the referee and, in senior games with limited substitutions and less side-line confusion, the referee will want to prevent such entry. However, he is not self-serving in any way if he makes a court case out of the genuine concern of a coach for an injured ten-year-old or turns an otherwise good game into a display of "Mickey Mouse calls" which are correct in terms of the tenets of the laws but which violate common sense at a given moment. Rather than peremptorily sending off such an offender, the referee might wave him on (even as he is coming on), legitimizing the act and avoiding a confrontation. He can then quietly tell the coach or player to wait till he is waved on next time around.

This clause is most frequently violated in connection with the injury of a player. Overzealous coaches will dash onto the field for the slightest scratch. The referee should not allow this. If a player is seriously hurt, the referee should stop play and see to it that he is administered to and, when it is safe to do so, moved off the field.

The true injury is often preceded by a foul and these are often, therefore, emotion-packed moments. The referee should be sympathetic but firm and, if he has decided that trainers should be brought onto the field, he is wise not to hover around the player but to stand a little off to watch for other problems. He should restart play as soon as possible. The provisions for all this are outlined in clause (g) prescribing stoppage for a seriously injured player and continuation of play when an injury does not appear serious, at least until the ball has gone out of play.

As with most of the other laws, it is *how* the referee administers this clause that matters. If I may be permitted yet another personal example: in a high school game, two team-mates knocked heads and went down like sacks of meal. I called "Play on" as the ball rebounded to an opponent who drove on toward the goal. He beat the last defenseman who tripped him from behind in the penalty area. I blew for a penalty kick and

Despite quick and decisive action by the referee, one coach is vehement. Surely the player who fouled his center half should be ejected from the game! (Horst Müller)

then held up play while the prostrate players were attended to.

After the game, the captain of the team which lost on the basis of the subsequent penalty kick came over to me and asked, "Aren't you supposed to stop play when someone is hurt?" I was on the point of explaining the basis of my decisions when his coach, having overheard the question, intervened and began, "The only trouble with that call was . . ."

"Here it comes," I thought. "Now he's going to lay into me, too."

". . . that the referee called the sequence of events just the way he should have from beginning to end."

I was grateful to that coach, not only for his support, but for his understanding of the spirit of the laws and the fact that there had been a crazy series of events that were not my creation but rather the spontaneous outcome of quite lawful player action.

On the other side of the coin, I witnessed one game in which the way the referee handled an injury, although technically within laws, was contrary to common sense and ultimately had an influence on the outcome of an important game. Team "A" was trailing an enthusiastic but underdog Team "B" by one goal with about five minutes to go in the first half. A player from Team "B" fell to the ground, bleeding profusely from the nose and mouth. He had apparently been hit in the face by another player's head or elbow while they went up for a high ball. The ball had then gone out over the end line for a corner kick and was, therefore, no longer in play. Two teammates of the injured player knelt over him, understandably concerned, and the captain ran over to the referee and asked him to hold up play for a moment as his man was hurt.

I was astonished to see the referee wave off the captain and call for the kick to be taken. The captain exhorted the referee to wait, but the referee ignored him and waved to the opposing player to take his corner kick. The kick was taken and a member of Team "A" headed the ball into the net almost unchallenged. "A" went on to score another goal several minutes later and added several more goals in the second half. Something went out of Team "B" after that tying goal which occurred when they were "short" four men: the injured player, the two men kneeling over him, and the captain who was desperately talking to the referee. The referee may have been within his rights, but it seemed to me at the time that he might have tempered his adherence to the laws with some compassion and wisdom.

Law 5 (i) is, on the surface, a rather evident-sounding clause. It calls for the referee to "Signal for recommencement of the game after all stoppages." This does not mean that he must blow a whistle, for hand gestures and "watchwords" can constitute signals, too. Familiarity with this clause is useful in dealing with the problem of the quick taking of free kicks in which the referee has not had an opportunity to signal. Some referees instruct players that if all other aspects of the law are conformed to — such as the ball being stationary — they may consider the whistle to stop play as a signal to restart play. I feel that this does not conform to the stipulation that he shall signal for the recommencement *after* the stoppage, but I understand that it is done in the interest of keeping the game moving and not penalizing the offended party. The whistle signals the first stoppage and therefore a signal coming *after* it cannot possibly coincide with it!

Be that as it may, the referee will have to learn from experience which method works best for him in a variety of situations and which games must be handled in which way. It is a good idea to signal quickly for the kick and not make the players wait around either for the defense to set up or for the referee, himself, to get into position; but, then again, there are times when — a certain delay having occurred anyway — the referee will prefer to opt for the ceremonial kick, making sure everyone is ten yards off and so forth before signaling for the recommencement of play. In order that the whistle retain its authoritative impact, hand signals should be used instead of the whistle when practical, as on the taking of goal kicks, throw-ins, and the like.

Law 5 (j) tells us that the referee must "Decide that the ball provided for a match meets with the requirements of Law 2." Thank God for this one! Every now and then a captain or coach will try to make a fuss or gain a forfeit on the basis that the only available ball is, in his judgment, inadequate and that he cannot be scientifically shown to be in error by the referee.

The referee should keep this clause tucked away in his mental hip pocket for quick retrieval. It bases the acceptability of the ball on the referee's decision and not on the raw figures of Law 2. If the referee uses the somewhat inaccurate but instinctive thumb-squeeze to verify pressure and hefts the ball in his hand to evaluate weight and then bases his decision on his findings, he is in compliance with the laws! The ball may be an ounce too heavy or a shade underinflated, but if he has *decided* it meets the requirements, so be it!

Before leaving Law 5 — inasmuch as we leave it at all in this book whose every page relates in some way to the first

The opposing coach, too, can see little justice in the call. Certainly the clash was unintentional. (Doug Schwab)

clause of Law 5 requiring that the referee enforce the laws — we must consider one of its little-known but important International Board Decisions. I am speaking of Decision 8 which, in tandem with the better-known "advantage clause", to some extent canonizes in the laws the intangible notion that the spirit of play may at times override the literal interpretation of the law.

In the preceding pages I have spoken repeatedly of the necessity to temper decisions with common sense and of the wisdom of not enforcing minute details of the laws in some instances when to do so will only harm the referee's image, as with the handling of a coach coming on the field to check a hurt player. My justification, within the laws, for such recommendations lies in Law 5, IBD 8. It warrants our careful consideration.

Decision 8 is also an "advantage clause", but it is not so generally known as Law 5 (b); however, properly applied, it helps to elevate the sportsmanship and the level of play on the part of both teams, although its application sometimes elicits dissent, too. It is the one other explicit instruction to the referee to refrain from punishing acknowledged infringements, in this case to the general advantage of the flow of the game itself. Decision 8 declares:

> The Laws of the Game are intended to provide that games should be played with as little interference as possible, and in this view it is the duty of Referees to penalize only deliberate breaches of the Law. Constant whistling for trifling and doubtful breaches produces bad feeling and loss of temper on the part of the players and spoils the pleasure of spectators.

This is a very important paragraph. It suffices as justification for the referee's seeing fit not to interrupt play for a goalkeeper's fifth step, an infinitesimal lifting of the foot during throw-in, or a goal kick taken from a foot outside the goal area. I would estimate that were one to stop play for every trifling infraction, the actual playing time of the game might be reduced to twenty-five or thirty minutes, and some junior games would be reduced to little more than alternate throw-ins!

If the players and spectators understand what the referee is doing and recognize his impartiality, they are bound to appreciate the fact that he is not bent on either taking the game away from the participants or on imposing rhythms or patterns of play on the game which are contrary to those otherwise developed by team strategy and the players' inspiration.

There are, then, two advantage clauses, not one. There is clause (b) benefiting a fouled player, and there is the equally important but less well known IBD 8 which ostensibly benefits the offender — by letting him go unpunished for a doubtful or small infringement — but which should be sensibly invoked to the general advantage of all the players and spectators alike.

To conclude our discussion of Law 5, the referee's *duties* are: to enforce the laws, to keep time and a record of the game, seeing to it that full time is accorded the game with allowances made for accidental delays and the like; to allow no unauthorized persons to enter the field; to report misconduct (failure to do so may result in suspension); to stop play in the event of serious injury; to signal for the restart of play after stoppages; and to decide on the legality of the game ball. The referee's *powers* include the authority: to decide any point of fact connected with play as far as the outcome of the game is concerned; to refrain at times from enforcing the laws, consistent with fair play and in keeping with the spirit of the advantage clause; to temporarily suspend or terminate play if he deems it necessary to do so for any cause; to caution or eject players for behavior which falls, in his opinion, under the several criteria provided in the laws and which dictate such cautioning or expulsion.

6

Law 6-Linesmen

Law 6 has two different interpretations, according to whether one has been assigned certified or "neutral" linesmen or has been sent alone to a game where he must rely on the benevolent co-operation of "club" linesmen who are usually cajoled by the coach into running the line.

Most of our consideration will involve neutral linesmen, but we should say a word first about club linesmen. The club linesman is not to do more than signal the moment the ball is out of play along the touchline. He shall not indicate direction of throw-ins, corner kicks, and the like; this due to the fact that many times these linesmen will be assistant managers, injured players, or relatives of players. The people pressed into service over a referee's career present a phantasmagoria of assorted types. I have had club linesmen whose energy, good will, and technical work surpassed that of some neutral linesmen. I have had excellent assistance from small children and inadequate assistance from middle-aged soccer veterans.

When inclement weather makes the turnout minimal, one is grateful for any help he can get although the laws state that there shall be linesmen. I recall one player's wife who was eight months pregnant who, for want of others around, agreed to run line. She laughed and said it would probably be good for her to have the exercise, and she proceeded to do an excellent job for the full ninety minutes.

On the other side of the coin, one day when the ground was cold to the feet, I had a game in which the players were beginning to grow difficult and were showing a tendency to dissent on minor calls. When a high curving ball appeared to go out and then back into touch, I glanced back to see if the linesman — the nattily dressed manager of one of the teams — had signaled. There was my flag, stuck handle-first in the mud near the touchline; the linesman was standing atop a bench some fifty feet from the field. Thereafter, all I could get him to do was wave the flag from the bench; I had to settle for that since he was the only person available, but I tried to stay near that line for the rest of the game.

It is wise to involve your club linesmen in the game to the degree permitted by the laws. I always make a point of thanking and congratulating those linesmen who have made a sincere effort to be of assistance. Although their duties are limited, those duties well-performed can improve the game, and club linesmen will, like anyone else, take pride in receiving appropriate credit for having done the job well. I always thank the linesmen and tell them I really appreciated the job they did. If they are excellent, I do not conceal that from them. They are an important part of many games but seldom receive the slightest recognition!

A free-for-all which occurred in a youth game I was officiating could, I realized later, be traced in part to my inexperience and in part to a club linesman. It was a rainy day and the lines were almost invisible. One father who agreed to run line looked fit, had a German accent, and appeared somehow to be a former soccer player. I started to instruct him about running line and he cut me short with such a confident "Yeah, I know!" that I assumed he would do an adequate job.

In the second half of the game there was some friction between the players of one team and this club linesman as to whether the ball was still in play or not. Things got worse and finally they argued openly and the language got strong. I went over and told the players that I could not see the lines and really needed this man's assistance and that they musn't give him a hard time. They said that he had been flagging as out-of-play several balls that had stayed in play. At that point

Play is resumed and the favored team is suddenly on the attack. A halfback brings the ball deep into enemy territory, searching for the open man.

the linesman said angrily, "Like hell, every one of those balls was more than half over the line!" I told him that the ball had to be all the way over all the line before it was out of play, but the damage, though subtle, had already been done. Play from that time on was rough, attitudes on the part of the losing team hardened and grew sullen, and just seconds before the game was over, a pocket of tight play in one of the goal mouths suddenly erupted into a melee of fist-swinging adolescents. Perhaps the whole thing might have been avoided had I been more experienced (it was about my tenth game as a referee and I was still loath to caution players) and had my club linesman been as experienced and knowledgeable as he appeared to be!

Hopefully such situations — in which one is not better but worse off for having a linesman's "assistance" — will not occur in those upper-level or championship matches in which the referee is provided the services of two certified officials to act as neutral linesmen, or assistant referees.

Law 6 consists of five sentences (*See* Appendix I). There then follow several Board Decisions and a cross reference to a two-page memorandum on co-operation between linesmen and the referee which is in turn followed by some ten pages illustrating the diagonal system of game control. All this material in the official referees' guide still fails to provide either full information regarding the customary duties of the linesman or how he might proceed in order to do a superior job.

Furthermore, very little has been written on the art of "running line" and training programs seldom give adequate attention to this difficult function either in theoretical sessions or in field exercises before a linesman is sent into the firing line. Every referee should read the two principal texts devoted to this art: Denis Howell's chapter on "Match Control" in his book **Soccer Refereeing** and Robert Evans' unique **Manual for Linesmen.** We shall return to them elsewhere in this book.

The proviso in the law stating that the linesmen "shall also assist the Referee to control the game in accordance with the Laws" is a Pandora's box. This phrase is an open-ended one involving the highly relative or abstract notion of what constitutes "assistance" and "control". For example, the specific law with regard to which Law 6 and attendant memoranda instruct the linesman to render assistance is that pertaining to touchline and end-line calls, namely Law 9 (Ball in and out of Play), but we all know a neutral linesman does far more than that.

The "memorandum" on co-operation reiterates the duties of the linesman:

> (a) To indicate WHEN the ball is out of play.
> (b) To indicate when the ball has crossed the goal line and whether a corner kick or a goal kick is to be awarded.
> (c) To indicate which side is entitled to the throw-in.
> (d) To assist the Referee in carrying out the game in accordance with the Laws.

Items (a) through (c) involve only two decisions: when the ball goes out of play and who last touched it. The appropriate signals will derive from those facts. Were the task of the linesman to be limited to this, he would be little more than a club linesman. The remaining duties and responsibilities of the neutral linesman would, then, presumably be subsumed in item (d).

However, the memorandum's next paragraph elaborating on item (d) scarcely widens the linesman's area of responsibility. It repeats the instructions in the first three clauses above regarding out-of-play and directional signals and then tells the linesman he shall also have the tasks of "Calling the attention of the Referee to rough play or ungentlemanly conduct" and "Giving an opinion on any point on which the Referee may consult him."

This last item involves a passive function since it can only be put into effect at the referee's instigation. The other item ("Calling the attention . . . etc.") is the only additional function allowed for in the memoranda and it does not indicate the extent to which the linesman should inject himself into the game. The relationship between the referee, sole authority on the field, and his assistant referees (the linesmen) will depend on both his pregame instructions as to their relative involvement and on how effective and reliable he knows them to be.

There is no reference to the linesman's responsibility in determining offside infringements, yet this is one of the traditional functions of lining implicit in the diagonal system of control in which the three officials move roughly along the following paths during the game, with a switch of sides at halftime:

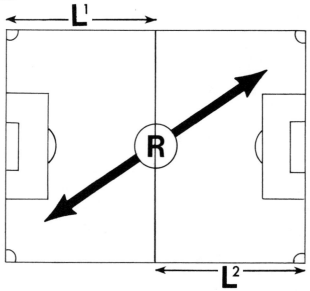

Figure 7: BASIC DIAGONAL

The various duties assumed by the linesman at one time or another in a typical soccer game may actually involve all of the laws. His pregame tasks may, depending upon the referee's instructions, include checking out conformity to field requirements (Law 1), making an initial inspection of the ball (Law 2), checking players' passes (Law 3), inspecting players' studs and other equipment (Law 4). Usually the referee will instruct the linesman to assist him, by appropriate position and flag signals, in determining certain things, such as foot faults and foul throws, goal-line calls on a free kick, ball placement in the taking of various free kicks, corner kicks, and goal kicks; so the linesman is also involved at times in enforcing parts of the laws governing goals scored (Law 10), direct and indirect free kicks (Law 13), penalty kick (Law 14), throw-ins (Law 15), goal kicks (Law 16), and corner kicks (Law 17).

In addition, the linesman is often asked to act as a back-up timekeeper who will make covert signals to the referee to confirm that the periods are drawing to a close or are over and he should also keep a full record of goals scored, cautions and the like; so the linesman is involved in Law 7 (Duration of the Game) and even in Law 5 (Referees) in that he keeps a record of the game and may, in addition, be called on to take the referee's place in case the latter is incapacitated.

The specific instruction that he watch out for rough play and ungentlemanly conduct suggests that there will, indeed, be occasions when the linesman must make decisions involving Law 12 (Fouls and Misconduct). The linesman may even become involved in Law 8 (Start of Play) since it may fall to him to signal an infraction such as a player entering the opponent's half of the field with the starting whistle rather than with the actual kicking of the ball into play.

We have mentioned all of the laws in connection with linesmanship save one, Law 11 (Offside). As they say, last but not least! We shall discuss the intricacies of this law when we come to it in due sequence, but I should mention here that, although not mentioned specifically in the rule book in connection with the linesman's tasks, signaling offside is one of his three major preoccupations, all of which essentially involve not an interpretation of contact (as with Law 12) but determination of the relative positions of player, ball, and boundary line at a given moment.

In short, the linesman will many times be in a better position than the referee to give a fair judgment on touchline and end-line balls going out of play and on offsides infractions even though the referee may have an unobstructed view of the entire area. The angle of vision is a major consideration.

Finally, the neutral linesman is involved — or should work towards being involved — in the totality of the laws governing the game by virtue of the policy laid down by Decision 1 which says that such neutral linesmen "shall draw the Referee's attention to any breach of the Laws of the Game of which they become aware if they consider that the Referee may not have seen it, but the Referee shall always be the judge of the decision to be taken."

I intend to dwell at some length on the linesman's role in my section devoted to technique and game control, and I shall also take up again the matter of linesmen's flags mentioned in the body of Law 6, but we should stress here that running line is important, is an oft-neglected skill, is often very interesting to do, and can, depending on how the job is done, make or break the man in the middle!

It is very difficult to run line. The dynamics and vantage point are quite different from those one experiences as the sole authority in the middle of the field. The new linesman will find that it will take him several games in that capacity to work some disastrous tendencies out of his system.

I know that I, when first assigned to the line, seemed to get worse the harder I tried. In my third game as linesman I experimented with a device by which I hoped to eliminate error. I placed rubber bands on my cuffs which coincided with the colors of the two sides. It was designed to make me point to the right (red band) if the ball went out of touch off the team defending the goal to my right (red jerseys), the opposite mechanics holding true if it involved the blue team to my left. I meant to make the basic functions of the linesman as automatic as shifting gears in a car, leaving my attention free to look for fouls in the field.

I did not realize that I was eschewing the best computer ever made — the human brain. I was a disaster that game. I got so involved in my rubber bands that I could not make simply and with authority the most basic out-of-touch call!

That night I called Roger Schott, the General Secretary of our referees' association, for consoling and for advice. He told me what I needed to hear and provided me with some practical advice. First, he assured me that in many ways running line is

The right wing dribbles quickly toward the goal. At the correct instant, he crosses the ball to his teammate. (M. Julius Baum)

more difficult than refereeing and that everyone has some trouble adjusting to its technique. I needed to know that; but I also wanted to know how to improve. He went on to advise me that for a few games I should concentrate completely on the three basic tasks expected of the linesman, not worrying at all about the fouls on the field. It was important, he added, to remain alert and dedicated to one's duties rather than to become engrossed in the flow of the game. If I were certain that I made all the touchline and end-line decisions and consequent signals and signaled for offside in my half of the field, the referee would no doubt be more than happy. When that was mastered, to call fouls would come by itself.

This was marvelous and sound advice. I spent one game in which I paid attention only to those three areas and by the following game I found myself unexpectedly making some additional calls as though by instinct when those calls were really needed. I found it more efficient than those blasted rubber bands simply to say repeatedly to myself in my mind as play moved downfield "White is defending" or "Stripes are defending" and the decisions and directional signals seemed to evolve automatically out of this fundamental conscious input. It was a device I had used from the start when refereeing but had not somehow thought to use it on the line!

I might add that my pleasure in running line was naturally related to my performance and that whereas I had not liked it when I started, I learned to love the job once I achieved a certain confidence in my ability to do the assigned tasks and to co-operate with any referee on a given Sunday.

I remember with pride a game in which I and a senior colleague, by doing our job efficiently and quietly, helped an out-of-town referee get through a difficult game. Suffice it to say that if the competent referee is seldom appreciated, the good linesman is never appreciated save by one man — the referee who knows how important he can be to the maintenance of game control.

Denis Howell, in reflecting on the notion of having permanent trios or teams of officials in which the referee would retain the same linesmen for a season, sums up the importance of the functions implicit in Law 6 and its addenda:

> I think that would be pretty boring for the linesman. He wants to advance, and the more varied the experience he gets the better for him. He could pick up bad habits as well as good. Personally, I would judge the question on a much more selfish consideration. I should be delighted to have two first-class linesmen with me throughout the year, but I can think of no greater purgatory than to be lumbered all season with a bad one. I can pay no higher tribute to our lining colleagues than to affirm again the great feeling one has when taking the field for a big match with absolute confidence in both one's lining colleagues. You are ready to take on the whole world, and, by heaven, you often have to![9]

Law 7
Duration of the Game

Law 7 deals with how long the game lasts and how its time is divided up with an eye to equitable exposure to field conditions, weather conditions, and so forth by both teams. It, like the three subsequent laws, is brief and to the point.

A game shall consist of two equal halves which shall be of forty-five minutes unless otherwise mutually agreed upon. This mutual agreement usually involves shorter halves for youth games and the addition of overtime periods in the case of tie scores.

Time lost is, as we have already seen in Law 5, to be added at the discretion of the referee, but he shall add time lost to each half, not for the entire game at the end of the regulation ninety minutes! There is only one other reason for extending time beyond the end of play. Time shall be extended to "permit of a penalty kick being taken at or after the expiration of the normal period of either half."

In other words, time can run out before a corner or other free kick is taken and it shall not be allowed to be taken, but the team charged with a direct free kick offense committed in its own penalty area while the game is still in progress and the ball is in play cannot be "saved by the bell." Time shall be added for the taking of the penalty kick, but time shall expire the moment the kick has run its initial course, unless it must be retaken for one of the reasons outlined in the law governing penalty kicks.

It used to be a relatively rare occasion when a postgame

The crossed ball is deftly trapped and boomed in one motion toward the goal. Was the man off- or on-side? (Doug Schwab)

penalty kick would be awarded, but it has become commonplace with the universal adoption of tie-breaker kicks from the penalty spot to determine a winner in certain matches, so it is important that the referee know well how to handle post-regulation-time penalty kicks. We shall deal with this matter under Law 14, but let me point out here that the referee should blow the whistle the moment the ball rebounds into play, goes out of play, or goes into the goal for a valid score.

If the ball is deflected by the goalkeeper, the post or crossbar, or both of these, in a continuous forward thrust into the goal, the goal counts. However, if the ball should rebound from the post out into play along the goal line, strike the goalkeeper and be redirected into the goal, there is no goal and the referee should have blown the whistle at the moment that it became apparent that the shot was rebounding rather than going on into the net of its own thrust. Again, the referee must practice judgment in this matter and it is important that he be alert to all factors on the field.

Unless there has been a prior agreement to the contrary in league or tournament play, a game that has been stopped by the referee before the completion of the specified time shall be replayed. Circumstances may lead to a forfeit on the basis of the referee's report, but the referee himself never has the power to grant a forfeit under international rules.

The half-time interval shall not exceed five minutes unless the referee so consents. On the other hand, should one or more players insist on having the five-minute interval, the referee is not empowered to shorten or forego the interval as he might desire to in the event of inclement weather, impending darkness, or the like. Decision 2 in Law 7 states that players "have a right to an interval at half-time," and the referee must accede to this right if the players exercise it. He may, however, insist that they be ready to play again exactly five minutes after the half-time stoppage has begun.

If there are overtime periods, the interval between the end of regulation play and the start of overtime play shall be left at the discretion of the referee. Such overtime periods shall be equally divided into halves, which is why the NASL sudden-death overtime of fifteen minutes is divided into two seven-and-a-half-minute periods . . . although in the case of a goal terminating the match, the provisions for equal halves will not, of course, be met.

8

Law 8
The Start of Play

At long last, with Law 8 we get to the rules of the game itself! Laws 1 through 7 involved things which must be established or are germane to every game prior to the first kick taken! Now the whistle can be blown and play can start. This very act of starting the game has its rules, however. Play actually starts not with the whistle, but when the ball has been kicked into play by the team designated to do so. To be in play, the ball must be kicked from the center spot, where it has been placed, into the opponent's half of the field and have traveled at least its circumference (no less than 27 inches). There are, however, a few formalities to be taken care of before this initial "tap-off" can take place.

Law 8 begins with the instructions that "at the beginning of the game, choice of ends and the kick-off shall be decided by the toss of a coin. The team winning the toss shall have the option of choice of ends or the kick-off." This coin toss can be made by the referee or a player. I personally make the toss, but many officials like to have the home captain flip the coin. The laws do not say that the visiting captain shall have choice as to the call of heads or tails, but it is customary to grant him that privilege as a courtesy. It is also customary for the person losing the toss to take whatever is left after the winner makes his decision. Thus, if the winner of the toss selects to defend a certain goal, the other captain will automatically be granted the kick-off.

This seems clearly intended by the wording "the team

winning the toss shall have the option of choice of ends or the kick-off," but I know one official who always asks the captain losing the toss — once the other team has chosen its goal — if he chooses to kick-off! The laws do not strictly exclude the possibility of such a choice which could actually give one side both the choice of goal and the kick-off, but custom simply does not allow it to be done that way.

Before the kick-off, the two teams must line up in their respective halves of the field and the team not taking the tap-off must not enter the center circle nor either team enter the opponent's half of the field until the ball has legally been put into play. There shall first have been a signal from the referee to start. If players violate these conditions, the kick-off shall be retaken. In other words, the referee should watch for early encroachment, another player or the kicker touching the ball again before it has moved the prescribed circumference, and a kick-off which travels along the midfield line or backwards into the kicker's own half of the field. These situations call for a retake of the kick-off and, if repeated, may justify the referee's cautioning the player.

Once properly kicked off into play, the ball may not be played again by the kicker until some other player has touched it. The punishment for this infringement is an indirect free kick awarded to the opponent at the spot of the infraction. This infraction occurs most frequently in matches played by younger children who have little experience, but I have had to call it at least twice in senior games! Since everyone must be behind the ball and in his own half of the field at kick-off, there can be no offside on a kick-off. It should be remembered that a goal is not permitted to be scored directly from kick-off. Such an event is unlikely, but with a small field and a heavy wind, such a direct shot is feasible.

The requirements outlined above which must obtain for the ball to be legally put into play shall also be in effect for the restart of play after a goal has been scored (the nonscoring team shall kick off to restart the game) or when a new period begins. The team not kicking off at the start of the game shall kick off at the start of the second half, exchanging ends of the field with the opponent. In the event of extra overtime periods, the coin toss ritual shall be done anew. This is also true in the case of choosing who shall go first when tie-breaking kicks from the penalty spot are called for, but in this last case the referee is expected to toss the coin and the player winning the toss does not have the choice of shooting first or second: his team *must* go first.

Law 8(d) is an important clause. It provides for restart of play for cases not foreseen elsewhere in the laws. Most stoppages will be made in connection with the end of a period (restart by a kick-off), an infringement (restart by direct free kick, indirect free kick, or penalty kick), or the ball going out of play (restart by throw-in, goal kick, kick-off, or corner kick), but if the referee has to stop play for any other cause, such as an injury or outside interference, which does not justify restarting play in one of the above manners, he shall recommence play by dropping the ball "at the place where it was when play was suspended." The ball will be considered in play "when it has touched the ground."

In the unlikely event that the dropped ball should go out of play over the end line or touchline before a player has been able to touch it, the drop ball must be retaken. If a player touches the ball before it has hit the ground, the referee shall drop the ball again.

There are only two Board Decisions accompanying this law. One stipulates, logically, that an infringement of the laws occurring before the dropped ball hits the ground cannot be punished by a free kick since the ball is not in play. If, for example, a player pushed his opponent away in order to have better access to the ball when it is about to hit the ground, the referee should caution or eject the player according to the circumstances, but he cannot award a free kick. He shall drop the ball again.

It is customary to drop the ball between two opponents, but the law does not stipulate that this be the case. There could be none, one, or several players around the ball, but the referee

Despite a diving attempt by the goalkeeper, the ball sails untouched into the back of the net. Goal! (Horst Müller)

should drop the ball in a manner consistent with fair play and expect similar attitudes of the players. It must be recalled that the referee is not required to preside over strategy procedures or stunts which bring the game into disrepute. He can, therefore, tell players not to crowd in on a drop ball if, *in his judgment*, a player or team is trying to gain an undue advantage over the other.

There is a tendency on the part of some referees to cast down the ball. This is not in accordance with Law 8 which says "drop" and not "throw". One can avoid premature action on the part of players and the unnecessary fuss which would ensue therefrom by contriving to drop the ball without telegraphing the gesture or by having the players step back to where they could not possibly hit the ball before it hits the ground.

This latter strategy is the one suggested by Diego De Leo, but I have tried it with poor results. Players are loath to step back. They are accustomed to "facing off" about two feet from the spot where the ball might be expected to hit the ground and they resented being forced back in what they felt was an arbitrary manner and even challenged my right to make them step back. I therefore discontinued this experiment in favor of another method which is very successful and which we shall discuss later in the section devoted to technique.

There is one other IBD. If the Nigerian Eagles of Washington, D.C. wanted the President of the United States to make the kick-off of one of their games and then duck off the field as play ensued, they could not do so, even were the President to agree.

The referee would not permit it, for IBD 2 states that "Kicking-off by persons other than the players competing in a match is prohibited." If a ceremony is desired, it must be done as a phony kick-off, like the throwing in of the first baseball. A fake tap-off may be made by the President, by Miss Tidal Basin USA, or whoever, after which they shall retire from the field in order that the referee might really start the game pursuant with the rules and with only the bona fide players on the field.

9

Law 9

Ball in and out of Play

The law is brief but widely misunderstood, witness my earlier account of my trials and tribulations with an ill-advised club linesman who thought a ball was out of touch when more than half over the line. (*See* Appendix I.)

Amazingly few players realize that the whole of the ball must be fully over all of the line for the ball to be out of play. A common quiz question is to ask how far shall the further edge of the ball be beyond the outer edge of the touchline or goal line for the ball to be considered out of play. A safe answer is: the full diameter of the ball. In the diagram below, only the ball in (c) is out of play:

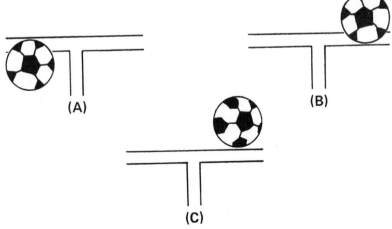

Figure 8: BALLS IN AND OUT OF PLAY

It should also be noted that, according to the law, if the ball goes out of play in the air and returns to the field of play while still in the air, play shall be stopped and restarted appropriately.

Another clause in this rule, which is sometimes not hewed to as it should be, is that stating that there shall not be a stoppage if the ball strikes the referee or linesman in the field of play. The referee and linesmen (when in the field of play) are part of the appurtenances to that field. They are neutral like flagposts and crossbars.

Recently there was heard before a local league arbitration a case in which the referee disallowed a goal which had deflected in off his leg. The goal in question would have been decisive in regard to the outcome of the game. The protest by the team deprived of the goal was upheld and the game had to be replayed. The referee had no business disallowing the goal in this case since no infraction had occurred and Law 9 is explicit in this question.

Lest one think that mistakes are the sole property of the lesser referees, he should recall the 1952 goal scored by Duquemin of the Spurs against Huddersfield. A corner kick by Eddie Baily knocked the referee flat. The ball rebounded to Baily who centered to Duquemin who headed the ball into the net for the only goal of the match.[10] Since the referee is considered part of the field, the kicker taking the corner rekicked the ball before another player had touched it and rightfully the defense should have been awarded an indirect free kick at that spot. The referee may not have seen what occurred, but when the opponent protested, it would seem sensible of the referee to consult his linesman.

No less important is the proviso that play shall continue in the event of a "supposed infringement" until a decision is given, usually by whistle. The referee is the sole authority who may render this decision during play. Players all too often pick up a ball when an apparent foul has occurred without waiting for the referee's whistle.

For example, there may have been a tripping infraction

just outside the penalty area but the ball may have gone out to a defender in a good position to thrust upfield on a counter-attack. The referee may decide to invoke the advantage clause despite the foul, and should the defender handle the ball it is he who will be charged with an infraction. This type of foolish reaction is found at a rather high level of play.

A typical case is the following which happened during a game of the National Amateur Cup preliminary round between defending National Amateur champions Philadelphia Inter and Schaefferstown of the Central Penn League. I was running line. A player was in an offside position on the right wing as the center midfielder moved the ball forward deliberately on the attack. I was poised to signal with my flag were the midfielder to send a pass anywhere toward the right wing. He rather passed the ball out to the left wing who was onside but raced into the free area to receive the ball.

The defending Schaefferstown captain pointed toward the right wing and started shouting "He's offside!" and when the left wing lobbed a center into the middle, yet another defender leaped up and caught the ball in his hands, thinking there had been offside. The referee signaled for a penalty kick, as he should have. The captain complained and the referee consulted me. I informed him that there had been a man in an offside position but he had been clearly out of the play and that I had made no signal indicating an infraction.

The referee, as a result of the information I had given him and consistent with the proviso of Law 9 under discussion, proceeded with the penalty kick. Except for obvious cases where the ball is way out of touch or buried in the back of the net, players should heed the common advice to "play the whistle."

A whistle need not be blown to indicate all decisions. If an obvious goal has been scored, it is sufficient to point to the center of the field and to take out your score card. If the ball is way out of touch and it is obvious whose throw it is, no whistle or directional signal is required. I recently had an amusing incident occur in a Second Division game. In the opening seconds of the game, a player of the "Blue" team tucked a long low shot into the far corner of the net. The players ran back to the center. One of the "Red" players looked at me hesitantly and asked, "Is it a goal?"

"Of course," I answered, my book already in hand to record the score.

"But aren't you supposed to blow two short whistles for a goal?" he asked.

Extraneous noises and gestures should be avoided and may even be misunderstood. One colleague told me that he co-refereed a game between a university team from England and an American college team, the latter winning by 2-0. He said that after the game the British captain came over to congratulate him and said that he had no quarrel with the way he called the game, but did think it a bit unseemly of the referee to show jubilation when the Americans scored.

When my colleague asked him what he meant, the Britisher referred to his having thrown his hands up in the air each time his countrymen scored a goal. The fellow had misunderstood the college signal for a goal — both arms thrust aloft — and it would have been a good idea to have used some more internationally recognizable gesture under the circumstances even if the game was being refereed under college rules!

There is only one IBD accompanying this law. In it we are reminded that the "lines belong to the areas of which they are the boundaries," information already given in Law 1, Decision 6.

10

Law 10
Method of Scoring

The text of Law 10 is quite brief (*See* Appendix I).

It is very important to note the criterion for scoring, in keeping with the logic of Law 9, that all of the ball must be beyond the rearmost edge of the goal line; in other words, the ball must be 100% over the line, on the ground or in the air. The lines are part of the area they delimit and must be the same width as the goal posts.

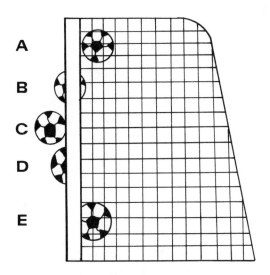

Figure 9: ONLY "A" IS A VALID GOAL

The first Board Decision simply forbids variations for determining a win or a draw. Thus international rules forbid deciding the winner by tossing a coin, drawing lots, counting corner kicks, or the like. The only exception is in the event failing light makes continuation of tie-breaking kicks impossible, in which case a coin toss decides the winner.

The two other IBDs deal with policy in the event of prevention of a goal by some "outside agency" (no goal can be given if the ball failed to go over the line; drop the ball or, in the case of a penalty kick, retake the kick) and in the event of a spectator interfering with play or touching the ball as it goes in the goal (disallow the goal and conduct a drop ball).

There are several facets of refereeing which become magnified in connection with scoring. Naturally, player reaction to alleged improprieties will be greater when a goal is at stake and it is more important than ever that a referee be sure of his casuistry and the facts before him when a goal is involved. The Baily corner kick just mentioned above would not have been retained as a major case in point had it not resulted in an important goal. Usually when there is a petition for a forfeit or rematch, it is on the basis of an incorrect call in connection with a decisive goal.

There are several items which bear underlining. The laws have long stated that a ball carried or propelled into the goal by the hand or arm of an attacker shall not be allowed as a score. A few referees construed this to mean that a goal could not be scored from an unintentional hand ball, so in 1974-75 the word *Intentionally* was added for precision. If the ball goes into the goal off the hand of the attacker but is not punishable as a hand ball — in other words, was not intentional — the goal is to be allowed.

The referee, it will be recalled, is considered part of the field. If a ball should go into the goal off the referee, it shall not be disallowed for that reason. One wag, when asked on his examination what he should do under these circumstances, replied with tongue in cheek, "Signal a goal and run like hell!"

A goal may not be scored *directly* from a kick-off, a goal

kick, a throw-in, an indirect free kick, a drop ball (that is, if no one plays the ball after it hits the ground and before it rebounds over the goal line, it shall be redropped), or directly into one's own goal on a direct free kick. Indirect or direct free kicks going directly into one's own goal from outside the penalty area shall result in a corner kick. If the ball has never cleared the penalty area before going into the goal, the kick shall be retaken.

We shall discuss the critical goal-line call in the second part of this book under positioning and running line, but there is no more important time for good positioning than when there is a shot on goal. The difficulty is that, when refereeing alone, one can never anticipate the moment a goal-line decision will be needed and yet the referee cannot get down to the goal line on every attack. Nor can he tell in advance whether the shot taken will be one like the controversial goal in the World Cup final held in England in 1966 which hit the crossbar, the ground on or behind the goal line (that was the controversy!), and came out again or will, perhaps, be a hard shot near the post that goes through a hole in the net.

In the first instance a goal-line position is ideal, in the second instance, the referee would be better off behind the play, directly out in front of the goal. There is no way the single referee can do everything that a referee with linesmen can do. He obviously cannot be in two different places at the same time.

He can just extend himself a bit more and hope his instinctive positioning will prove satisfactory. With or without linesmen, goals will be scored from time to time on an undetected hand ball. On a corner kick it is sometimes very difficult for the referee who is standing at the far post to tell if a ball deflected into the goal by the near post was played off the attacker's chest or upper arm. I have once or twice had players claim the latter and they may have been right, but I had been screened by the player in question and had not personally seen any evidence of an infraction and could not disallow the goal.

As I have been analyzing the various laws (in my head and sometimes in print), I have slowly sifted out a personally workable and — to me at least — logical approach to just about all of them. There is, however, one item that still bothers me. Its interpretations from "the top" vary considerably, and the various approaches can all be more or less rationalized. I find that I lean one way but am subject to nagging doubts when I see others persuasively justify another approach.

I am referring to the situation (involving both Law 3 and Law 10) in which one finds twelve players on the field when a goal is scored. I have seen or heard three different interpretations: (1) a violation being in effect at the time of the goal, the goal is disallowed; (2) if the twelfth man touches the ball or is involved in the play leading directly up to the goal, the goal shall be disallowed, but if he was not "involved" in the scoring play, the goal stands; and (3) the twelfth player is, according to De Leo, an "outside agent" rather than a bona fide substitute and consequently a goal would have to be disallowed only if this "outside agent" interfered with play or touched the ball prior to the score, play being restarted with a drop ball in accordance with the stipulations of Law 10, Decisions 2 and 3.

I personally lean to the first option but can see how one would favor the second. De Leo's position is incompatible with that which he, himself, and other authorities have generally adopted regarding a reserve player on the side line committing an infraction inside the field of play. In the case of, say, tripping, there shall be a direct free kick since the more serious penalty shall prevail between an indirect free kick for illegal substitution and a direct free kick for tripping. Were we to adhere to De Leo's reasoning regarding the twelfth man on the field, we should then also have to consider this "twelfth" reserve player who did the tripping in the field along the side line to be an outside agent and administer a drop ball.

The elation of a well executed play and the jubilation of first goal are registered on the face of the player who drove the ball past his opposing goalkeeper. (John Marconi)

The offense of illegal substitution without surpassing eleven players occurs when the player enters the field and, if the infraction has gone unnoticed, the infringement can technically but not very practically be punished after a significant amount of time has elapsed. The referee would look foolish and tend to subvert his own game control if he suddenly stopped play in the second half to administer a caution for an illegal substitution which he suddenly realized had occurred in the first ten minutes of play. However, the extra-man infringement remains in effect continuously until the man is removed.

For example, one might claim that a stoppage can legitimize some aspects of a nonreported substitution of a player from the sideline during play. That is, if Player No. 12 enters the field during play and takes the place of Player No. 11 who goes to the bench and then a stoppage of play occurs, the referee should still caution the players, but he can consider that the new player is thenceforth in good standing if he wishes and need not make the players return to their original places and resubstitute properly — for to do so would be a farce under the circumstances.

On the other hand, no amount of time lapsed or number of stoppages and cautions can legitimize the presence of a twelfth player on the field. In short, I would consider the presence of a twelfth player on the field an unfair advantage obtained in violation of·the laws of the game. I would maintain that the extra player — whether he came on without realizing he was *de trop*, as in Ken Mullen's "Case in Mind" No. 17, or had sneaked onto the field surreptitiously — simply has got to be interfering with play, either directly or indirectly.

We have all seen evenly played games in which, upon the loss of a player through ejection, the scales have tipped in favor of the opponent. In today's style of total soccer, many goals are scored by defenders who, finding themselves free for a moment, race up to add an attacker to the front line. Some years ago, many Americans saw a player in a nationally televised British cup final limp around the left wing for much of the game, hobbled by what turned out to be a broken leg! In those days you could not substitute for injured players in such games and, although this man was manifestly useless, his very presence, inefficient though it might be, meant that the other team had to keep a defender out in that area. Conversely, his presence prevented the opponent from assuming sole dominion there.

Even if the twelfth man has not touched the ball, who can say categorically that he did *not* cause a defender either to hesitate between two attackers or to leave his customary post or did *not* cause a forward instinctively to hang back to help the beleaguered defense rather than stay forward in an effort to exploit a loose ball or a long center pass? Anyone who has seen the immediate, even if fleeting, advantage that occurs when a two- or three-on-one situation develops in soccer, hockey, basketball, or any other sport, will understand that a goal scored under such circumstances cannot be fairly allowed if this advantage has been gained through an infringement of the laws. Twice I have stopped play because I ascertained that there were twelve players on one side and both times what aroused my suspicions was a sudden inexplicable surge in dominance of play on the part of the team in question.

In this case, Law 3 is being violated, for it will be recalled that there shall be two teams, "each consisting of not more than eleven players." To allow the goal to stand is tantamount to granting summarily a temporary waiver of Law 3 and giving an illegal "power play" to one of the teams. The goal should only stand in the event that the referee has restarted play — aware of the extra player or not — but the referee should be sure to relate the entire incident in his game report should he realize the infraction after he has restarted play.

Were I, as the official, *certain* that the twelfth man was a "player" at the time the goal was scored (as opposed, say, to a reserve running across a remote corner of the field to get a drink of water), I would deem it a point of fact connected with the play that he was interfering with play as an illegal substitution in violation of the first clause of Law 3 and disallow the goal, caution the offender, and award an indirect free kick to the defenders, to be taken on the goal line.

It is the referee's responsibility to determine points of fact, to judge the all-important factor of the intent of the player (Is he on the field because he intends to play or because he intends to chase a stray dog away from the center of the field?), to be fair to *all* players, and to evaluate what constitutes "interference with play." Needless to say, were the team with eleven players to score against the twelve-man team, the referee would invoke the "advantage clause" and allow the goal to stand, although he would still caution the unlawful twelfth man and make him or some other player leave the field.

In answer to the question: "What action should the referee take if he discovers that more than eleven men had been actively playing on one of the teams at the time it scored a goal, assuming (a) play had not yet been restarted and (b) that play had been restarted?" Mr. Rene Courte of FIFA replied as follows: "(a) Disallow the goal and request, through the team captain, that one player leave the field . . . [and] (b) Stop the game and ask for one player to leave the field. The goal would stand." (Letter dated August 15, 1975)

11

Law 11- Offside

Ah, the offside rule! Yes, this matter is what an administrator of my acquaintance is wont to call a "can of worms." The offside infringement is unlike any other and must, therefore, be considered from a unique viewpoint by the referee. It is the only infraction which is, so to speak, committed by remote control, triggered by a teammate at some distance.

The basic reason for having an offside law is obvious. It is there to balance defense against attack and to permit each player to contribute to the contest to the level of his ability whether his specialty is attacking or defending. I personally feel that defense is half the game and that the offside law does a good job in providing interesting soccer. I firmly believe that a magnificent save by the goalkeeper is as thrilling and admirable as a beautiful goal.

Over the past twenty years, however, a trend toward defensive tactics at times placing nearly an entire team in its own penalty area has alarmed some fans and club officials who want more goals scored. These critics of defensive soccer might do well to consider what has happened in other sports where the number of goals has been increased. Basketball is a case in point. The games that end in a 101-99 score have proved even more stultifying than the old 65-60 games of pre-24-second-clock vintage. It is a fact of life that any device, such as larger goals or the elimination of offside, which will make a typical soccer game end in an 8-6 score will soon find the fans undergoing a "spiral of expectation," clamoring for more goals when the thrill of those few extra ones has worn off.

When goals become too easy to get, we find ourselves hankering back after an "interesting" time when there was the possibility of winning through brilliant defense, of shutting out the opponent! Even as we hear talk of making soccer goals larger, there is talk in basketball circles of raising the basket to put some challenge back into scoring. What is more grotesque than some behemoth with huge paws dunking the ball in the hoop as though he were stuffing a piece of paper into his pocket!

In any case, I feel that the idea is to maintain *balance* between the offense and the defense so that the players and fans can enjoy ninety minutes of soccer and not just those few minutes in which actual goals occur. New methods of attack should be derived to neutralize the strongest defense. Total soccer is perhaps the answer. There are, after all, eleven men on each side. Players will have to be physically able to press hard when they can and drop back when they must, regardless of their position on the field. Just as the milers are ever nicking away at the record time and high jumpers soaring ever higher, so must soccer players extend themselves a bit more. In other words, rather than eliminate the offside rule, one might better consider allowing additional substitutions so that players have more stamina and speed while on the field. Freshness inevitably abets the attack.

There have been experiments in changing the offside law, such as the one in the North American Soccer League in which the player cannot be offside if he has not passed a line parallel to and thirty-five yards from the opponent's goal line. Indeed, in the past the law has been changed, no doubt because it is a subtle law to administer and is at the center of much controversial debate. In 1863 the original laws did not permit a player who was nearer to his opponent's goal than the ball being played by a teammate either to touch the ball or to interfere with an opponent. This was changed in 1866 with the institution of a rule basically resembling the modern offside rule, to the effect that a player became offside if he found himself between the ball and the opponent's goal unless he had three opponents between himself and that goal. In 1907, the player was given sanctuary from offside in his own half of the field.

The important proviso that a player who is not interfering with play shall not be penalized was added in 1924 and, in the

After working more than 30 minutes for a goal, the entire team is overjoyed by success. (Horst Müller)

following year, the number of defenders who had to be between the player and the goal line was reduced from three to two.[11] Most of these changes were made to neutralize tactical gimmicks by which certain clever players learned to take advantage of the existing rules and thus disturb that vital and delicate balance between attack and defense.

Law 11 appears straightforward at first glance, but we shall see that it is, nevertheless, subject to much misinterpretation and controversy.

> A player is off-side if he is nearer his opponent's goal line than the ball *at the moment the ball is played unless:*
>
> (a) He is in his own half of the field of play.
>
> (b) There are two of his opponents nearer to their own goal line than he is.
>
> (c) The ball last touched an opponent or was last played by him.
>
> (d) He receives the ball direct from a goal kick, a corner kick, a throw-in, or when it was dropped by the Referee. *Punishment:* For an infringement of this Law, an indirect free kick shall be taken by a player of the opposing team from the place where the infringement occurred.
>
> A player in an off-side position shall not be penalized unless, in the opinion of the Referee, he is interfering with the play or with an opponent, or is seeking to gain an advantage by being in an off-side position.

There follows but one IBD which provides not so much additional information as an elaboration of something already understood in the law itself, namely a reminder that the infringement is assessed at the moment the ball is played by a teammate and not when it is received by the infringer. It goes on to specify that a player who is onside when the ball is played does not then become offside if he moves forward past the defenders when the ball is in flight.

Every one of the conditions of Law 11 contains something that merits our attention. For some reason, even seasoned referees find areas of difficulty in this law. The first clause contains one such difficulty because of confusion with the clause about the two opponents. It does not say that a player must be *behind* the ball, rather that he must not be *nearer* his opponents' goal line. A player *even* with the ball cannot be in an offside position:

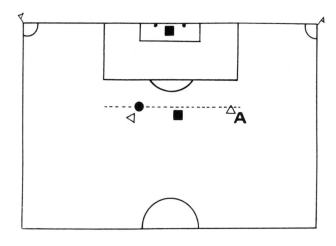

(△ =ATTACKER; ■ =DEFENDER; ● =BALL)

Figure 10: PLAYER "A" NOT OFFSIDE, BEING EVEN WITH THE BALL

He cannot be offside in his own half of the field, which includes the midfield stripe itself. He is not subject to offside unless part of his feet are beyond the line and extending into his opponent's half of the field. In other words, the stripe belongs to either half as the half becomes alternately "his own half" for one team or the other. See Fig. 11 on page 124.

The referee should, however, remember Law 5, Decision 8 in this case and not overstress doubtful or trifling breaches of the laws.

The clause in which it states that a player cannot be offside if he has two players between himself and his opponents' goal line is difficult to assess in practice on the field because of the constant flow of the players, but in principle it is clear enough. It must be remembered, however, that if one is safe if he is even with the *ball*, this is not true when it comes to

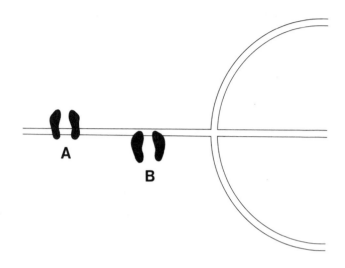

Figure 11: PLAYER "A" SUBJECT TO OFFSIDE

the next to the last defender. The law says he shall have two men *nearer* and being even with one or both of these two does not satisfy this proviso.

The referee will do well to remember this when it comes to the taking of free kicks near the goal. If an attacking player stands on the goal line in the middle of a defensive goal-line wall when a free kick is taken, he *must* be in an offside position since no one can be nearer to the goal line than he! Many times players wring their hands and claim that they couldn't have been offside because they were exactly even with the penultimate defender, not realizing that they are unwittingly defining an offside position and corroborating the referee's decision!

The clause stating that a player cannot be offside if he receives the ball directly from a goal kick, a corner kick, a throw-in, or when it is dropped by the referee is self-explanatory. Some referees think that a dropped ball may be kicked by a player up to a teammate in an offside position without there being an infringement. This is not so, of course. The man who first plays the ball when it is dropped may do so with impunity even if he is standing in an offside position, but after he does so, the regular rules prevail.

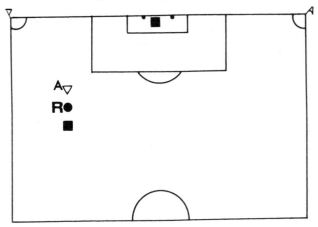

Figure 12: PLAYER "A" NOT GUILTY OF OFFSIDE WHEN REFEREE DROPS BALL

It is a sad fact that many players, despite the clarity of clause (d), do not realize that a player cannot be offside if he receives the ball directly from a throw-in. I have frequently seen even Major Division players shout to a teammate, "Don't worry about him! Play him offside!" about an attacker all alone down by the corner, although a throw-in is being taken.

Less frequently, but often enough, one will have the reverse of this situation in which an attacker being called offside will proclaim himself innocent since there is no offside on a throw-in when in reality another teammate (B) has played the ball between the time it leaves the thrower's hands (C) and the time it reaches our disgruntled forward (A); see Fig. 13 on page 126.

There are certain offside situations which are more likely to elude the referee and he should remember to be alert for these infractions. It is easy to fail to call offside when a corner kick is passed back to the kicker who is now offside. The quick rebound from a defender's clearing shot which instead hits an

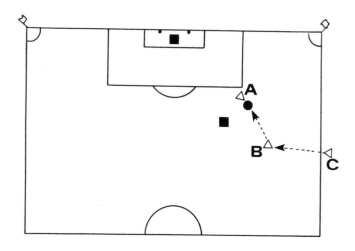

Figure 13: OFFSIDE

attacker and bounds up to a man caught offside happens so quickly that it can go unnoticed if one is not careful, or it happens so quickly that one freezes up and fails to make the call. One of the most difficult calls is that in which all the indications of offside have long since disappeared although nothing has happened to clear the infringer of his guilt. This sort of infraction can even escape an alert linesman.

Examples are the shot on goal which hits the post and bounds out to be played by a player who was offside at the time of the shot but was judged to be out of the play when the shot was taken. Similarly, a player who is offside and runs back into an onside position after the ball was played may be guilty of an infraction even though some time has elapsed. This will often occur when a forward who is coming slowly back upfield speeds up to contest a high punt or clearance coming down near midfield.

One of my finest calls as a linesman went unheeded because the referee presumably did not expect a signal at that point and failed to notice my flag. A long clearance by the fullback went up to midfield. A player was in an offside position at the other end of the field and so far from the action that I considered him out of the play and did not raise my flag. The midfielder to whom the kick came completely missed on his trap and the ball rolled on downfield untouched. The offside player ran back upfield and played the ball. I raised my flag for offside. It was a classic case of a player coming back onside to play a ball and, since no one else had touched the ball since it was kicked, the offside was not even open to debate. However, at least ten seconds had elapsed and there had originally been some 100 yards between the kicker and the infringer. Such are the situations which can give even the experienced official some difficulty.

The referee's difficulties are compounded by the fact that savvy players on the senior level and some junior levels try to use the offside tactically. Some years ago the Hungarian team patented a method of moving suddenly forward all along the rear defensive line a split second before the moment the ball was played, with an eye to placing the opponent's forward line offside. This device is used effectively by older or slower players who are in this way able to make the swifter forwards lag an extra moment before cutting into the area behind the defense. The referee must be careful, for players will sometimes try to fool him if they see the opportunity. When a high forward pass occurs, the referee should quickly turn to see where the ball will land, for that is where the imminent action is. He should only wait to turn his eyes if there is some reason to suspect hostilities or infringements at the spot whence the kick came. It is then still wise to look quickly downfield and then back at the source if necessary.

There surely is no point in watching the flight of the ball through the air. I was once refereeing two very evenly matched and fairly strong teams. The "Blue" team centered the ball, from about forty yards out, up and over my head toward the penalty area. I whipped my head about just as a player on the "Green" defense yelled "Offside!" and jumped forward. The only problem was that he was taking his tactical broadjump forward *after* the ball was played. As he saw me looking right at him, the offside call faded from his lips even before he landed and he scrambled as fast as I have ever seen a player scramble in order to get back around the opponent who had a clear run on the goal because of this defender's unsuccessful ruse.

One colleague told me of a game he refereed in which a British team from a ship in port would string its forwards out along the forward line, just onside, and the midfielder would yell "Now!" just as he passed the ball. The forwards cut in between the defenders like the arrows on a football play diagram and three goals were scored before the host team knew what had hit them and endeavored to take some steps to counteract this tactic.

There are some tactics which are good soccer, and others which are contrary to the spirit of fair play. One such action is for a defensive player to leave the field in order to place an attacker in an offside position. This is not recognized, and the defensive player shall be judged as though he were on the field of play and is even subject to being cautioned for deliberately leaving the field without the referee's permission.

If the defender cannot tactically leave the field to exploit the offside law to his advantage, it is also true that the attacker cannot automatically take himself out of the play merely by being out-of-touch or over the end line. The status of an attacker in the goal itself or over the goal line outside the goal posts — whether he got there through natural momentum or stepped there in an effort to remove himself from the play — has been the subject of much discussion.

In essence, my position is that the player momentarily off the field of play shall be judged as though he were on the field of play; namely, he shall be guilty if interfering with play or seeking to gain an advantage at that position and he shall not be guilty if the criteria applied in the field also apply to him there — for instance, if he is, in the referee's judgment, out of the play or if the ball was kicked back to the goalkeeper by his teammate while the forward is on the ground inside the goal mouth.

Several interpreters (De Leo, for example) recognize that

the presence of an attacking player inside the goal may constitute an infringement, but argue that since the infringement occurred off the field of play, play should be restarted not with a free kick but rather with a drop ball on the goal line. This would be patently unfair in the instance of an offside infringement accompanied by the goalkeeper's deflecting the ball over the crossbar. According to the "off-the-field-of-play" notion just mentioned, the referee would either have to impose the offside and have a drop ball on the goal line or else invoke the advantage clause and award a corner kick to the offending team! A curious and obviously inequitable set of alternatives in this particular case.

In a question and answer session reported in **Soccer America**, Ken Aston gives a genial justification for the clearly fair decision, in this instance, to award the defense an indirect free kick:

> Question 15: Situation: An offensive player is inside the other team's goal. In the referee's opinion he is distracting the GK. The off-side is whistled. The offending player is *outside the field of play*. Is play resumed with an IFK? If so, from where and why? . . . or is play resumed with a DROP BALL from the point the ball was when the distraction was first noticed?

> "Solution 15: Indirect free kick. Comment: There is no official decision on this point. There are many circumstances where common sense must be used in the light of circumstances. A referee should carry out the spirit of the Law and the spirit of the Game and should not be called upon to justify his every decision to 'lawyers' of the game. In the above-mentioned case:

>   a. an offense was committed.

>   b. a drop-ball would give clear advantage to the offending team.

>   c. an indirect free kick off the field is impossible.

> SO — my action would be to restart the game with an indirect free kick from the goal line. If pressed for the logic, I would say that the goalkeeper (on the goal line) suffered the distraction, i.e., that was where the offense occurred.[12]

As we have said, Law 11 is unique in that it finds a player guilty of an offense contingent upon the actions of a teammate.

Most players will be called offside before they have even touched the ball. It is at the instant that the first player "plays" the ball that the relative field positions of the ball, the attackers, and the defenders become relevant to Law 11, for we should never forget that offside and all of the listed exceptions come to bear only "at the moment the ball is played."

To take a simple example, Player A is advancing with the ball and his teammate B has only the opposing goalkeeper between himself and the goal line. Even if B is standing right beside the goalkeeper, he is not guilty of offside until the moment that A actually plays the ball forward to him.

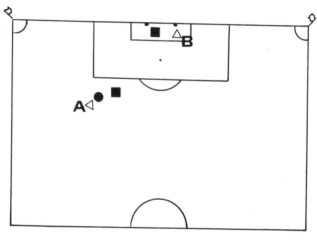

Figure 14

If A simply never passes the ball but dribbles out to the touchline and loses possession of the ball, B never becomes liable for being in his offside position.

Permit me a homely analogy. In school laboratories, one of the simple experiments which amazes young chemistry students is that in which more and more sugar is dissolved until at a given moment whole crystals are precipitated around a string. I like to think of the offside situation in a similar vein. Just as the addition of a few final grains of sugar at the top of the beaker can cause crystallization near the bottom of the solution, so player B is suddenly involved in an infringement because of the instigating action of A, who might be a full sixty yards away.

The notion that A can, by his pass, implicate B in an infraction indicates that there are invisible but binding lines of force between them just as there is an infinite atomic network of interaction in the dextrose solution which only ceases to be theory and becomes reality at the actual moment of precipitation. There is, on the field, a saturated play situation in which offside can, at any moment, be precipitated. It is the network of potentially activated lines of action which govern offside and the referee or linesman who is alert and cognizant of these lines of force will be in a good position and frame of mind to detect infractions.

The invisible triangle suggested by the interaction of passer (A), offside receiver or interferer (B), and the next to the last defender can, of course, extend beyond the field of play, and it is on the basis of this geometry that I would justify a certain stand with regard to decisions involving players who have momentarily left the field of play. It is generally accepted that a defender who steps outside the touchline in an effort to isolate an opponent in an offside position shall be treated by the referee as though he had remained on the field of play; that is, the attacker will not be considered offside as a result of the defender's sly manoeuvre.

And, as we have already mentioned, a player who has gone into the goal proper or over the end line may still be guilty of offside. This contradiction is found nowhere else in the laws save in such matters as stopping play to caution a reserve player − a foul, such as tripping, committed off the field of play cannot be penalized with a direct free kick or penalty kick on the field of play − and merely underlines once again the fact that Law 11 is, indeed, a law unto itself and must be dealt with in terms of its own spirit.

Similarly, in the figure below, the offside infraction committed by D actually involves both C and D due to the interaction already discussed. Thus, although D is a yard outside the field of play, the crystallized interaction implied at the moment C plays the ball forward covers twenty yards. In that case, although the player penalized is a yard out of play, the infraction in which he is involved occurs 95% on the field of play, pursuant with a logic not unlike that which inspired Aston's answer above.

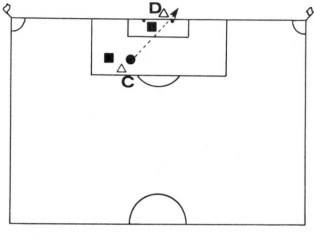

Figure 15

In short, if pressed to justify the free kick, one could use Aston's good argument or argue similarly that the infraction is not the sole responsibility of the forward player and that the lines of force that made his position illegal occurred in part on the field.

I have left one clause — that most argued by top-level referees — till last: clause (c) which states that a player is not guilty of offside if "The ball last touched an opponent or was last played by him." Some referees take this as a very literal phrase, ignoring the spirit of the game and failing to consider through reverse logic which eventualities might have caused the sentence to be written into the law.

At first sight it would appear that any ball touching an opponent will *ipso facto* legitimize the player in an offside position if the whistle has not already been blown. Many referees adopt this position and either allow play to continue regardless of the relative fairness of such action or else try to avoid the problem by blowing the whistle very quickly.

Denis Howell, in his **Soccer Refereeing**, expresses bewilderment in applying this clause and says that he finally figured out a rule of thumb by which he considered that a defensive player *trying* to play the ball and touching it lifted the onus of offside from the offside attacker, whereas if the ball played the defender, play would continue and the forward man would be guilty of offside. This rule of thumb is obviously not in accordance with the laws since one or the other of the calls must be incorrect, in addition to which it rewards indolence and punishes initiative, but I cite it to show how the phrase gives pause to even the most qualified referees.

I have even seen one interpretation which seems to suggest that the "last played by *him*" refers back to the person playing the ball, covering the eventuality of a player running ahead of the ball he himself is dribbling. This eventuality is merely left to common sense, however, and the syntactical intent of the clause is clarified by consulting some of the foreign-language versions of it which translate (in French, Italian, and Swedish) as "If the ball has been last touched or played by an opponent." This syntax makes it all the more apparent that Howell's split criterion is untenable.

"All right, then," one might ask, "What eventuality is covered by the clause if you will not allow a touched ball to legitimize an offside position?" Well, I go on the assumption that the law means what it says not only in this clause, but also in the prior proviso that offside infringements occur "at the moment the ball is played."

In other words, when the ball is played and a player is offside, an infraction is instantly in effect unless certain conditions existed at that moment. Usually it is a teammate of the offside player who plays the ball, but it is possible that an opponent was the one who played the ball, such as when passing back to his goalkeeper. If the ball *at the moment the ball is played* is, in fact, *played* by a defender, there is no

While the sun shines brightly on one side of the field, the beaten goalkeeper finds life somewhat less exciting. (Stan Pantovic)

offside. This is one of the conditions which had to be covered in the law or the law would be unenforceable.

There is one other loophole which this clause plugs, namely that in which a player is in an offside position but judged by the referee to be "out of the play" at the moment that his teammate plays the ball. Should the ball then touch an opponent — perhaps even bouncing out to that very offside player — there is no cause for stopping play. In short, in this instance there was no infringement since, as with the previous case, it is the defender who last played the ball. In summary, if the "moment the ball is played," refers to play by a defender there is no infringement, and if the ball subsequent to being played by an attacker touches a defender, an offside player considered not to be involved when the ball was first played shall be free to play the ball.

Essentially, my view is that if the referee would have blown the whistle for offside had he had the time to blow it and is only prevented from doing so because a defender has intervened and touched the ball too soon, the referee should go ahead and blow the whistle. The F.A.-endorsed "crack-down" memorandum of the Football League in 1971 says that under these circumstances if the whistle has not been blown in time, one shall not blow it:

> Having decided that a player is, in fact, offside, the referee should blow his whistle immediately and not await the result of the pass. If, however, the ball touches, or is played by an opponent, whilst he is going to blow his whistle (but has not already done so), he should not blow it. (The action of the ball touching or being played by an opposing player brings into effect the 'unless' clause, and referees are not entitled to ignore it.)[13]

In direct contradiction to this, Diego De Leo apparently recognizes that the "unless" clause is not needed for those cases where the player is offside and interfering with play. In such a case there is an infraction regardless of the timing of the whistle and it can only go unpunished if unnoticed or through an application of the advantage clause. As far as De Leo is concerned, the clause permits a player to get involved in play or seek to gain an advantage from his offside position once the ball has touched an opponent as long as the player in question was out of the play at the moment his teammate originally played the ball. De Leo deals with the subject in the following dialogue which I have translated from his **Regole del Calcio:**

> Q. Is an attacking player who is in an offside position in every instance put back into the play if the ball is last touched by an opponent?
> A. The illegal position of an attacking player is remedied by the intervention of a defender touching the ball only if, in the referee's judgment, this attacking player was not taking an active part in the action. Otherwise the offside should be punished, even if the referee's whistle is not blown in time.[14]

Thus Howell and the Football League memorandum are plainly at odds with De Leo. I personally feel that the latter's view is the only one consistent with the logic of the law and the chronological priorities established during play; the punishable event by definition *precedes* the intervention which supposedly made it not punishable! In this vein, a defender's hand ball on an offside pass is not possibly punishable as the more serious of "simultaneous" infractions since, no matter when the whistle blew, the offside infringement has perforce preceded the hand ball.

Diagram 10 in the FIFA rule book might appear to contradict the argument I set forth, but these diagrams give no notion of distance. For example, the position of the Player B in diagram 8 would seem to suggest that he is offside on the initial play and not only after the ball rebounds from the post. The book must consider B to be out of the play on the first shot on goal in diagram 8 and in diagram 10, B is even further away from the play and the line of the shot, so diagram 10 — viewed in light of diagram 8 — supports rather than contradicts my contention. In other words, had A's shot on goal not been touched by D, the referee would presumably not have called offside on B.

12

Law 12
Fouls and Misconduct

The most important law other than Law 5 and Law 11 is Law 12 which, for the first time, provides some guidelines for player interaction on the physical rather than the strategic plane. Law 12 deals roughly — no pun intended — with two major aspects of the game. First, it lays down the rules and punishments for specific fouls not to be tolerated in the game of soccer and then it describes, in a kind of supplement to Law 5, the circumstances under which the referee should caution or eject a player for misconduct. Law 13 (Free Kicks) and Law 14 (Penalty Kick) deal with the mechanics of implementing the punishments accruing to the enforcement of the clauses of Law 12.

As with the other laws, Law 12 is designed to permit the player to demonstrate his soccer skills for his own pleasure and that of his teammates and his fans. It is especially Law 12 which, if correctly enforced, prevents brute strength from prevailing over ability, might from becoming right.

Inevitably a player who substitutes strength for ability will commit fouls and run the risk of disqualification. This is a good thing, and referees must see to it that the player with ability is not made the subject of pre-emptive physical action on the part of less skilled players. If Law 12 had been more strictly enforced in the 1962 and 1966 World Cup games, Pele would not have been brutalized as he was and forced to sit out some games to the regret of the many fans who loved to see him play. The laws are so constructed that a 5'2" player can compete with a six-footer on equal terms, that is on the basis of his skills.

The excitement of scoring easily transfers to those spectators supporting the team now ahead. When played before more than 100,000 fans, soccer can become an emotional experience. (Doug Schwab)

The fouls are broken down into two categories according to alleged severity: what we might call major and minor fouls. We shall consider them in the order in which they are presented in the law (*See* Appendix I).

There are nine major offenses. If a player is judged guilty of one of these offenses, his opponent is granted a direct free kick (i.e., one which may be sent directly into the opponent's net for a score) at the point of infraction; however, if the infraction is assessed against the defense in its own penalty area, the referee shall award a penalty kick.

Of the nine major fouls, eight are against the opponent's person and one involves the player and the ball. The nine offenses, which must be judged by the referee to be *intentional* to be punishable, are (1) kicking, (2) tripping, (3) jumping at an opponent, (4) charging in a violent or dangerous manner, (5) charging from behind, (6) striking, (7) holding, (8) pushing, and (9) handling the ball. Some of these fouls are difficult to assess and it is important to recall that, except for handling, they must be directed at an opponent to be considered fouls and, in all nine cases, they must be judged intentional.

The referee has, then, three things to decide when a suspected incident has occurred. First, he must decide if an infraction has occurred (for example if a charge was a legal shoulder-to-shoulder nudge or was hard enough to be considered violent); second, he must decide if the action was committed intentionally (once again, this is a matter left to the referee's judgment as one cannot rely on players to attest truthfully as to their intention and it is impractical to submit the player to a polygraph test after every foul!); and third, he must decide if contributing circumstances of play warrant his invoking the advantage clause and allowing play to continue. His task is not an easy one, for the incorrect decision may lead to an eruption of hostilities between players or toward the referee himself, either case not making the remainder of the game any easier to officiate.

Before discussing the fouls one by one, we should remind the novice referee that it does not necessarily mean that there has been an infraction if someone goes down or is hurt. The referee must first ask himself if the cause for the opponent's falling or being taken out of the play was (1) intentionally provoked by an opponent, (2) mere by-play to a legitimate move, or (3) simply a bit of histrionics on the part of the would-be "victim" desirous of drawing a direct free kick or penalty kick for his team. Ruben Navarro of the Philadelphia

Spartans in the old NPSL would time after time "dump" an attacker without committing a foul. He had uncanny timing and could run shoulder to shoulder with a player and send him flying by giving him a slight nudge at a moment when the man was off balance.

Every referee has had situations in which a player has been injured, even seriously, without a foul having occurred. When legitimately contesting control of the ball a player can, through mistimed effort or sheer enthusiasm, bump heads or upend an opponent. The referee has a thankless task of deciding dozens of borderline cases of intent every game.

I remember one coach becoming outraged when I did not call a foul on a player who had apparently tripped that coach's man. In fact, the player had tried to leap over the legs of the other man who had committed himself physically to a sliding tackle. He did not jump high enough, however, and tripped himself much as a horse will when not clearing a jump. The sliding player had not raised his leg to trip the other player or it would, of course, have been a foul.

In another game, two opponents simultaneously blasted a ball that was about waist high and one of the players went off in a dramatic cartwheel. The spectators booed when they heard no whistle, but neither player had committed an infraction, nor had they even touched one another, making contact exclusively with the ball. The player who spun off was simply the victim of an extraordinary transference of kinetic energy. Keeping in mind that teammates cannot technically "foul" one another (although certain behavior may constitute misconduct), the referee must be careful not to blow the whistle if a player commits one of the bodily fouls on a teammate.

A careful reading of the law reveals that several of the nine offenses do not require that contact be made between players for the foul to be signaled. It is sufficient to *attempt* to strike, kick, or trip an opponent for the referee to whistle for an infraction; and to jump at a player does not mean that the infringer must actually make contact.

Some referees use a mnemonic device to remember the

nine major offenses: two 'with the feet, three with the body, four with the hands.

HOLDING
PUSHING
STRIKING
HANDLING

JUMPING AT
OPPONENT
CHARGING IN
A VIOLENT OR
DANGEROUS
MANNER
CHARGING
FROM BEHIND

KICKING
TRIPPING

Figure 16: THE NINE MAJOR OFFENSES
two with the feet; three with the body; four with the arms

The first clause states that it is an offense if a player intentionally "Kicks or attempts to kick an opponent." This is a serious infringement because the condition that the infraction be intentional to be considered punishable means that to call this foul at all is to accuse a player of an ungentlemanly or violent act. Although it is conceivable that it could be a foul without misconduct, the player charged with kicking or attempted kicking should generally draw at least a caution and possibly an ejection.

Figure 17: KICKING AN OPPONENT

A player who intentionally "Trips an opponent, i.e., throwing or attempting to throw him by the use of the legs or by stooping in front of or behind him" is guilty of committing a foul. One seldom calls attempted tripping unless it is at least partially successful, but from time to time a definite gesture to trip which only fails because the infringer couldn't quite bring it off, will be called.

Tripping is generally done by hooking the foot in the legs of the opponent, but it also is the charge leveled if tripping is done with the body. Some people laugh or look dismayed when the referee indicates "tripping" by word or a swing of the foot after someone has been sent tumbling over an opponent's back; but that is, indeed, the call to make, and not some coinage like "low bridge" which is never mentioned in the laws! In enforcing this law about tripping, the referee must be doubly sure to ascertain intention and the timing of contact and what sort of contact has been made. Often a player brings down another when tackling him and the following reasons might cause the referee *not* to assess a free kick:

1) the referee might have seen that the tackler made contact with the ball first and that the dribbler fell over the ball or over the opponent's leg after the latter had secured the ball;

2) he might have understood that the dribbler changed direction after the challenger had committed himself to a tackle and decided, therefore, that the tripping was unintentional;

3) he may decide that the dribbler has "taken a dive" in an effort to make it look like he was tripped.

These are cases in which there had, in fact, not been an infringement, besides which the advantage clause might be appropriate if there was a real infringement but the offended team had a chance to score which would be diminished by stopping play.

The clause which follows makes it an offense if a player "Jumps at an opponent." This does not mean that a player cannot jump into the air to play the ball. The possibility of there being some misunderstanding here no doubt prompted the addition of the advice to referees in the **Chart** that "it is jumping at an opponent, and not jumping for the ball, that is a foul," to which they add that there is "no such thing as accidental jumping at an opponent." If the referee sees a player jumping at an opponent, he must call the foul, unless he invokes the advantage clause, although he could in marginal cases charge the player with the lesser offense of "dangerous play."

There are two frequent forms which this jumping at a player will take. There is the foot-first broad jump at a player, and there is the sideways flying leap at the player who is going up for a head ball. See Fig. 18 A-B, pp. 144-5.

Charging "an opponent in a violent or dangerous manner" is an offense. Only the referee can decide the borderline here. It is on the basis of this clause and the general spirit of the game that I would discredit Ted Smits' unfortunate assertion, in an

(18a) Feet First
Figure 18: PLAYER JUMPING AT OPPONENT

otherwise pleasant enough book called **Soccer for the American Boy,** that

> It is always possible to be rough in soccer within, or at least
> almost within, the rules. In the charge, for instance, it is legal
> to hit hard with the shoulders an opponent who has the
> ball.[15]

Furthermore, Smits defines "Charge" in his glossary as a "legal, sometimes violent, attack on an opponent who has possession of the ball." This is a nonsequitur as any "violent" contact is forbidden by the word and spirit of the soccer laws and is even likely to lead to the ejection of the offending player.

(18b) Sideways

It is legal to charge shoulder to shoulder when within playing distance of the ball and when definitely competing for control of the ball, and it may be done fairly hard, but not violently or so hard as to become pushing. Furthermore, the hands should not be used to hold off or restrain the opponent, an infraction Pele has frequently gotten away with committing. It is also not fair to take advantage of this privilege by doing such things as charging the player when he has his feet off the ground and cannot control his body. Such a charge, even shoulder to shoulder, can be construed as dangerous.

Frequently players think they can charge an opponent with the shoulder, regardless of the position of that opponent. Once when I called a foul on a player who had just charged with his shoulder right in the opponent's spine, the infringer looked at me in genuine astonishment and exclaimed, "I charged him with my shoulder! Our high school coach said we could charge with the shoulder!"

The charge in the back is especially common, enough so that the next clause specifies that a player is guilty if he intentionally "Charges an opponent from behind unless the latter be obstructing." The tail end of this clause is sometimes misinterpreted to the disadvantage of one player or the other. What it permits is a charge from behind if the player with the ball turns his back to protect the ball as when he is dribbling or is shielding a ball to let it go out of bounds. Although he may, under such conditions, be charged from behind, he may not be charged violently or dangerously or pushed or pulled off the ball. One of the IBDs (No. 2) pertains to this sort of contact: "If a player deliberately turns his back to an opponent when he is about to be tackled, he may be charged but not in a dangerous manner." See Fig. 19, page 147.

It is perhaps appropriate to point out that it is almost impossible to tackle a player from behind and get the ball without committing some kind of infraction if the man is not obstructing. Depending on how the player approaches his opponent, he is apt to commit tripping, jumping at the player, kicking, or charging from behind; and even if the referee is

*Figure 19: PLAYER SHIELDING BALL MAY BE
CHARGED FROM BEHIND*

certain that the player intended to tackle the ball and just
mistimed his slide, unless he does get the ball first, he shall be
judged guilty of dangerous play (indirect free kick).

If a player is dribbling along at normal pace, pursued by an
opponent, the latter might be able to hook his leg around or
between the legs of the man in possession of the ball and take
or flick it from him without first hitting the man or endangering
him, but it is a very difficult feat indeed. If he so much as grazes
the player on his way through from behind, assuming the player
with the ball is not obstructing, I feel an infraction should be
called, because such tactics are generally successful not in
securing the ball but rather in causing serious injury to the
dribbler and should, therefore, be discouraged. Charging from
behind was one of the fouls which the famous Football League
memorandum of 1971 aimed at eliminating.

The offense of a player who "Strikes or attempts to strike
an opponent" is like that of kicking. If intentional it will
normally draw a caution or very possibly an ejection, as well as

the direct free kick. The referee's action will depend on the circumstances.

I recently had a situation where a player struck an opponent with his elbow while they were up heading the ball. It was not premeditated like a dirty trick or deliberate like a swinging punch in a fight, but rather a nasty reflex of the kind that brings the game into disrepute. In this case I cautioned the player instead of ejecting him; but many times striking will be done in a manner so as to constitute grounds for ejection. Again, even attempting to strike an opponent is a foul, and should a player take a swing at an opponent and miss, the referee should take the appropriate action.

The clause against holding an opponent was abbreviated in 1974-75 in order to encompass any kind of holding, not just with the arms and hands. A player who is on the ground will sometimes put a scissors grip on an opponent's leg to prevent him from pursuing a loose ball. This is holding. Sometimes two players will collaborate to immobilize or "sandwich" a player and deprive him of his freedom of movement. This is generally interpreted as holding. An arm held out to prevent an opponent from passing is holding rather than obstruction.

Pushing an opponent is an infraction. This can be with the hand, the body, or any part of the anatomy. Pushing is generally not too difficult to detect, the only problem being in deciding when a legal shoulder charge or back charge against an obstructing player goes beyond the acceptable limit and becomes pushing. And, as we have mentioned, some players in possession of the ball have a tendency to push off challengers with their hands; this must be distinguished from a normal protective gesture to avoid undue contact or injury. Experience is the best mentor in this matter.

One of the hardest calls to make is that when the goalkeeper pushes away a player from in front of the goal. The attacker is not allowed to obstruct the goalkeeper, but even should he be obstructing — and it is possible that he is not — the goalkeeper has no right to push him away, any more than a fullback would. Sometimes, however, goalkeepers think that their privilege of using the hands extends to infighting in front of the goal.

The unfortunate thing is that the goalkeeper might find himself facing a penalty shot for pushing whereas he might rather have been taking an indirect free kick for his team had he played the ball instead of trying to take care of the man first! Referees might understand, however, that the goalkeeper feels stymied and frustrated during the taking of corner kicks and indirect free kicks near the goal if a player or players get close to him and crowd and jostle him as he is getting set to await the kick; it is important that the referee be alert for obstruction and intervene in favor of the goalkeeper if necessary as soon as the kick is taken and the obstructive action becomes a factor.

A player is guilty of an infraction if he "Handles the ball, i.e., carries, strikes or propels the ball with his hand or arm," excluding of course the goalkeeper in his own penalty area. This call is very often misunderstood. Attackers think that every ball hitting a defender's hand or arm is an infraction and every ball hitting their own hands an accident! Indeed, the requirement that the fouls be intentional includes hand balls.

The ball must be played by the hand, either by definite gesture or by a willed refusal to move the hand out of the way. It is somewhat like the hit-batsman rule in baseball. The player might be expected to make a reasonable effort to get his hand out of the way of the ball; if despite that he is struck by the ball, play should continue. For example, if the players in a defensive wall held their arms high over their heads and did not move them and the free kick hit an arm, one could technically say that the ball played the arm, but it is obvious that an infraction has been committed, the players having placed their arms in an unnatural position in an effort to gain an unfair advantage contrary to the spirit of the game.

Conversely, a player running with his back to the ball, as in an effort to get back into a defensive position on a quick free kick, could hardly be said to have intentionally played the ball if the ball strikes him in the triceps when he is not even facing the action, even if his arm happens to be on the backswing at the moment it is struck. A foul would be in order, however, if the player swung his arm out and back in a blind effort to stop the ball and miraculously succeeded in hitting it.

The arm is considered to be an area up straight through the shoulder joint, as in the illustration, and players sometimes do not realize that a ball hitting the upper arm or shoulder bend falls under the handling clause.

Figure 20: "HANDS" ALL THE WAY TO SHOULDER JOINT
Broken Line depicts area considered

There is a sequence in the Pele Pepsi-Cola training films which shows the maestro juggling the ball variously on his instep, thigh, head, chest, and shoulders. At one point he bounces the ball from shoulder to shoulder and whereas some of the balls are in near the collarbone and quite legal, others are out beyond the line extending up from the ribs and would constitute "handling" in a real game.

There is a fine line as to whether hands should be called or not. New referees tend to call it more often than seasoned referees, the latter having come to realize that few hand balls in a game are intentional. The hand ball used as a tactic is another matter and should be dealt with severely. For example, the hand deliberately knocking a ball into the goal, the grabbing of a high center to thwart an attack plan, or the hand ball which knocks a sure goal out of the goal mouth before it crosses the line (or even if it has crossed the line, for that matter, but the player thinks the referee may not have seen that it did), should draw a caution for ungentlemanly conduct.

However, if a goal is scored off the hand or arm and the referee is certain it was an accident and that the ball was not intentionally propelled, the goal should stand. Like the valid goal deflected off a referee, this one going in off a hand or arm is bound to· provoke dissent and the referee must not only be sure of his decision but must also remain steadfast in that decision once he has made it. It is one of those courageous and, at least from one team's viewpoint, unpopular calls that a referee has to make from time to time.

The punishment for these nine fouls is a direct free kick, as we have said, with the exception of inside the penalty area on the part of the defense: then it is a penalty kick. It is especially important, within that area, that the referee be certain his punishment fits the crime. I do not mean that he should call hand balls anything less than that; but he must remember that he is granting an almost certain goal to the offense when awarding a penalty kick.

He must, in short, be certain that the charge from behind was not legitimized through obstruction on the part of the

Second half action becomes a case of midfield play. Neither team seems able to penetrate near the opponent's goal. (Horst Müller)

other player, he must be certain that the hand ball was not inadvertent, and he must be sure that what he is about to call jumping at the player is not perhaps rather a case of dangerous play by an over-zealous neophyte. Once he has made his decision he should not hedge on the call or on the location of the infraction. If the defender intentionally trips an opponent out by the corner of the penalty area but clearly inside the area — or clearly on the line, for that matter — the referee should not place the ball just outside, but should call a penalty kick. He should only place it outside if he is sure of the foul but uncertain as to whether it was committed inside or outside the area. In such doubtful cases, one should give the advantage to the defense, doing so impartially at both ends of the field.

It is important to remember that the point of the infraction is what counts and not necessarily where the ball or the body was when it occurred. For example, a player in his own penalty area strikes an opponent while the ball is at midfield. This calls for a penalty kick and ejection of the player.

It is to be recalled, however, that the ball must be in play for such a foul to be punished by a free kick. In other words, had the incident I have just mentioned occurred in the penalty area while the ball was out of touch, the referee could discipline the player (ejecting him for violent conduct) but could not award a free kick; play would rather restart with the throw-in as though the incident had not occurred.

One of the closest calls I have had to make involved this factor of the ball being in or out of play. The "Red" attacker had beat the "Blue" defense and was driving on goal. A "Blue" player was running behind him and it was obvious he was about to trip the "Red" player in a desperate effort to prevent a shot. Just after the "Red" player got off a shot, he was taken down. The shot missed the goal by a foot. I awarded a penalty kick as the ball had not yet crossed the line out of play when the tripping infraction occurred. Had the tripping taken place a split second later, I should not have been able to award the penalty kick as the ball would have been out of play. The "Blue" coach was upset and maintained that since the player had taken a shot, I should have applied the advantage.

As I have said elsewhere, the referee should go on the assumption that there can be no advantage greater than a penalty kick, save perhaps a goal actually in the net. As the shot was taken I could not see where it was going and had no reason whatever to feel that a goal was inevitable and therefore I did not invoke advantage. Had the ball entered the goal in this instance I should have been obliged to disallow it and have the penalty kick taken since I had blown the whistle before the ball went over the line. In this case my instincts proved right and the fact that the shot the player got off was close rather than a clumsy slice out to the sideline should not make the tripping less of a foul. The defender had deliberately — I might even say flagrantly — tripped an opponent in his own penalty area while the ball was in play. These criteria warrant the awarding of a penalty kick even if the ball is on the goal line on its way out of play at the instant the infraction takes place.

There are lesser infringements, punishable by an indirect

free kick (which must touch another player before entering the goal for a valid score) awarded to the opponent, whether the foul occurred in the penalty area or elsewhere in the field of play. These are enumerated in Law 12 and I shall reiterate them one at a time with accompanying commentary.

"Playing in a manner considered by the Referee to be dangerous, e.g., attempting to kick the ball while held by the goalkeeper." This infringement, usually called simply "dangerous play" covers a multitude of sins. The most common examples, aside from the example given in the clause, are the high kick, the low head, and reckless play which might endanger others.

Dangerous play must be done in the vicinity of an opponent to be assessed. The high kick, low head, and hitch-kick (a variation of the high kick) are usually considered dangerous within a yard or two of an opponent, it being at the referee's discretion to judge this matter. Often two opponents will go for a ball, one with a high kick, the other with a low head, and the referee shall judge which is the offender. In the event of equal infringement here, I penalize the high kicker as he is endangering others whereas the low header is endangering himself. Some referees would, in such an instance, give the benefit of the doubt to the defense. The important thing is that one be consistent in his policy.

It is a shame that some beautiful goals, such as a diving head shot, must be disallowed due to dangerous play, but were one not to enforce this concept, one could hardly blame defenders who then tried to kick clear the ball even though they might hit the opponent in the head.

Reckless play endangering others is an umbrella for a variety of acts which are dangerous but don't quite fall under the nine major offenses. Disregarding the safety of others when making a running leap to head a ball is a good example. Playing with enthusiasm is one thing, playing with wanton abandon is quite another! The law is vague and thus it is up to the referee to determine what is dangerous in a given situation on the field. The referee may judge that a player did not deliberately charge from behind or jump at a player, but that he did intentionally leap through the air in what is, in fact, a dangerous manner; he need not have set out to make the leap or charge dangerous.

This foul ("dangerous play") is a useful one to call when the referee cannot unhesitatingly call a major foul because he is in doubt about the intentions of the guilty player. If a player crashes into an opponent and the referee is not sure the player has intentionally committed a violent charge, he may call, instead, an indirect free kick for dangerous play. As we have said, a player can be called for dangerous play without his having *intended* to be dangerous, as with a high kick near the head of an opponent whom he has failed to realize is near at hand. He certainly *intended* to kick high. Similarly, a player can be judged to have intended to run fast where congestion would have dictated caution, and so forth.

It is not unlike telling a policeman you went through a red light because the light changed when you were too close to it to stop without ending up in the middle of the intersection; to which he properly answers, "You would only end up in the intersection if you were driving at a speed excessive for the conditions at hand." Catch-22!

There is no description in the laws of what constitutes a high kick or a low head. Some referees will say that stomach-high in either direction is a good gauge, but such rules of thumb can prove lamentably inadequate, especially in juvenile games where a tall gangling player may kick knee-high in relation to himself and the foot will be in the chest of a tiny adversary. You must protect all the players and yet you cannot forbid the tall player to kick the ball. The referee must make a decision in each instance on the basis of the action at hand.

"Charging fairly, i.e., with the shoulder, when the ball is not within playing distance of the players concerned and they are definitely not trying to play it." This is a relatively infrequent offense since the contact away from the ball, if intentional, will usually be obstruction rather than a fair charge. The punishment being the same for these two, the distinction is perhaps academic. This clause makes illegal the act of riding the player off the ball with a legal shoulder skirmish if the ball is not within a distance that is considered playable, say six or ten feet and in line with the direction the players are running. In other words, if the ball were within playing distance, the action punishable under this clause would be considered legal.

"When not playing the ball, intentionally obstructing an opponent i.e., running between the opponent and the ball, or interposing the body so as to form an obstacle to an opponent." Obstruction takes several forms. It is the act of blocking a player out of the play when you yourself are not playing the ball. This kind of obstruction cannot be justified. It is done when one player blocks for another who is dribbling by him or when a player passes off the ball and then steps sideways or backwards to block an opponent who might pursue the ball.

A common variation is the action taken by a defender when an opponent has kicked the ball forward and tries to run around the defender only to have the latter step sideways into his path. What I like to call "cuttin' them off at the pass" is also a form of obstruction: namely running across the path of a player to slow him down or to obscure his vision. This action is often taken by a defender who runs between his goalkeeper and an advancing striker.

It is common practice for backs to try to provide some protection for their goalkeeper, but they are subject to penalties if they do not obstruct in a legal manner. Legal obstruction is the shielding of the ball when it is within playing distance. It is a good tactic to keep rotating or pivoting around the ball when dribbling in a tight spot so as to interpose the body between the ball and one's opponent.

Similarly, if one is technically playing the ball, he may hover over it and slow down his pace so as to prevent an opponent from getting it before it goes out of touch or reaches the goalkeeper's outstretched hands. The person so obstructing is not allowed, however, to back into a player in an effort to keep him from charging through to the ball. The referee must remember that the player being thus legally obstructed may charge the opponent from behind, albeit not dangerously.

Decision 7 states: "If a player covers up the ball [by this they mean hunching over the ball when dribbling so as to protect the ball with the body, not covering it on all fours, for this would constitute dangerous play if an opponent were in the vicinity] without touching it in an endeavour not to have it played by an opponent, he obstructs but does not infringe Law 12 para. 3 [here under discussion] because he is already in possession of the ball and covers it for tactical reasons whilst the ball remains within playing distance. In fact, he is actually playing the ball and does not commit an infringement; in this case, the player may be charged because he is in fact playing the ball."

"Charging the goalkeeper except when he − (a) is holding the ball; (b) is obstructing an opponent; (c) has passed outside his goal-area." This section of the law is tricky and requires wisdom in its use. If one were to misread this section of Law 12, he might allow the attacker to run up and stand shoulder to shoulder with the goalkeeper as long as the latter is holding the ball. This is obviously not what the law intends by (a) above! Elsewhere, in Decision 9, the rule book indicates that it is a cautionary offense to attempt to prevent the goalkeeper from putting the ball into play, and we have already noted that it is dangerous play to attempt to kick the ball whilst it is held by the goalkeeper.

In other words, there is a brief instant when a fair charge on the goalkeeper is allowable in the goal area. He may not be *charged* before he has secured the ball, presumably because he is vulnerable when concentrating on catching or deflecting the ball. The **Chart** advises the referee to "See that the goalkeeper is not unfairly charged, as he has so little chance of protecting himself when his attention is engaged with a coming shot."

Once he is firmly in control of the ball he may not be prevented from getting rid of the ball promptly as the next clause will demand that he do, so the attacking player can make legal shoulder to shoulder contact with the goalkeeper in his goal area only during the brief time that the ball is held but before firm possession is established. This means that a player, if his timing is good, might legally go up for a head ball in competition with the goalkeeper and not be afraid that if he touches the goalkeeper after the keeper catches it there will be a foul assessed.

The slight possibility of a goalkeeper being legally nudged off balance in that split second after he has caught hold of the ball and is falling into the goal is, no doubt, why many world-class goalkeepers will never handle a high cross or corner kick coming across the goal mouth but will rather deflect it over the crossbar. They could often easily catch the ball but would, in so doing, come down on or near the goal line.

If the keeper is obstructing a player, he may be charged in his goal area, even if he is not holding the ball. This sometimes results during byplay in the goal mouth on a corner kick although it is more frequently the goalkeeper who is obstructed.

Outside his goal area the goalkeeper may be charged fairly. However it is rarely possible to do so, for to charge him fairly the ball must be within playing distance and if that is the case the goalkeeper will often be stooping, diving, or in some other way tending to his duties in the expected fashion. Under such circumstances a fair shoulder charge is not easy! There is a certain contradiction in roles held by the goalkeeper and the regular player, and when these roles clash, it is usually the goalkeeper who is fouled. Despite the clause that he may be charged outside his goal area (if he is not holding the ball), the proviso against impeding obtains and further limits the allowable body contact.

We shall return to a discussion of the relative rights of the attacking player and the defending goalkeeper in a moment, for such jousting in front of the goal, if not properly supervised, can bring the game into disrepute and provide the referee with unwanted and unnecessary headaches; but first let us review the last of the five paragraphs devoted to lesser fouls.

"When playing as a goalkeeper (a) takes more than four steps whilst holding, bouncing or throwing the ball in the air and catching it again without releasing it so that it is played by another player, or (b) indulges in tactics which, in the opinion of the Referee, are designed merely to hold up the game and thus waste time and so give an unfair advantage to his own team."

The four-step rule was designed to avoid the goalkeeper's dribbling the ball by hand all over the penalty area delaying play while he seeks a better place whence he might send the ball downfield. The rule has produced some problems, however, because the goalkeeper can legally roll the ball along the ground without the accompanying steps counting towards his four. In other words, if the goalkeeper takes one step and then rolls the ball along before him, he may upon picking it up again take three steps while getting rid of it. If he has taken two, he has two left, and so forth. Many goalkeepers are not familiar with the subtleties of the law in connection with the roll-out. It is a "step" for example if the keeper taps the rolled ball with his hand to make it move a little further or faster. The same goes should he pick up the ball and roll it anew without taking any steps while holding it.

With much of the soccer action and strategy compacted into one area, the referee keeps a close watch for fouls. (Raff Frano)

There is one paradox to the roll-out which causes enough problems that I would like to see the roll-out steps count just as the ones while carrying or tossing in the air now count: the goalkeeper is considered in possession of the ball with regard to his total steps remaining, but the ball is a free ball (that is, he is not *holding* it) as it rolls at his feet. He loses the protection of the paragraph which forbids preventing the goalkeeper from getting rid of the ball, but he may not be charged in his goal area when not holding the ball.

If he rolls out past the goal area he may be legally charged and fouls and injuries needlessly occur. The goalkeeper invites a particularly swift and dangerous charge if he rolls the ball in the vicinity of an opponent who will understandably grow frustrated at being teased or taunted and will try to catch the goalkeeper off guard with a quick and unexpected tackle or shoulder charge. Furthermore, it can be disastrous! I have seen at least one instance in which the forward stole the roll-out from the goalkeeper and scored.

There is no time frame beyond which a goalkeeper is guilty of delaying tactics. Sometimes a goalkeeper is so overwrought by an annoying attacker standing in front of him that he just stands there confused, waiting for the attacker to leave. When such an incident occurs, and it is obvious that the goalkeeper is not using "tactics . . . *designed* to hold up the game and waste time," the referee might call "Play on!" or "Let's keep it moving!" so as to break the tension.

I have heard of referees granting an indirect free kick when an injured goalkeeper lies on the ball. Unless the man is obviously faking with an eye to wasting time, the referee should rather call time and then restart with a drop ball. I usually allow time for the injured keeper or his teammates to realize the consequences of a stoppage, however; and it usually dawns upon them that they had better get the ball out from in front of the goal line.

The laws do not prescribe such a gesture of fair play on the part of the referee, but it would be contrary to the spirit of the laws in their entirety to reward a goalkeeper for his valor and skill with a drop ball on the goal line should he have the misfortune of sustaining a serious injury. Sometimes the referee will have no choice but to drop it there, but he should make every effort to restart play further out if the defense catches on and clears the ball, or by a free kick if there was the slightest chance there was an infringement on the part of the attacker.

This is in conformity with Decision 3: "In case of body-contact in the goal-area between an attacking player and the opposing goalkeeper not in possession of the ball, the Referee, as sole judge of intention, shall stop the game if, in his opinion, the action of the attacking player was intentional, and award an indirect free-kick." As for the amount of time he shall permit before taking some action, the referee may take into account several relative factors and use his own judgment since Decision 12 is couched in relative phrasing replete with judgmental words like "opinion", "longer than necessary", etc.: "If, in the opinion of the Referee a goalkeeper *intentionally* lies on the ball *longer than necessary*, he shall be penalized for ungentlemanly conduct . . ." Indeed, how long is *necessary* in the instance of a broken arm?

If in doubt, the referee should protect the goalkeeper. The latter does not, however, have exclusive rights to the penalty or goal area! The art of jousting for position in front of the goal is a rather narrow one and should not be allowed to get out of hand. Both players have certain privileges and those should be vouchsafed by the referee.

Forwards often stand right in front of the goalkeeper who has gotten possession of the ball. This is done — sometimes on specific instructions from the coach — in an attempt to confuse the goalkeeper and make him get off a bad kick or take too many steps. The clear-cut privileges and territorial rights of goalkeeper and opposing forward differ considerably in FIFA, intercollegiate, and Federation rules, but a uniform interpretation of what may and may not be done to one another by these adversaries once the keeper has gained possession is clearly needed.

I am submitting some food for thought in this matter and

a suggested attitude to adopt in calling infractions and thus regulating these critical moments. That they be handled decisively and with consistency is imperative as they constitute moments of friction which, if allowed to crescendo unchecked, can lead to anger, ungentlemanly conduct, violence, injury, and loss of game control. The two areas most fraught with potential difficulty are the roll-out, already discussed, and impeding the goalkeeper, two acts which contribute little to the game but can do a great deal to make it deteriorate.

Much bad blood is created between players and even entire teams by a tenacious striker's habit of standing in front of a goalkeeper who has just gained possession of the ball. An ill-advised reaction on the part of an irritated goalkeeper can even draw a penalty kick and violent conduct can easily erupt. I have even seen a goalkeeper angrily kick the ball at the rear end of a bothersome forward only to have the ball rebound over his head into his own goal!

The FIFA interpretation of the goalkeeper's right to clear the ball unimpeded is found in Law 12, Decision 9:

> If a player intentionally obstructs the opposing goalkeeper, in an attempt to prevent him from putting the ball into play in accordance with Law XII, 5(a), the referee shall award an indirect free-kick.

The NCAA rules (and, with slightly different wording, the Federation high-school rules) state that the goalkeeper "must not be interefered with or impeded in any manner by an opponent while he is in possession of the ball until he releases the ball. Possession includes the act of dribbling the ball with the hand and also the dropping of the ball for the kick."

The problem involves interpretation of "prevent", "impede", and "interfere" in connection with the goalkeeper's effort to put the ball into play. Some spectators, coaches, players, and even referees feel that a player can never stand in front of the goalkeeper; it is, therefore, the act of simply standing in front of a goalkeeper, making no gestures or movements, which often draws unwarranted dissent from players and coaches.

It seems to me that in interpreting the forward's actions, one must adhere, on the one hand, to the wording and the spirit of the laws of the game while vouchsafing, on the other, a general principle of games like soccer, hockey, basketball, etc., that one player cannot lay claim to exclusive territorial rights to a portion of the field which he does not occupy but must rather compete for the territory within the framework of the game's laws as otherwise stipulated, whether it be while going up to head the ball or while keeping a watchful eye on the goalkeeper with the hope that he might bobble the ball or make a miskick.

The referee must distinguish between (1) psychologically annoying but lawful activity and (2) ungentlemanly acts and actual impeding or interference. Running alongside a goalkeeper is not an infraction if the latter is not prevented from getting rid of the ball properly, but running in such a way as to impede or obstruct him during his "clear" is an infraction, obviously. To stick up a foot nearby as the goalkeeper punts the ball may constitute an attempt to prevent the punt or even dangerous play, although the referee may, of course, wish to invoke the advantage clause in marginal cases where game control is not in jeopardy.

As for the player standing still in front of the keeper: It seems to me that the player who, through normal movement of play, finds himself standing face to face with the goalkeeper, is in no way obliged to yield his ground as long as he makes no impeding gestures; but if he deliberately runs over to stand before a goalkeeper who is already in possession of the ball and is about to start his punt or throw, he is attempting to prevent the clearance and impeding, for he cannot contend that it is his innocent intention to contest control of the ball in a lawful manner, for to try to play the ball would by the laws constitute dangerous play (kicking at the ball in the goalkeeper's possession).

In the first case, where the player simply remained where he had landed through normal play, should the goalkeeper then move sideways and the opponent also move to remain in front of him, he may be judged to be preventing clearance and guilty of ungentlemanly conduct. The referee must decide whether the forward had ulterior intentions or came to his position in front of the goalkeeper through the flow of legitimate play. At some game levels, as in games between fifteen-year-olds, the referee may find it wise to inform goalkeepers and team captains before the start of the game as to their respective rights. Nor is it a bad idea to remind them — in keeping with the **Chart**'s "Advice to Players," paragraph (g) — that "the best advice possible to a goalkeeper is to get rid of the ball at once."

There are several situations falling under Law 12 which present the referee with the possibility of an infraction by either of two opponents. He must assimilate in a twinkling the data and decide which way the foul is to be assessed. I am not speaking of offsetting penalties such as one player pushing while the other is holding his jersey. I am speaking of contact of the irresistible-force-meets-an-immovable-object variety when the referee must determine whether the force or the object is guilty of an infraction, or perhaps neither.

There are especially two situations where the referee can be misled by the superficial effect of the player contact and blow the foul the wrong way, if he is not careful. Inexperienced referees find these two situations particularly hard to assess and they sometimes fool the experienced ones, as well.

First, there is the situation in which one player is playing the ball or attempting to play the ball and his opponent will not yield ground. See Fig. 21, page 165.

As we averred earlier, no player has territorial rights to any spot on the field; but, by the same token, he may not be removed from it by foul play or dangerous or violent means. Spectators and fellow players often feel that an opponent has charged their teammate and are dismayed to see that the passive "innocent" teammate is charged with obstruction or even tripping the opponent with his body.

There are many variations of the relationship between a player going up to head the ball and another player waiting for the descending ball. If the leaping player can go up and play the ball without endangering or bullying the opponent, it may be

Figure 21: CHARGING, OBSTRUCTION, OR FAIR PLAY?

judged a fair play. There is no law that says a player must jump to meet a high ball, but if the player who is waiting for the ball to come down to him is not really concerned with playing the ball but rather with restraining his opponent, he is guilty of an infringement. Much depends on the way the players look, the angle of their body movements, and the degree of force in their actions. What may appear to be climbing on a player's back may be deemed obstruction on the part of the opponent. Some referees try to watch for the eye movement of players in such situations. If a player awaiting the ball is not watching the ball but rather the opponent, chances are he is bent on playing the man rather than the ball!

A refinement of this situation is the legal shielding or

covering of the ball within playing distance while stalling so that the ball can go over the touchline or the goal line. As we have mentioned elsewhere, the referee alone can determine whether the action deserves to be punished or constitutes good tactics.

The last portion of Law 12 pertains to misconduct on the part of the players which can lead to their receiving a *caution* or being *ejected*. It is important that the referee be familiar with the relationship between various misconducts and the action called for when they occur. He must measure the extent of the misconduct and determine the appropriate disciplinary action.

The law stipulates that a caution shall be issued to a player who "enters or re-enters the field of play to join or rejoin his team after the game has commenced, or who leaves the field of play during the progress of the game (except through accident) without, in either case, first having received a signal from the Referee showing him that he may do so."

This matter is dealt with in this section rather than as an illegal substitution under Law 3 because no actual substitution is involved, only the return of a player out for a moment, a late-arriving starter, or a unilateral departure without someone replacing the player. Unlike substitutions, such actions may be approved by the referee during the flow of play.

Since a 1975-76 emendation, the restart after a stoppage for failure to report as a late or returning player or as one leaving the field without asking the referee's approval is the same as in the case of illegal substitution, the referee awarding an indirect free kick to the opponent at the place where the *ball* was when play was stopped.

The three other categories of misconduct warranting a caution are those most commonly cited. They are not specifically fit to misdeeds as was the case we have just finished discussing. They are rather umbrellas covering a multitude of deeds, and the three are sufficiently sweeping to permit discipline in an infinite variety of unforeseen circumstances. What they do not cover, the causes for ejection will!

A player shall be cautioned if, in the judgment of the referee, he is guilty of (1) persistent infringement, (2) dissent, or (3) ungentlemanly conduct. The laws state specifically that he shall be cautioned if:

(k) he persistently infringes the Laws of the Game;
(l) he shows by word or action, dissent from any decision by the Referee;
(m) he is guilty of ungentlemanly conduct.

If play is stopped *solely* to administer the caution for any of these three offenses, it shall be restarted with an indirect free kick to be taken by the opposition from the place where the offense occurred.

In all these instances, the matter of what constitutes cautionary behavior is left to the discretion of the referee. As with matters of poor weather, he will somehow know when to act, especially when he has had some experience. The new referee is loath to caution, but he will learn that there are times — fully sanctioned by the laws — when a caution in time will save a player nine stitches. For instance, a caution is generally in order if an attacker deliberately attempts to impede the goalkeeper when he is getting rid of the ball, and the referee should not feel he is being an ogre to administer the caution in such cases.

Persistent infringement can be two fouls by the same player in close sequence or an accumulation of numerous minor infringements. Dissent can be a cynical shake of the head or a subtle case of talking "over the head" of the referee, or it might be downright angry disagreement. Ungentlemanly conduct is a passepartout accommodating hundreds of potential things which may or may not be taken care of under the laws and which may or may not occur when the ball is in play.

Sometimes the referee will be able to choose; for example, a player throwing a little tantrum might be cautioned for dissent or ungentlemanly conduct, and a player might behave in such a way as to be cautioned for persistent infringement and ungentlemanly conduct. The referee may prefer in some instances to talk to the player and alert him to the fact that he is in some jeopardy, but no prior warning is necessary before he administers a caution just as he need not give a caution before he ejects a player for good cause.

The important thing is to keep the wording and the punishment in concord. If the player is to be cautioned, he must be guilty of one of the prescribed offenses or three general areas above. The referee should remember that it is within his power to caution a player for actions detrimental to the spirit of the game or which tend to bring the game into disrepute, but such actions must be dealt with under one of the three headings mentioned.

There are three grounds for ejection of a player: (1) violent conduct or serious foul play, (2) use of foul or abusive language, or (3) persisting in misconduct after having been cautioned. If play has been stopped *solely* in order to administer the ejection, it shall be restarted the same way as after a caution, viz., the other team shall be granted an indirect free kick from the place where the infringement took place.

Major and minor fouls could only be committed against an opponent, but misconduct can be directed at anyone and even when the ball is not in play. Some referees call dangerous play for action taking place between teammates, but such a decision is not in keeping with the laws. If the dangerous action involving a teammate is severe enough to warrant a caution, then the referee may whistle for the misconduct; but he must be sure then to administer the caution since to do so was his sole justification in stopping play!

There are several important interpretations and Board Decisions along these lines. Decision 11 states that "Any player, whether he is within or outside the field of play, whose conduct is ungentlemanly or violent, whether or not it is directed towards an opponent, a colleague, the Referee, a linesman, or other person, or who uses foul or abusive language, is guilty of an offense, and shall be dealt with according to the nature of the offense committed."

Unlike the major and minor fouls, these disciplinary problems are punishable no matter at whom they are directed or even if they are directed at no one in particular. The intent

After many minutes of parry and thrust action, a forward finally breaks momentarily free and shoots. (M. Julius Baum)

and the degree of the misconduct shall be a factor. If the referee overhears a player muttering a curse at himself for having missed a trap, it is technically punishable by ejection, but any referee who would eject a player under the circumstances could not have once been a player or else he would be hypocrisy personified.

I occasionally work out in scrimmages to keep fit for the coming season and I have found myself uttering fricatives and sibilants at my own awkwardness. It is a different matter to curse in a loud manner bound to offend the spectators or to direct foul or abusive language at the referee or another person. Such behavior cannot be justified and requires prompt action of one kind of another. I try to catch the first tendency toward foul language and to alert the player that we will have none of that sort of thing on the field.

There is another important Decision stipulating that the offense of "spitting at opponents, officials or other persons, or similar unseemly behavior shall be considered as violent conduct."

Examples of the various categories of misconduct which warrant ejection are fighting (violent conduct), a vicious deliberate tackle from behind (serious foul play), swearing at the referee (foul language), berating an opponent with cutting racial or ethnic slurs (abusive language), leaping up and handling a high ball to thwart an attack — in itself a cautionary offense — after having already been cautioned for this or some other cause (persisting in misconduct after a caution), spitting in someone's face (specified in Decision 13), and dissenting in an irrational and infantile way, rolling on the ground and chewing the grass (unseemly conduct).

Consider the following news item carried by several soccer magazines and daily newspapers:

> Four months' prison, that was the punishment given to the Greek national player Angelis of Olympiakos of Athens because he exposed his bare backside to the referee during a match! A severe punishment for a 'football streaker'!

Severe, indeed, and difficult to understand if there was no physical contact or assault made on the referee. Some people would maintain that to stifle this gesture is to deny one the right to free speech! Leaving aside the civil action, this offense certainly is punishable according to the powers given the referee by the laws of the game. It would presumably call for ejection on the grounds that to drop one's shorts and wave his derriere in the referee's face is unseemly behavior.

It should, at the very least, draw a caution although I don't quite know whether one should construe the gesture as dissent (clearly it is that) or ungentlemanly conduct (clearly it is that, as well). The referee must, in such a provocative situation, above all be sure to resist the obvious urge to give the player a swift kick in the posterior!

Sometimes players who are being cautioned for dissent take advantage of the fact that they are going to be punished to get everything off their chests or, when about to be cautioned for ungentlemanly conduct, they will begin to argue the point. Recently a Decision was added which permits the referee to cut short such prolongations of his disciplinary problems. If he is about to caution a player and the player commits another offense which merits a caution, the player is to be sent off.

When I am cautioning a player and he continues to argue and I see no end in sight, I sometimes say slowly, "That is enough, NOW!" and slowly lower one hand to the palm of the other like a cutting blade as though to say "That cuts it short, any further discussion will be a new cautionary offense and off you go!" One will tolerate a certain amount of "natural" dissent, but players invite a caution when they try to make a fool out of the referee.

In a Seattle-Cosmos game televised by CBS, the referee bent over backwards not to discipline Pele who was constantly disputing his calls. Finally, when Pele began to point to his head as though to tell the whole world the referee was crazy, there was no choice but to caution him. I was glad to see it done, otherwise all the youngsters watching would think that that is the way you treat referees in soccer. The referee carried him along the way he did in all likelihood because he understood the enormous pressure on Pele to deliver skillful feats and goals, but the great player went too far and he knew it, for his behavior was exemplary thereafter and he embraced the referee at the end of the game.

13

Law 13-Free Kick
(Direct and Indirect)

Law 13 is the sequel to the punishing action inherent in the first part of Law 12. This law distinguishes between the direct free kick (for the major offenses) and the indirect free kick for the lesser offenses and after stoppages to administer cautions and ejections.

The direct free kick is one from which a kicker may score directly in his opponent's goal without anyone else touching it. As we have already mentioned, indirect free kicks may not be scored against one's own team if the ball has not been touched by another player (a corner kick would be given if the kick came from outside one's own penalty area, and it is retaken if the kick came from inside). Indirect free kicks must be touched by another player before they may go into the goal for a valid score. If sent directly into the goal, a goal kick is awarded (a corner if it is sent into one's own goal from outside one's own penalty area). The referee shall distinguish these two kinds of kick by holding an arm aloft to indicate an indirect free kick and making no such sign when it is direct.

The referee *never* grants a direct free kick inside the guilty player's own penalty area but rather opts, in that case, for a penalty kick, which is a direct kick escalated to a more deadly level by virtue of the fact that the kicker is then only opposed by the goalkeeper. This does not hold true for indirect free kicks which may be awarded right on the guilty player's goal line if that's where the infringement took place.

When a direct free kick or indirect free kick is being taken, the opponent must remain at least ten yards away from the ball and may not encroach inside that distance until the ball has been put into play. The only exception to this is when an indirect free kick is being taken within ten yards of the goal line, in which case the defending players may stand *on the goal line between the uprights.*

As with kick-offs, throw-ins, goal kicks, and corner kicks, a player who has put a free kick into play and who touches it a second time before it has been played by another man shall be punished by an indirect free kick. Free kicks taken from within one's own penalty area must clear the penalty area into play before they may be touched or played by anyone. All opposing players must remain outside the penalty area until the ball is in play. This holds true as well for goal kicks. Unlikely events which crop up repeatedly on referees' tests are the following mind-teasers:

Q. If the goalkeeper takes a direct free kick from inside his own penalty area and the ball goes out of the penalty area but is carried back into the goal by a gust of wind without anyone touching it, what is the decision?

A. No goal since a team cannot score directly against itself on a free kick. A corner kick should be awarded.

Q. What if the goalkeeper had lunged and touched the ball just before it entered the goal?

A. Indirect free kick to the opponent from where he had touched the ball, for the ball was in play and he touched it a second time before anyone else played it. One cannot apply advantage in this instance.

Q. What if the kick did not clear the area but blew back into the goal?

A. If the ball does not go over the penalty area line into the field of play it shall be retaken, whether it is touched again, goes into the goal, or over the end line within eighteen yards of the goal post.

The greatest problem for the referee in Law 13 involves the requirements for the execution of a legal free kick — which

The shot is lofted into a melee of attackers and defenders in front of the goal. The ball is cleared, but there is much pushing and shoving. (Horst Müller)

if shunned will cause the kick to be invalid so that it must be retaken — and the behavior of the defensive team at this critical moment. The free kick is awarded to a team which has been the victim of foul or ungentlemanly play, and it is not appropriate to make the players wait inordinately while the defense sets itself up to cope with this new threat; but the laws must be enforced and, therefore, some delay will often be necessary. The referee's role at these moments will be discussed under game control in Part Two of this book, but he should not let players eschew the law even as he makes certain that he does not delay play for the sole purpose of letting himself get into a better position on the field.

The ball must be stationary and at the place where the infringement occurred before it may be kicked. The referee need not place the ball down, but he should clearly indicate the spot where it should be placed. He should not tolerate free kicks being executed when the ball is still rolling, just as he should not tolerate opponents dallying in front of the ball. If the referee permits the former, how can he blame the opponents for doing the latter? If the ball is in the right place and immobile, the player may kick the ball.

Law 5 stipulates that the referee shall signal for the recommencement of play after *all* stoppages, but many referees permit players to take a quick free kick if other conditions are met, but the players do so at their own risk and if the ball hits an opponent who is only five yards away, they cannot ask for a retake of the kick. The kicker opted for the quick-kick advantage and must live with any adverse results. The referee should only stop play in this instance to administer a caution or ejection if he feels the kicker tried to hit the opponent with the ball, not unlike the situation encountered when a goalkeeper punts the ball into the back of an opponent dallying in front of him.

The kicking team may wish to wait and even have the referee move back the defense if it is clearly within the ten yards. The referee should remember that the offended team is within its rights when it asks that the law be enforced. He should also know that he must be careful lest clever players try to "psyche" him and the other team with picayune tactics during the taking of free kicks. We shall have a good bit more to say about this later. Suffice it to say, here, that much friction develops because one side or the other tries to cheat on the clauses of Law 13 and that sometimes their strict and painstaking enforcement is the referee's best possible ally in maintaining game control.

If players encroach into the penalty area or within ten yards of the ball (or the distance from the ball to the goal line if that is less than ten yards), the referee should wait for them to quit the area before permitting the kick to be taken. If they do not withdraw to the proper distance or if they repeat their encroachment, the referee should caution them.

14

Law 14 - Penalty Kick

Law 14 is another part of the sequel to Law 12. The referee shall punish any direct free kick offense committed by the defending team in its own penalty area by awarding a penalty kick to the opponent. This is a dramatic and important moment in many games, for the percentage of goals resulting from penalty kicks is very high, even on the lower junior levels. The referee must be certain that the foul was deliberate before he signals for a foul, but having done that he must be firm in his decision as this is no time to show timidity and uncertainty.

The ball is placed on the penalty spot — if it is not visible or is known to be inaccurate, the referee shall pace off the twelve yards. Even if the spot is in the middle of a puddle of water, the ball may not be placed elsewhere, say two yards to the left on dry land. The kicker and the goalkeeper, who may not move his feet and shall remain on the goal line until the kick is taken, are the only players allowed inside the penalty area and within ten yards of the ball until it has been put into play. It should also be remembered that all the players must be not only outside the penalty area but also *on the field of play*. Once in awhile a player will have the bright idea to stand just over the goal line by the goal post so as to recover a goalkeeper's fumble. This is not in conformity to the requirements of the penalty kick and he must return to the field before the kick may be taken.

The first Board Decision of this law states that "When the Referee has awarded a penalty kick, he shall not signal for it to be taken, until the players have taken up position in accordance with the law." The main text of the law does not say that he must signal, but this IBD makes it clear that without the signal he has not expressed his satisfaction that all is ready and therefore a kick taken prematurely shall not count but be retaken. This reinforces the notion set forth in Law 5 that the referee shall signal a recommencement of the game after all stoppages; and, in the case of a penalty kick, he should not ever forego signaling, preferably with the whistle.

A number of things can happen. Naturally, all can proceed smoothly with the ball going into the net, missing, or being saved. Play will continue accordingly in this happy event. The problems can obviously occur when an attacker or defender infringes on one of the many criteria for a lawful penalty kick. If the person infringing benefits from the result, it shall be disallowed, and, if necessary, be retaken. For example, if the goalkeeper moves too soon and a goal is not scored, the kick is retaken. If a teammate of the kicker encroaches and a goal is scored, the kick shall be retaken and the player cautioned.

The referee shall not signal till everyone is legally set up for the kick, but once he signals he shall do nothing until the kick is taken and then act accordingly if there has been an infraction. The only time he is to intervene even if he has whistled for the kick is if the goalkeeper moves his feet *and* a colleague of a kicker encroaches or if a player from each side encroaches. In this instance, the IBDs state that "the kick, if taken, shall be retaken." It was this ruling that saved me some embarrassment, as I mentioned earlier in this book.

Law 14 is a minefield of latent trouble for the referee. Difficulty arises not so much from the fact that the laws are vague but rather from the sheer multiplicity of variables packed into a few seconds of highly charged action! So much can happen in so brief a period of time! The referee must, aside from overseeing the kick, be on the lookout for possible incidents unrelated to Law 14, such as foul or abusive language, ungentlemanly conduct, and, most frequently, dissent. The referee, in enforcing Law 14, must observe infringements by the kicker, the goalkeeper, and these players' respective teammates. The action to be taken by the referee in the event of such infringements is clearly laid out in the law.

There is only one minor area which is repeatedly debated and which is basically a lacuna in the scope of the law. It recently came up again at our local Eastern Pennsylvania & District Soccer Referees' Association monthly meeting – as it does every year or so – and, as usual, was the basis for a lively discussion.

Here is the situation: after the whistle has been blown but before the kick has been taken, a teammate of the kicker encroaches within the penalty area. The referee shall, in accordance with the laws, "nevertheless, allow the kick to proceed," and now the goalkeeper deflects the shot over the crossbar. The action to be taken by the referee in this situation is not specifically referred to in the laws but must be adopted by the referee according to whether or not, in his judgment, several things have happened.

In the situation described, had the ball gone in the goal, the kick would have been retaken and the encroaching player cautioned (IBD 4,b). Had the ball rebounded into play from the goalkeeper, the goal posts, or the crossbar, the referee would have stopped play, cautioned the player, and awarded an indirect free kick to the defending team (IBD 4,c). The case of a deflection is not dealt with in so many words but must be inferred as falling between (1) the notion of continuing play if a goal is not scored, which is the implicit obverse of *Punishment (b)* which stipulates that for any infringement of the basic law "by the attacking team other than the player taking the kick, if a goal is scored it shall be disallowed and the kick retaken," and (2) the specifics of IBD 4(c) which states that if, when there is encroachment by the attacking team, "the ball rebounds into play from the goalkeeper, the cross-bar or a goal-post, the Referee shall stop the game, caution the player and award an indirect free-kick to the opposing team from the place where the infringement occurred."

Much as absolute noontide does not exist save as a

hypothetical and timeless juncture between the two measurable antemeridian and postmeridian concepts, the problem of a ball deflected by the goalkeeper must be judged by the referee *either* to fall under that unwritten negative corollary of *Punishment (b)* — in which case play continues if a goal is not scored — or to fall within the condition of a ball rebounding into play. The expression of substance in the interpretation of this matter is "rebounds into play" and, as is also the case in applying so many other clauses of the laws, it is ultimately up to the referee to determine the points of fact involved.

The invisible line analogous to my image of exact meridian is that involving the judgmental dividing line between whether the ball did, in fact *rebound into play*, or not. If the referee considers that the ball did so, the laws clearly instruct him what to do (stop play and give an indirect free kick to the defense or apply advantage, cautioning the encroacher right away or when the ball goes out of play), whereas if the referee considers that the ball did not do so, there is no other possible action but to allow play to continue and to caution the player the next time the ball goes out of play, which in this case will necessarily be almost immediately. If the ball touches the goalkeeper without rebounding into play and proceeds over the goal line outside the goal post or over the crossbar, a *corner kick* must be granted, but the player who encroached shall be cautioned.

Just as he was to evaluate such things as what constitutes "within playing distance of the players" (Law 12), the referee has it left at his discretion to judge what constitutes "rebounding into play." It should be remembered, however, that the dictionary defines "rebound" in terms of bouncing back, springing back upon impact with another body, and returning to a previous or similar state.

I personally could not judge that a penalty kick slightly deviated from its original course by the goalkeeper as it went out of play over the end line outside the goal had "rebounded" and would signal for a corner kick. The only gray area would be the one involving a ball redirected out along the end line and which remained in the field of play for a short while before eventually going out over the line under its own steam. Is it a deflection or a rebound?

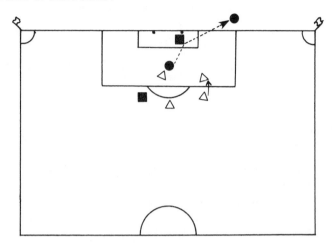

Figure 22: REBOUND OR NONREBOUND?

The referee will simply have to make the decision in such instances as to whether the trajectory of the ball constituted a rebound into play from the goalkeeper or a continuous motion or thrust of the ball — in short, a nonrebound.

If a penalty kick is being taken or is to be taken and time runs out at the end of the game or between periods, time shall be extended to allow for the kick to be taken. This is only done for penalty kicks, and time is only extended long enough for the kick to be taken and, if necessary, retaken. The referee shall blow for the end of the extended time as soon as the outcome of the immediate kick is clear. If it goes right in the goal or bounces in off the goalkeeper and/or the goal post or crossbar in a direct thrust of its momentum, it shall count, assuming all the conditions of Law 14 have been met. If it rebounds into play or goes out, the game ends forthwith.

The only marginal cases will be those in which the ball could be judged to rebound or to be going in under its own direct thrust. As with the deflection shot already discussed, the referee will simply have to decide the matter. If the ball were to hit the post, roll back along the goal line, and bounce in off the goalkeeper's back, it would probably be judged "no goal" — its thrust having been redirected by the goalkeeper whereas it would have presumably rolled on out of the goalmouth if untouched by him — and if that is so, the referee should have already blown his whistle for the completion of the game before it got into the net!

Kicks from the penalty spot are being used more and more as a tie-breaker in tournament competition. When first introduced, they were referred to as "penalty kicks", but this was, of course, not proper as no offense had been committed. The rule was emended to call these special tie-breakers "kicks from the penalty-mark" in the memorandum accompanying the laws. This memorandum explains in detail this procedure of post-game kicks. It has been criticized by some, but one can say that it is no more brutal than flipping a coin or drawing straws to see who goes on to the next round and it does, at least, permit one to conform to the condition of Law 10, Decision 1 that scoring properly across the line is "the only method according to which a match is won or drawn; no variation whatsoever can be authorized."

The kickers shall be those lawfully on the field of play at the end of the game or overtime. The teams shall take alternate kicks pursuant with Law 14, being dealt with as one would an extended-time penalty kick. Five players from each team shall take kicks unless an inevitable winner is produced earlier. If Team "A" leads Team "B" by three kicks to none after three turns for each team, the tie-breaker is over. If after five turns, both teams are even, the kicks shall continue alternately until a team scores and its opponent does not or has not. The players shall all take turns as kickers, even the goalkeeper, and a player may not take a second kick until every other player on his team has taken his turn. No substitutes will be permitted except for a goalkeeper who has been injured and is unable to continue.

Several things should be remembered by the referee. Unlike the start of play or regular overtimes, his coin toss is not for option. He shall toss the coin (not one of the players) and the winner *must* shoot first. The players are to stay in the center circle until their turn comes, and the goalkeeper who is temporarily idle is to remain just outside the penalty area out by the corner of the area until he exchanges places with the opposing goalkeeper. While there he must in no way distract his opposite number who is busy trying to protect the goal mouth.

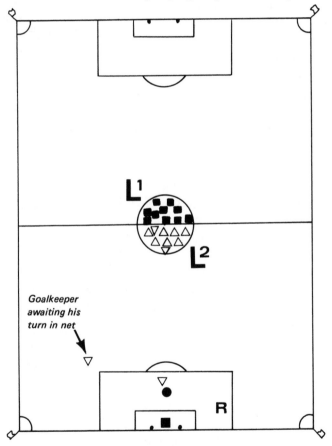

Figure 23: DEPLOYMENT FOR TIE-BREAKER

It is important to know all these things since these postgame kicks are not only used in the NASL but also to determine tournament advancement and winners in the youngest youth tournaments.

I heard of a case in which the referee got himself into a jam because he did not follow proper procedures. I learned of the situation in the form of a question submitted for an interpretation:

Q. During tie-breaker kicks — tied at 4-4 — the first kicker trying to make it five for his team is successful, but the linesman has noticed that a teammate of the kicker is standing inside the penalty area by at least a foot and he has raised his flag. The referee consults the linesman and the kick is ordered retaken. This time the player misses. The opponent successfully scores its fifth goal and is declared the winner. Should the kick have been ordered retaken?

A. This is a weird one! First of all, the players should all have been in the center circle and not lined up at the penalty-area line. There is no possibility of playing a rebound, so in this instance — granting that the referee has made a mistake in letting the players come forward — the linesman should not have raised his flag for the technical fact of the player encroaching within the penalty area, but only if the player in question was guilty of ungentlemanly conduct during the kick, was distracting the goalkeeper, or something like that. "An ounce of prevention . . ." as they say! Had the referee followed the proper procedure and insisted that all the players save the goalkeepers and the kicker remain in the center circle he would never have had the problem.

If darkness falls before the kicks have resulted in a winner, a coin shall be tossed to determine a winner, but since this provision is somewhat at odds with Law 10, IBD 1 regarding how games may be won or drawn, the referee should make every effort to complete the postgame kicks if he has allowed them to start. One can hardly expect two teams to return hundreds of miles to a neutral Cup game site in order to take two or three kicks to complete their competition, whence the ultimate expediency of the coin toss.

15

Law 15-Throw-in

Anyone who has attended a rules interpretation meeting or witnessed a soccer match in the company of several referees has noticed that the seventeen apparently simple laws of the game contain ambiguity enough to fuel endless lively discussions over the application of these laws to situations on the field of play.

A colloquium of medieval scholasticists arguing the number of angels that could fit on the head of a pin, or the ratiocinations of high-browed Sophists in quest of the Absolute, never generated more heated debate. Generally disagreement among top-ranking referees can be pinned down to the interpretation of one or two words in a clause. There are two areas of particular importance, involving actions of high frequency in most games, in which I have found the standard authorities to be of two minds. One is the offside question already discussed, the other is Law 15 on the taking of throw-ins. Law 15 contains only five sentences but has caused much ink to be spilled in discussions regarding what is and is not a valid throw-in. (Before proceeding, read Law 15 in Appendix I.)

Pursuant with the standards of Law 9, to be out of touch the whole of the ball must be over all of the line, on the ground or in the air. The law states that the throw-in shall be taken by a player of the team which did not last touch the ball before it went out of play. It states that the throw shall be made from the point where it crossed the line. Some players think that as long as they are upfield from the point where the ball went out of play they are in order. This is a persistent myth. The player standing ten yards out of touch or ten yards along the line towards his own goal is *not* at the point where the ball crossed the line.

A sensible rule of thumb to be used by the referee is to consider approximately one yard as an appropriate distance. Intent is very important here. A player edging back to throw to his goalkeeper is behaving in a manner contrary to the spirit of the laws, whereas a player at midfield who inadvertently runs a few yards beyond the appropriate spot in his eagerness to get the ball back into play is not out of order. The referee must be judicious in enforcing this part of Law 15, tempering it with our "old saw", that is Law 5, Decision 8, lest he irritate the players and fans alike for no good reason.

There are two principal parts to the throw itself, which is a very unnatural act not quite like any other in sports unless you could say it is twice as awkward as the stiff-arm overhand delivery of the cricket bowler. I am sure it is meant to be awkward lest the throw-in become such a powerful weapon that it would tend to supplant footwork for a major portion of the game. It is really meant merely to put the ball back into play, not be a powerful attack weapon as it would be were throw-ins to be executed in any way, such as in the manner used by goalkeepers. The two principal parts are, then, the foot action and the throw itself, that is, the movement of the arms and torso during the delivery.

According to Law 15, for the throw-in to be legal, the thrower "at the moment of delivering the ball must face the field of play and part of each foot shall be either on the touchline or on the ground outside the touchline." This would seem crystal clear, yet there is room for debate in the word "or", "ou", "o" and "eller", to mention only the four languages in which I have checked this rule.

Some interpreters appear to feel that the wording "a part of each foot" refers exclusively to the fact that some part of the feet must remain on the ground, in this case within an area defined as "on or behind the line." This group would disallow a throw-in with any part of the foot inside the line, on the field of play.

The opposing school takes the phrase as a whole: ". . .part of each foot shall be either on the touch-line or on the ground outside the touch-line." They argue that one can conform to the wording of this phrase and still have part of one or both feet inside the line and on the field of play. It would appear, at the very least, that the law should be rephrased to remove this ambiguity whichever way the International Board of FIFA sees fit.

Two books by outstanding referees maintain that it is an infraction if the thrower has his toes extending into the field. Denis Howell writes, in **Soccer Refereeing**, that the thrower "must not have any part of either foot over the touch-line inside the field of play."[16] No less an authority than Diego De Leo, an official FIFA instructor, provides, in his **Regole del Calcio**, an illustration of what he considers foot faults with the foot or feet partially in the field of play. Furthermore, De Leo links his illustration to an official Federazione Italiana Giuoco Calcio decision that it is not permissible "to have one or both feet in the field of play, over the touch-line,"[17] although this wording in itself is ambiguous and could mean the entire foot in the field, which is of course an infringement.

Now, some books, such as Stanley Lover's, make no reference to this specific situation of the feet partially in the field, but two official publications of the British Football Association mention it — in contradiction of Howell and De Leo! **The F.A. Guide to the Laws of The Game** asserts that a diagram with both feet partially over the line represents a legal throw-in.[18] In a pamphlet called **Association Football — Know the Game**, billed as "The Football Association's Illustrated Handbook", there is a drawing of a player's boots which, as a result of the heels being lifted off the line, have contact only with the ground inside the field. The text states that players "who have one or both feet on the line when throwing may, by raising their heels, have the part of the foot touching the ground in the field of play and not on the line, which is infringing the law."[19] The implication is that were the heels not raised from the line the throw would be legal, even though part of the foot would be in the field of play. This echoes the **F.A. Guide.**

It seems to me, personally, that the latter interpretation makes sense, for it is physically and logically possible to adhere to the law while still having the tips of the shoes on the field. To demonstrate this, let us consider the following diagram.

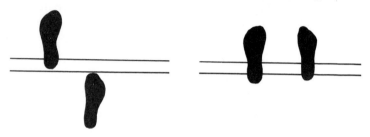

Figure 24: TAKING THE THROW-IN

Notice that the positions meet the requirements of the wording of the law since part of each foot is *"either* on the touch-line *or* on the ground outside the touch-line." If we ask of either situation the questions, "Is part of the left foot either on the line or outside it?" and "Is part of the right foot on the line or outside it?" the answer must, in both cases, be "Yes"; hence the foot positioning is admissible. One last cavil: those who would not allow the foot to extend into the field of play but would let the toes be on the line are actually permitting part of the foot to be on the field in the very technical sense that the line constitutes part of the area it delimits.

Finally, in reply to my question asking if it is a "foot fault during a throw-in to have part of the foot over the line protruding into the playing field," Rene Courte has succinctly answered: "No" (Letter dated August 15, 1975).

No less complex is the matter of throwing faults. I had always assumed that the wording to the effect that the thrower "shall use both hands and shall deliver the ball from behind and over his head" pertained to the motion of delivery and that as long as the delivery is correct and the ball is thrown and not dropped, it can be released in front of the head. Now, Denis Howell avers that the "player throwing in must deliver the ball — that is to say he must release it — over the head. He cannot release it in front of his face."[20]

I must confess that I had always interpreted the word "delivery" as an American. When you speak of the smooth delivery of a pitcher, you mean his entire throwing motion and not just the way in which he relinquishes the ball. Both Webster's and the Random House dictionaries contain clauses which bear me out in this: "To direct; throw; *to deliver a blow; deliver a fast ball.*"

Conceding that Mr. Howell's language is British English and in a benevolent effort to overcome the legendary insurmountable obstacle of a common language, I turned next to the **Oxford English Dictionary** which yielded this: "To give forth, send forth, emit; to discharge, launch; to cast, throw, project"; furthermore, two of the usage examples then given by the **OED** certainly indicate that the verb "deliver" can suggest to a Britisher the totality of a gesture and its immediate result that we derive from the American definition: (1) "The Earl of Kent, as he was delivering his bowl upon the green at Tunbridge Wells last Wednesday, fell down and immediately died," and (2) "In delivering his harpoon he lost his balance."

Finally, in this instance, Howell's interpretation is contrary to that given in the F.A.'s booklet **Know the Game** which provides a ready answer to Howell's assertion: "It is sometimes wrongly assumed that the player must release the ball whilst his hands are over his head. In a natural throwing movement, the hands will always be in front of the vertical plane of the body when the ball is released. The throw *starts* from behind the head and there should then be a continuous movement to the point of release."[21] In fact, were "deliver" to mean exclusively "release" as Howell maintains, the thrower would require two soccer balls and four arms, like some exotic goddess, in order to be able to simultaneously execute releases "from behind and over the head."

Here, more than ever, one must be ready to invoke Law 5,

After a foul, the ball and goalkeeper end up over the goal line. What call should be made? (Jai Pleskacz)

IBD 8 about not whistling constantly for trifling and doubtful breaches of the laws. Many referees feel that if the ball spins or if a player exerts more pressure with one hand than the other, it is a foul throw; but each throw-in has many contributing foot, arm, and body gestures and the legality of the totality must finally be determined by the officials.

American players — weaned on baseball and other sports in which one throws with one arm — tend instinctively to favor one arm or have one arm much stronger than the other. Law 15 does not say anywhere that pressure must be identical or that the ball may not spin or curve. It merely states that the player shall *use* both hands and the **Chart** advises referees to see to it that the player "taking the throw-in *really* uses both hands; some players are apt to throw with one hand only, using the other simply as a guide." Thus, as long as the delivery really uses both hands, comes from behind the head and is over the head (not over the ear), is made in a continuous motion, and the ball is not dropped but clearly thrown, the throw-in is legal, assuming the footwork is correct and the player facing the field.

Several misconceptions, such as that in Howell's book, cause referees to whistle and many players to claim a foul throw whenever a throw is directed downward at a sharp angle toward the ground, is thrown hard, is thrown very softly, is released in front of the head, is thrown one way while the face is turned another, is thrown while the player's body is twisted, is thrown as the player is slowly falling forward, or is thrown so the ball spins or curves. In all of these instances, however, it is possible for the throw-in to be quite legal, even if it is not necessarily elegant. The referee must decide whether the throw is foul or not and whether it is incorrect in so trifling a manner that he should allow play to continue. That most players and coaches are basically unaware of what constitutes a lawful throw-in is attested to by the fact that they often claim that an opponent's throw is foul but seldom argue in their own behalf when the referee has charged them with a foul throw.

Let me insert a mildly relevant story. I once heard tell of a coach of younger players who noticed that 75% of both teams' throw-ins went to the opponent. He therefore instructed his players to deliberately make foul throws and, if boxed in on the sideline, not to kick the ball out off the shins of the opponent as one is wont to do but rather to kick the ball straight out of touch. These tactics were adopted in order to exploit the percentage factor when the ball was put back into play. Not very good soccer training, no doubt, but this coach's strategy bears out the notion that − with a few notable exceptions − the throw-in is seldom the major contributing game factor that players would make it out to be as they wring their hands in despair over a referee's directional signal in favor of the opponent.

Some referees contend that the advantage rule applies here, but the foul throw occurs, perforce, before the ball enters the field and comes into play and, therefore, a special clause (a) stipulates that as punishment if the ball is "improperly thrown in the throw-in shall be taken by a player of the opposing team."

16

Law 16 - Goal Kick

The last two laws (16 and 17) cover restarts after the ball has gone out of play over the goal line without a goal being awarded. If the offense last touched the ball before it went over the end line, the game is restarted with a goal kick; if the defense last touched the ball, play resumes with a corner kick.

The goal kick is to be taken by a member of the defending team from a point within the half of its goal area nearest to where the ball went out of play. Thus the prescribed area for the goal kick is made up of the goal-area markings on three sides and an imaginary line perpendicular to the goal line and bisecting the goal area. See Fig. 25 on page 194.

When a goal kick is taken, the ball shall be considered in play when it has gone out of the penalty area (i.e., completely and wholly crossed the penalty-area line) into the field of play. If a player from either side prevents the ball from crossing the line, if it goes over the end line before going into play, if it is deflected or touched by another player after it is kicked but before it clears the penalty area, or if it simply stops short of the penalty-area line as sometimes happens in children's games, the kick is to be retaken and, if circumstances dictate, a caution administered. If a caution is issued to a player who deliberately and repeatedly prevents the ball from crossing the line into play, the referee cannot restart play with an indirect free kick but shall have the goal kick retaken since the ball had not been put into play. One will also recall that a goal may not be scored directly on a goal kick and that a player cannot be offside on a goal kick.

I once argued that, a goal kick being "kicked . . . from a point within that half of the goal-area nearest to where it crossed the line," the ball must be standing on a point no further out than the line itself; however Rene Courte, Press Secretary for FIFA, has corrected me and averred that if any

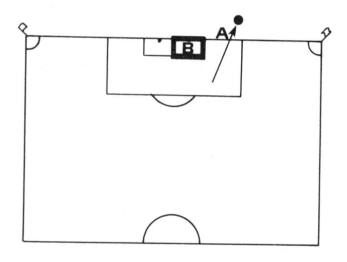

Figure 25: BALL WENT OUT OFF ATTACKER AT "A";
GOAL KICK TO BE TAKEN FROM "B" AREA

part of the ball is over the goal-area line, the placement for a goal kick is lawful. I accept this, and with it the logic of another correspondent, Henry Georgi, whose explanation is the only one that can maintain some fidelity to the wording of the law and still permit us to follow Mr. Courte's instructions. Namely, the emphasis is to be placed on the verb "kicked" which would now have the *point* within the goal area be not where the ball is placed but where the point of the kick occurred.

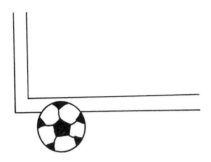

Figure 26: LAWFUL GOAL KICK

Play is quickly resumed, but tempers are hot. Two players push each other for possession of the ball. Another foul, or "Play on." Which? (Raff Frano)

17

Law 17 · Corner Kick

If the ball last touched a defender, a corner kick shall be awarded the opponent. The ball must be placed within the corner arc and kicked from it into play. Opponents are to remain the prescribed ten yards from the ball until the ball is kicked. The ball, as with throw-ins, kick-offs, goal kicks, and free kicks, may not be played a second time by the kicker until another player of either team has touched it. In all of these instances of playing the ball twice on the kick, if the ball has not traveled into play (e.g. more than its circumference), the kick shall be retaken, but if it has gone into play, the opponent shall be awarded an indirect free kick.

As we have said, the ball shall be placed *within* (not kicked from a spot within, as with the goal kick) the corner quadrant. Thus, no part of the ball should protrude beyond the outer edge of the line delineating the quadrant. See Fig. 27, page 198.

A goal may be scored directly on a corner kick. It is a relatively rare occurrence — I have had corners go into the goal untouched by another player only on two occasions — and when it happens, there is a moment's hesitation and dismay and then the players look at the referee and ask if it is a goal.

The referee should remember that if the corner kick curves out completely over the end line and back onto the field of play, the ball shall be called out and a goal kick indicated. The referee should be sure that he or his linesman has good positioning to make this decision. Contrary to some players'

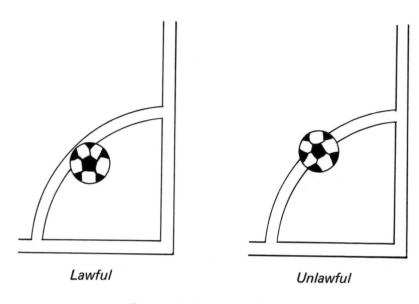

Lawful   *Unlawful*

Figure 27: CORNER KICK

obstinate belief, time can expire as a player is about to take a corner kick; some referees prefer to end the game the instant after the kick is sent into play to avoid unnecessary confrontation, so persistent and deep-rooted is this misconception!

18

Law 18· Common Sense

Law "18" does not officially exist but is referred to by referees on many occasions. It is the all-important law of good old-fashioned common sense. It is the one unwritten law which contains cross references to all the other laws. If Law 5 instructs the referee to "enforce the laws", common sense should be applied in liberal doses where needed to temper the rigorous cold print of the laws.

Grammars were not written so that people could learn to speak, they were written to describe what already existed. The laws of scansion describe what a poet's inspiration has told him is right; if he has slavishly composed a verse on the basis of the laws of scansion without any consideration for spirit, adhering solely to the mathematics, the resulting poem will be a sorry affair indeed! Similarly, a slavish obedience to the laws was never intended when the game was designed and improved. The rules were implemented to assure that players might give free reign to their sense of fair play without being stymied by opponents who will resort to unfair play in order to stop them. Common sense dictates not only the use of the advantage clause − admittedly, experience helps in this case, too − and the winking at trifling breaches of the laws, but it also tells the referee when too many yellow cards will undermine rather than assert his authority, when too intransigent an attitude on some matter may cause him more problems with game control than turning the other way. Sometimes the referee will be able to de-fuse a dangerous situation better with a quip or a word muttered to the player during the flow of play than with an official caution.

The very act of stopping play is to deprive oneself of one of the best de-fusing devices: it is good to keep the game moving as players who are playing soccer will not have time to stand around fuming and fussing at the referee or they will be left out of the play and perhaps let a goal be scored or find themselves in an offside position.

Only the referee — assisted by experience and a fundamental sense of self-preservation which only the most obstinate referee will fail to take into account — can tell when an action technically called for by the laws will be countereffective. It is appropriate to remember that the players are human too, and must be respected as you would have them respect you. Putting yourself in their shoes will sometimes tell you what course to take. I once had a situation where I did not take any action when a player was guilty of what could easily have been considered dissent or even abusive language, given the tone of voice he used. I could, however, understand the player's reasons for being upset and knew his feelings were not directed at me.

A player was fouled from behind as he shielded a ball going out of touch. The player was hurt and fell to the ground where he lay writhing in pain. I cautioned the offending player. The coach and some teammates of the injured player were attending to him and were understandably concerned and angry. I went over to them and simply told them to move him to the side line as soon as it was possible so we could resume play. One player kneeling over his teammate shouted at me something like, "Come on, get out of here, our man is badly hurt!" It would have been foolhardy to inject myself further into this hornet's nest. All I could have succeeded in doing would have been to transfer the team's anger to myself! I quietly withdrew and rather concentrated on seeing to it that there were no reprisals against the player who had committed the foul. I made a mental note, however, to learn from this experience that players righteously distraught but minding their own business are better allowed to simmer down, and that it is

The pushing was enough to result in a direct free-kick and a caution to both players. (M. Julius Baum)

foolish to divert innocent anger toward oneself. This kind of restraint has many variations, as every referee soon learns.

Recently a FIFA referee was discussing the role of the referee in regard to fighting between players. He said that he used to jump in and try to prevent fighting as it started or looked imminent, acting the policeman. It is natural for the referee to feel that a fight occurring in one of his games might discredit him as a sign of poor game control and, unfortunately, many spectators feel that way about such an incident.

All is relative. A hockey fan told me that So-and-So was the best referee in ice hockey and that he never had trouble with players, there seldom occurring more than one or two fights when he was officiating a game! I replied that that was one or two too many. Strong action is called for when violent conduct occurs on the soccer field, but the laws do not state that the referee shall "prevent players from committing violent conduct", merely that he shall punish them for it.

The FIFA referee I mentioned above said that you are apt to be so busy fussing with the two fighters at close quarters that other fights will break out behind your back; furthermore you may even have difficulty identifying the fighters after it is all over. He claims that players determined to have a go at each other will not be deterred no matter what you do and sometimes you have to let them get their emotions out *on each other* if that is what they are bent on doing. If the referee thwarts it, they will return to do something vicious later in the game. In short, he should let the safety valve work wherever possible. If the two players insist on fighting, throw them out for violent conduct and get on with the game.

If players are arguing, the referee should not inflame them but calm them. Perhaps coming up to them slowly after they have had their little verbal exchange ("Hey watch out, Fellow!" – "Yeah? *You* better watch out!") and saying something like "Okay, are you two guys finished now?" will provide the relief needed all around. Similarly, if players are fighting, the referee should concentrate on printing indelibly in his mind the pertinent data: numbers and teams of fighters, their faces, who started the fight, reasons for the eruption, and so forth. Obviously, the two players will be going off and the referee should be concerned about their safety, but also about the safety of others. If he leaps in and then can remember no details about the guilty parties when it comes time to mete out discipline, he has served neither himself, nor the sport, nor the other innocent players who want only to play soccer.

I said above that the laws do not state that it is the referee's task to prevent violent conduct but to punish such misconduct. It is quite true that nowhere does it say that it is a foul to commit violent conduct or to spit or the like. It is rather a misconduct to behave in this way. However, the single most important quality in a referee is his ability, in fact, to maintain control over the game in a very broad and general way, preventing a mood from setting in which will lead naturally to misconduct and behavior demeaning to the game of soccer and contrary to the spirit of sportsmanship in general.

Good game control, which will be the trade-mark of the outstanding referee, will in part depend on his ability to have and to exploit psychological insight, but it will also be fostered by certain learned or acquired techniques of officiating. To put it in another way, the referee must communicate with the players, which means he must, on one plane, understand them and know how to act toward them as people; and, on another plane, he must communicate with them according to various procedural customs. To take a specific example: to caution a player at the right time to prevent further problems requires psychological insight and communication on a high level, but the comments the referee makes and the holding aloft of the yellow card constitute communication and procedure on a much more technical level. The referee must also, in dealing with players, understand the difference between talking *to* them and talking *at* them!

In the next part of this book, I shall consider these two intertwined areas of technique and game control, of procedure and psychological insight as they affect the performance of the referee.

Part Two

It is difficult to separate conclusively technique from game control. For example, the *technique* of co-operation between the referee and his linesmen is the basis of the diagonal system of game *control*. I am taking a very special view of what constitutes "game control" for the writing of this book, limiting the term to psychological matters, personality factors, the effects of timing, and so forth. Everything else which does not pertain to the laws will be properly considered technique. In this present section we shall discuss some of those many things one can learn that will help him improve his performance from a technical viewpoint. Whereas many of the qualities properly pertaining to game control which are laudatory in a referee are intangibles and cannot be consciously learned — already being present or not — the things discussed here are, for the most part, learnable and should become part of the working repertory of every referee. We shall deal with everything from the referee's whistle and linesmen's flags to approaches to physical conditioning.

As I said at the beginning of this book one can break down officiating into three broad categories: knowledge of the laws, technique, and game control. The ultimate aim is consistently perfect game control and one can only strive to achieve that goal through a complete and sensible understanding of the laws of the game and near-mastery of effective technique. True, one can imagine a referee doing almost nothing and yet never losing game control — as in a match in which the players were in accord on all throw-ins and committed no fouls — but normally a referee's consistent game control will hinge on his technique (I shall assume throughout this discussion that our referee knows his rules).

Webster's dictionary defines technique as follows: "Expert method in execution of the technical details of accomplishing something (...); manner of performance with respect to mechanical features or formal requirements..."

Technique should not be confused with mechanics. The latter is subordinate to the notion of technique. It is that which technique must have as its formal common denominator. Thus, the laws of the game and such things as the dimensions and playing surface of a given field fall under the heading of mechanics (which Webster's defines as "mechanical details") while technique is the way in which the laws are interpreted and enforced and the way in which those other things like field conditions are taken into account as one sets about accomplishing his purpose. The diagonal system of control is an example of what might be termed *standardized technique*, and the personal way in which one handles situations such as the coin toss, a drop ball, corner kicks, or single-referee positioning provide examples of what might be termed *individualized technique*.

Game control — or more precisely whether or not play tends to become disreputable — is used by many spectators as the sole criterion for judging a referee. The spectator will see a game in which several players are ejected for serious foul play and say to himself that the referee is not doing a good job. It may be, however, that the players have been playing a poor game and that the official has not only been doing an excellent job, but has even demonstrated excellent technique in making the ejections when and how he did.

The first-rate French referee Michel Vautrot, upon my congratulating him for an impeccable performance in a First Division game between Red Star and Nantes, wrote back that he thought my remarks too generous since "refereeing will, perforce, be good when the players behave correctly." Although

I feel that Vautrot was being too modest in this particular instance, his statement is valid and one can, indeed, imagine a game in which the official has to do little more than whistle for the start at kick-off, half time, and after goals. I once refereed a children's game in which there was only one infraction during the entire game. We should remember, not without some nostalgic longing, that referees were only introduced into the game after years of more or less gentlemanly self-enforcement of the laws.

Thus, although good technique should ultimately lead to good game control, the latter is relative, for no two games are alike, and standardized technique will never reach a point where it yields standardized games. For example, had an official of inferior technique handled Vautrot's game, it might have turned nasty, or if an official so superb that his technique included many personal ways of de-fusing explosive situations had handled the above-mentioned hypothetical "bad" game involving several ejections, the level of misconduct might never have reached a point requiring such drastic action; although any referee will, of course, periodically have his abilities tested to the limit by malevolent fans, coaches, or players.

An official who is unpopular in a given game but whose technique is flawless is, in the long run, better off than the fleetingly popular official whose calls tend not to reflect the realities of play on the field. Anyone can be a "nice-guy ref" during an easy game; the true test comes when adversities having nothing to do with him personally make the game hard to handle. To work on technique is to develop greater consistency which will, in turn, win the respect of those who know the game.

We have already referred to the adage "Presence lends conviction," and if you are in a position to see foul play or that the ball is kicked away from the goal line in the nick of time, your call will not only be more accurate but more credible, as well. In short: positioning, which is part of technique, is vital in performing satisfactorily and, in turn, in maintaining game control. Referees should, in attempting to improve their game control and overall performance, concentrate on improving technique: appearance, use of equipment, conditioning, consistency, positioning, knowledge and interpretation of the laws, directional and informational signals, preventive manoeuvres, ability to communicate with players, and the like. Coaches and assessors, when evaluating an official, should concentrate their attention not on the outcome of the game or whether a good time was had by all, but on the official's technique, for that is what will, in the long run, determine his ability to achieve consistent game control under the most varied conditions.

I would be the last person to counsel against book-learning, but it is important that the new referee realize that he must exercise a blend of study and analysis of the laws with a lot of experience in the field. As a young man, my father read a book on swimming and practiced the strokes lying across a chair and then went into the water and swam. But another time he read a book on how to drive and maintain a car, then bought a car and set out to drive from Minneapolis to Philadelphia. He had somehow skipped the pages about changing oil at certain intervals and he burned out the engine in Indiana and had to sell the car for the price of a train ticket for the remaining portion of the trip. He received an expensive object lesson! But it was one that had obviously stuck since he used to tell it to us kids years later. No amount of reading or thinking about refereeing can take the place of game experience. They only serve as a valuable adjunct to it, for one will learn a great deal from his mistakes as well as find out which techniques conform to his personal temperament.

19

Tools of the Trade

Every professional has his tools. The weaver has a variety of knives, combs, and reeds to use in his craft, the plumber his wrenches and torches, the cowboy his lasso and chaps, and so it goes, on and on. The referee is no exception, and the condition and quality of his equipment is as important to him as the quality of a saw or drill is to the carpenter.

The referee must have a certain minimum of equipment when he takes to the field. Some of it is apparent and in constant use, some of it is emergency equipment. The referee's equipment should, aside from his uniform, include the following items: two watches (one with stop action), a notebook or scorecard, two pencils, two whistles (one for use, the other to be used if the first one fails or is lost), a coin or two, two plastic cards of about 3 x 5 inches (one yellow, one red), and a set of linesmen's flags. He will, in addition, find it useful to have in his kit-bag a small knife, cellophane sandwich bags and rubber bands (to protect from rain and sweat the player passes he may have to keep in his pocket), a tape measure, and a copy of the latest edition of the **Laws of the Game** or pertinent rule book.

The uniform is important. The saying goes that the "clothes make the man." I will not go so far as to suggest that the uniform makes the referee, harkening back instead to another saying: "Handsome is as handsome does." It is important both how one looks and acts in the initial stages of a match, for the interaction of referee and players is a superficial one and the ninety minutes together provide little time or opportunity for the eradication of conclusions to which others have jumped in the first few minutes. It is like a job interview — one has to get the job before he can demonstrate what he can do. Similarly, the referee has to work unnecessarily — in addition to the normal workload — to overcome poor impressions of him due to slovenly clothes, poor posture, questionable behavior, or downright improper behavior like drinking or smoking publicly on the field before the game.

The international referee's uniform consists of black shorts, black shirt or blouse with white collar and cuffs, black stockings with white tops, and black soccer-style shoes or officials' shoes. If a cap is worn, it should be black and of an appropriate style. The same goes for gloves in the event of very cold weather. There are different styles of uniform for different climates and to provide different tailoring. There are nearly indestructible nylon uniforms from England, lightweight flimsy uniforms from Sweden, form-fitting polyester uniforms from California, shiny uniforms with fancy collars from France, and short-sleeved shirts for summer use. I have four or five different types of uniform, but I prefer the polyester double-knit since it is comfortable and will stretch rather than rip when you burst into a sprint, especially after a two-month snow-out of soccer and Christmas dinners galore have made your uniform shrink an inch or two around the waist. In selecting a uniform be certain that the shirt has two pockets, one preferably having a button-down flap, and that the shorts have four pockets, one of the hip pockets having a button or flap. I bought one pair of shorts in France that had no hip pockets and two very shallow front pockets and they have proven to be useless.

The uniform should be kept clean and neat. The badge is to be affixed over the left pocket. The badge may be kept fresh-looking by removing it when washing the uniform. I find that the time it took to sew snap-ons onto the badge and on my various shirts was time well spent since I can interchange my various amateur, school, and college badges (USSF, EP&DISOA, PIAA, and NISOA!) and shirts and remove them in seconds when it comes time to launder the shirts.

Despite considerable rough play, the referee is able to keep the flow and spirit of the game intact. (M. Julius Baum)

Functionally the most important part of the uniform is the footgear. One must be certain that the shoes are comfortable in the store as an ill-fitting pair will give sore feet or even cause one to go lame. Once I had a brand-new pair of shoes which always hurt my ankles and made my Achilles Tendon ache. It had something to do with the lateral angle the shoes assumed when I ran on a soft field. I finally broke down and bought another pair, cheaper than the first, as it turned out, and they were excellent. I now keep the first pair with an extra uniform in the trunk of my car should I be pressed into service at a game where the official has failed to appear.

Shoes should be kept neatly polished for all games. I personally like, as well, to smear them with grease waterproofing if the field is very wet or muddy. If one covers them carefully and is sure to treat the entire seam around the sole, the shoes will stay dry through the entire game. I find nothing more annoying and enervating when officiating than to have water sloshing around in my shoes when I run around on the field.

The two watches one adopts will depend on one's finances and personal preference in techniques of time-keeping. There are expensive chronographs and cheap timers. One gets more or less what he pays for. I personally do not like to have the stopwatch in my pocket, but some referees do keep it in the shorts pocket or on a lanyard and in the shirt pocket. I find a wrist chronograph best. I have a Seiko stopwatch on one wrist and a Timex time-lapse watch on the other. I thus have two regular watches, one stop watch, one time-lapse ring that shows the number of minutes which have elapsed and another which shows how many minutes are left — all in these two instruments on my wrists! I have a tendency to forget to note down the time when the game ends — information required on our game reports — so the time-lapse ring is invaluable in that it shows me the end of running time, even hours later when I sit down to write my game report.

The whistle is the referee's trade-mark. He should have a good supply of them available and the new referee should experiment till he finds one that suits him. I have found that metal ones have a richer resonance but hurt the teeth and are cold in winter, so I generally use plastic whistles. There are rubber covers for the metal whistles, but I found that I did not like the feel of them. There are few whistles readily available (there is an Italian whistle that outblasts them all, but it is hard to procure) which can top the wide-mouthed Acme Thunderer in plastic.

There are three ways to carry the whistle: on a neck lanyard, on a finger grip, or on a wrist thong. The finger whistle is uncomfortable and one can strike his teeth when bringing the whistle up quickly to the mouth. The neck lanyard is preferred by many referees and it leaves the hands free for signaling, but it has one major drawback. One has a tendency to carry the whistle in the mouth when using a neck lanyard. This leads to premature signals and even to inadvertent whistling.

One colleague said that he gave up running with the whistle in the mouth after a bug flew in his nose, causing him to snort and blow the whistle by mistake. When I started officiating, I used a neck lanyard and I found that I tended to get set for a call although I did not run with the whistle in my mouth. That is, I anticipated end-line calls, putting the whistle in my mouth in order to be ready when the ball went over the line. The result was that I once called the ball out too soon, only to have the ball hit the post and bounce back into play. I took care of this irksome habit by switching to a wrist thong. I am convinced that this is the only way to carry the whistle, for you cannot run with the whistle in the mouth and you have a slight lag before signaling which avoids the telegraphing mentioned above and allows for a better application of the advantage clause. If one is switching to a wrist thong, he will find it a bit uncomfortable at first − I almost pulled out my incisors until I learned to hold the whistle in the hand all the time − but once he makes the adjustment, he will be better off than he was before.

A wrist thong can be purchased or easily made from a heavy-duty shoelace cut to length. A loop which measures about nine inches when stretched taut is appropriate and a slide can be contrived from a knot or a tube of plastic, rubber, or wood of appropriate calibre to slide when pulled but not slide down by itself. An adequate slide can be made by rolling a bit of index card material into a tube about one inch long and wrapping it with Scotch vinyl tape.

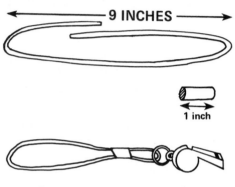

Figure 28: WRIST THONG

Another advantage to the wrist thong is that the whistle, being held in the hand, is less likely to freeze up in cold weather.

There is an art to using the whistle. Jack Hyde has a fine essay on referee Jack Taylor, the man who officiated the 1974 World Cup final between West Germany and Holland. Hyde speaks of Taylor's authority and stage presence, and how, right from the beginning of the game, his whistle speaks as though it were an extension of the voice and mood of the man. Hyde writes:

> "His opening whistle to call the captains to the center circle for the coin toss was a direct blast and seemed to say, 'OK, guys, I've decided to get the proceedings underway,' with the emphasis on 'I've decided.' The previous week I'd watched another 1st Division game where the proceedings were started with two short whistles, and not very direct sounding ones at that: 'If you don't mind, I think we ought to start,' they seemed to say. 22

Just as the referee would not want to sound or appear either overly timid or garrulous, his whistle should be neither pusillanimous nor overbearing. The whistle should be used only when necessary or when its use helps the referee forestall a problem, as when he feels that a player will perhaps dispute that a ball went out of touch. In the case of routine signals, he should make them firm, but in a "normal voice", so to speak, that is, at a volume near the middle of his register. He should save the full blast for severe fouls when he would want his whistle to take on a special edge, as though to say, "Knock it off! We're not having any of that business today!"

Next to the whistle and the watch in importance is the referee's booklet or scorecard where he keeps a record of the game. I have yet to meet two referees who use the same technique in this matter. Some use a plain book, as in the case of one of our finest referees who puts game records down in a little book in which he indiscriminately enters addresses, appointments, and everything else in his work-a-day life as well. Some like to use a long pencil and stick it in their stocking top, others prefer the short pencil stub attached to the booklet. Some prefer to keep a scorecard in a folder. This is the method I quickly found to suit me.

I have experimented with various types of cards in an effort to reduce to an absolute minimum the sheer mechanics of noting goals and documenting cautions and ejections. After a goal has been scored and especially after a caution, the referee does not want to delay the restart of play more than necessary because he is fumbling around with pages, yellow card, pencil and the like.

Below is a scorecard layout which allows one — whether referee or coach — to keep a record in a clear, concise, and efficient manner. The record thus kept may also be conveniently stored away in a small file box. During the game, the 3 x 5 inch scorecard is kept in a vinyl or plastic folder of the sort covering pocket planners or calendars. The card is slipped under the right-hand pocket, and one can keep caution and ejection cards, line-ups, and so forth in the other pocket. The scorecard has only one half exposed to eliminate confusion and may be reversed at half time. It is easy to contrive a pencil holder by attaching a suitable caliber tube of card material to the vinyl holder with black Scotch vinyl tape. A few turns of tape around the top, or a broad eraser, will keep the pencil from slipping through. Reverse the direction of the pencil in the holder at half time and you will be less likely to open the holder upside down. I have used such a folder for more than a hundred games without its having deteriorated a bit.

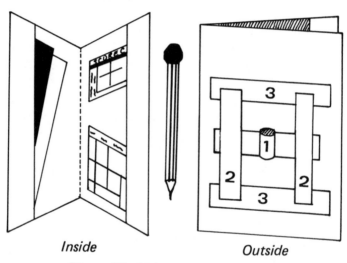

Inside   *Outside*

Figure 29: SCORECARD HOLDER

The card itself allows for the recording of all the information required later when the referee files his game report or which a coach might need to recall at some later date when reviewing the match. If overtimes occur, box scores can be entered under "Comments" on the back of the card. It is suggested, however, that a special second card be prepared to record postgame tie-breaking kicks from the penalty spot if the particular rules of competition call for such an eventuality.

The scorecards can be drawn up individually by hand or a rough version can be mass-produced by preparing a linoleum block or by cutting a stencil with an X-acto knife and then

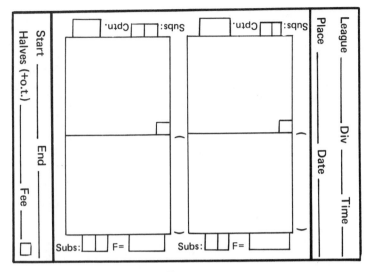

Front

Cautions:	Ejections:	Injuries:

FIELD a) Surface b) Markings	Comments:
Weather:	

Back

Figure 30: SCORECARD

running a felt-tip marker over the slots. The cards can also be duplicated commercially (as was the example shown here) at a moderate cost.

As we have seen in dealing with several of the laws, the referee is called upon from time to time to issue cautions and to eject players. The technique by which these cautions and ejections are administered can be of great importance. It is important, among other things, that the referee make it quite clear to the player, his coach, and the interested fans, that he is booking the player officially. To this end, the referee carries a yellow caution card and a red ejection card. When administering the caution or ejection, the referee is to hold aloft the appropriate card for all to see.

These cards can be made of construction paper and the players' names written right on them, or of more durable plastic. They may be purchased from any of several major soccer outlets if one prefers. I carry a set of them in my vinyl scorecard holder and an extra yellow one handy in my shirt pocket, for I believe that as soon as the referee has decided to caution a player he should forthwith produce the yellow card.

It is as a part of his duty to "enforce the laws" that the official administers cautions and ejections, and he should do so much as he would signal infractions, firmly but without personal malice. Just as the referee should not wax furious at a player for committing a foul (some referees seem to think it an outrage that a player would dare to trip an opponent when he is officiating), he should not become overly emotional in the administration of his form of justice for misconduct. The one time I do let the player know my displeasure in no uncertain terms is when he touches me. If a player lays his hand on my arm when protesting a call, I tell him to take his hands off me immediately, even if it is not meant as a menacing gesture. In the same spirit, I *never* touch a player, such as when moving a defensive wall of players back to a distance of ten yards from the ball.

I have seen referees shove and push players around like chess pawns; this seems to me to be an invitation to the players

Action near the goal-mouth can challenge a referee. Was the ball all the way over the line? Did the foul prevent a score? (M. Julius Baum)

to respond physically. The player to be cautioned or ejected should, after the card has been held up, be told why he is thus being punished and — if it involves a caution — informed that he will be ejected if there is further cause for discipline. The referee should note the player's jersey number and team, and have him give and spell his first and last name. The referee should enter all this on his card or in his book and make a note of the time the incident occurred. Time should be entered not as "2nd half, 20 minutes" but rather as "65 minutes." He should then restart play in accordance with the laws. All this should be done calmly and play restarted as quickly as possible.

Many referees feel that the best way to maintain game control is to keep the game moving; idle players can easily become disgruntled players. Stoppages should, therefore, be kept as short as possible in general and especially when they are the occasion for disciplinary action or after a goal where some dissention appears imminent. "Get the ball back into play," is sound advice.

I like to let the player know that I am not personally angry at him and that what I am doing is rather part of my job. If I am not angry about it, he will perhaps better understand that the caution or ejection derives directly from his conduct and not from my low tolerance for, say, dissent or violence. Usually, as I pull out my yellow card and scorecard, I quietly say something like: "OK, that's enough now, let's get the paper work over with so we can get on with the game." In other words, I want it understood by the players that certain actions on their part will automatically draw cautions and that I need not be goaded to some point where I whip out the card in vengeance. I hope, too, that they understand from my behavior that I do not necessarily think that a caution puts them in a bad light should their behavior be exemplary thereafter. What I want to say with my tone of voice is that the future standing of the player in the game will depend on him, not me! Clearly to be avoided is the following scene which rightfully upset Robert Evans:

> At a First Division game in Mexico, I was horrified to see the procedure used by one referee when he chose to caution a player. He ran straight at the offender, wildly waving the yellow card under his nose. The player backed off in surprise, obviously shaken by the attitude of the official. It was apparent to all that the referee was so emotionally involved in that game that he took the offense personally.[23]

It is not from such a man that one might expect justice to be done in a cool detached manner.

In regard to cautions, the referee must remember that the players have their rights, too. All too often one hears referees tell of issuing a "team caution" or a "captain's caution". These are interesting ideas, but they are unsupported by anything specifically laid down in the laws and are contrary to the fundamental spirit of fair play. To send off a previously innocent man for a cautionary offense because of a prior general team caution is, it seems to me, unlawful; and the "captain's caution" is an abuse of the traditional but uncanonized notion that the captain be expected to assist the referee in seeing to it that his players observe the laws.

What do these phrases, in fact, mean? The choice of words is most important. One topflight writer has described a "team caution" in the following terms:

> It is sometimes necessary to issue a general caution to the whole team, which means that any player who thereafter commits any one of the major offenses, as stipulated in Law [12], shall be sent off the field.[24]

I do not know where this oft-held idea had its genesis,* but the semantic confusion between the terminology of the international rules and that of the rules applying to school and college games has certainly not helped matters any. The school referees talk about official "warnings" (their version of the international-rules caution) and to caution a player in those circles has no official impact but is mere finger-wagging. Conversely, if the FIFA referee "warns" a player, it means he is not officially booking him but merely telling him to watch his step.

The referee is perfectly within his rights if he notifies an entire team or both teams directly or through their captains that, in the interest of game control, he will take a very narrow and rigid view in regard to any future marginal activities on their part. He must not, however, subsequently tell a player that he is ejecting him for "dangerous play", "ungentlemanly conduct", or "persistent infringement" if he has not specifically cautioned and booked that player previously. The referee *may*, of course, view as "violent conduct" or "unseemly conduct" — calling for ejection — something which prior to the general notification he might have considered less provocative and warranting, therefore, only a caution. In short, the referee can serve notice that he is not going to put up with any nonsense and will make full use of the authority granted him under Laws 5 and 12.

It is as inequitable to give a "captain's caution" as it is to

---

*I have heard that the policy of team cautions was adopted at one of the World Cup Finals — apparently with some success — but that the practice was subsequently abandoned as inequitable.

give a "team caution", with the further drawback that it specifies the injustice in the person of one player as a scapegoat. The referee can exhort the captain to assist him by having his teammates desist from encroaching or handling the ball, for example, and he is even within his rights to tell the captain that he will terminate the game (for "other cause" as laid out in Law 5, d) if the activity continues, but he cannot fairly or by any extension of the laws of the game caution and book the captain for an offense committed by another player. Again, he can alert him to the consequences should the captain's players not co-operate, but those consequences must, in turn, be *ad hominem* and according to the norms laid down in the laws.

How, then, can one deal with the messy situation of generalized misconduct that tends to bring the game into disrepute, such as when one player after another encroaches on free kicks or handles high passes through to the attackers? The referee can do one of three things or a combination of these things: (1) the referee can ignore some of the offenses in the interest of maintaining dignity and game control quietly coping with the situation by talking to the player as play continues (with regard, say, to encroaching); (2) the referee can caution each player as he encroaches, handles, and so forth; (3) the referee can officially caution every team member for ungentle-manly conduct or the like, being certain that every player has been guilty of some cautionary offense.

The referee can use variations and combinations of these solutions of which only the second is clearly prescribed by common sense and the laws, the first solution being dangerous, and the third one a sure path to perdition if slavishly followed!

Clearly, the referee cannot let everything ride when a generalized problem begins to develop, nor can he preside over a circus in which he trots around booking every team member. Every referee recognizes that he must on occasion desist from cautioning in order to make the yellow card retain some real impact and importance on the field and in the eyes of the arbitration board. Norman Burtenshaw describes one of his matches in which almost the entire Benfica team committed dissent, ungentlemanly conduct, or violent conduct. As he concludes, he could not gracefully caution or eject the entire team but entered the details in his game report:

> Some players grabbed my arms, pulled my shirt and pushed me. One spat in my face. It was impossible to caution any particular player or send one off because the whole team seemed involved. If one went, the whole lot would have to go.
> "It was four minutes before we were able to control the Portuguese players. Normally Portuguese footballers are most disciplined, but when they go, they really go! I reported the whole team to UEFA with the exception of the goalkeeper.[25]

On the other hand, to caution only one player seems all too often to have little effect on the behavior of teammates. Often the referee will caution a defender for standing in front of the ball on a free kick, only to have some other player do the same thing next time around and be genuinely astonished when cautioned. This is an especially frequent occurrence in junior and high-school games. It is at such moments that one must resist the temptation to issue a collective caution.

The method prescribed by Robert Evans and others for coping with tactical encroachment, as when a defensive wall refuses to move back to ten yards before the kick, is to caution methodically one player after another until they move back. This is, of course, a last resort in which the referee must demonstrate that he is not abdicating his authority. The early exemplary caution (not against the captain, but against an offender) with a firm but courteous word or two might be more effective. One colleague whom I respect a great deal suggests that if one is going to caution, he should caution early, in the first ten or fifteen minutes.

It is fascinating to see the way in which the defensive wall at a distance of less than ten yards brings out the qualities or styles of players and officials alike. I saw radically different approaches to situations in two games in Sweden, in 1963 and in 1972, respectively. In a First Division game played at Stockholm's old stadium on Storagatan, one team set up a wall about six yards from the ball. The attacker asked the referee to move them back. The wall was formed around a once great player who was now "over the hill" and whose jersey stretched comically over his big stomach. The obese player was apparently a much-loved joker and surely a crowd-pleaser. The referee marched to a spot ten yards from the ball and the wall backed up. As the referee marched back toward the ball the players in the wall took back two of the yards in step with the referee. I cannot condone the behavior of the players in the wall, and surely the referee should not have turned his back, but I must admit that the whole incident was very comical. The crowd laughed with genuine amusement; not at the referee, but at the players' cancan motions. The referee, even with his back turned, surely could tell something had occurred, but he called for the kick to be taken. The attacker was sensible enough to realize that nothing could be gained by making a fuss out of the two yards, and he took the kick and the game went on without further incident.

The other game was between AIK of Stockholm and Partick Thistle in a summer tournament called the "July Cup". The referee put down the ball for a free kick for Partick Thistle and began to run over to judge the offside. The player took a quick kick and, when the referee turned around, the ball was already well into play. He whistled, placed the ball back at the same spot and wagged a finger at the player. He ran back towards the offside position and the player took the quick kick again, without waiting for the whistle. I don't know if he understood what the referee wanted, but the referee now had no choice but to caution the Partick Thistle player. There was a great deal of officiousness displayed and considerable time wasted. The official might have let play continue the first time, remembering, for future reference, that this team likes to take quick kicks, or, at the very least, he might have backpedaled the second time around and given a quick whistle for play to resume. The law states that the referee shall signal for the recommencement of play after all stoppages and this official was technically in the right but he was not self-serving in this instance. It is possible that the second official was the more qualified of the two referees I am talking about, but on the basis of the two games I saw, the former handled his free-kick situation far better.

The referee must conscientiously evaluate the extent and nature of each situation and invoke a blend of authority and self-restraint, avoiding over-reaction. He should, if necessary, caution or eject the guilty party or parties only; he should not caution or eject one player as a proxy for another. He should not, furthermore, think that he can give a blanket "team caution" which carries official cautionary status regarding a further offense; and he should realize that to truly and officially caution or eject a whole team is tantamount to abandoning the game.

All too few referees bring a set of linesmen's flags to their games without neutral linesmen. In matches officiated by three officials, the flags with which linesmen signal their opinions are a fixture of the game. However, club linesmen — appointed from among the coaching staff, players, or spectators — are usually seen gesticulating with a towel, sweatshirt, or handkerchief, if not with a bare hand.

There are two references to these flags in Law 6, and no distinction is drawn between their adoption by neutral certified linesmen and club linesmen. Law 6 contains only five sentences, the last of which states, "The Linesmen should be equipped with flags by the Club on whose ground the match is played." The third IBD following the law itself adds: "In International Matches Linesmen's flags shall be of a vivid colour, bright reds and yellows. Such flags are recommended for use in all other matches."

Since there is no exclusion clause exempting club linesmen from this law and its attendant Board Decision, it would appear that *all* home teams should provide satisfactory flags for both neutral and club linesmen. This is seldom the case, so it is wise for the referee to bring along a set of flags, one red and one yellow. (In a game with neutral linesmen, the senior linesman carries the red flag and it is he who normally replaces the referee if the latter is incapacitated.) Club linesmen will usually do a more efficient job with proper flags and their use makes it easier for the referee to make decisions with accuracy and authority. Just as fields which are well marked and equipped with corner and optional midstripe flags tend to foster better officiating and, thus, better soccer, so does the use of linesmen's flags add a touch of care and professionalism which can only improve performance all around.

There is no reason why every club and every referee cannot have a good set of flags. They can be had for a few dollars from sports outlets handling soccer referee uniforms and supplies. Furthermore, if none are available an excellent set of flags can easily and inexpensively be made with several dollars' worth of material and an hour's labor.

Materials: Two 3/8-inch dowels; four cheap thermos-type corks; two small picture-hanging screw-eyes; half a yard each of red and yellow polyester or nylon material; a yard each of red and yellow hemming material.

1. Cut the 3/8-inch dowels to an appropriate length of about 19 or 20 inches.

2. Drill a 3/8-inch hole through two corks and about 3/4-inch into the broad end of the other corks. Glue the broad end of the pierced cork to the broad end of the half-drilled cork and insert the dowel into this handle and glue. A piece of vinyl tape may be applied around the middle of the handle to reinforce the joint.

Handles may also be carved from balsa wood or contrived from padding and vinyl tape. A handle can be improvised by forcing a four-inch length of rubber tubing (of the sort found on hand showers) over the end of the dowel. Replacement tool-handles, bought in a hardware store, may also be used, but they take a smaller dowel and therefore tend to split.

3. Screw the eye into the dowel about four inches above the handle. Be sure to predrill the dowel to avoid splitting.

4. Cut a rectangle of polyester or nylon material (about 14 x 10 inches); the final shape, after hemming, should be such as to allow the linesman to clasp the end of the flag with his thumb while holding the handle.

Fold a narrow hem around the piece and machine sew. Then take a piece of color-matching hem material and run it up along the edge of one end of the rectangle, fold it over the top and run it down the other side (as shown in the illustration). Machine sew up the outer edge, across the top of the little piece and down the inner edge of the hemming material. Be sure to leave the bottom unstitched, forming a long thin pocket, and leave some of the strip hanging so that it may be shaped with scissors and hemmed to make strings with which to secure the flag to the staff.

Now slip the pocket over the dowel and tie the end-straps to the screw-eye. This attachment allows the flag to be removed for laundering and also prevents the flag from riding up the stick. Other methods, such as drilling holes through the dowels or nailing material to the dowels, are less satisfactory and increase the likelihood of the flagstaff splitting or breaking. It is just as well to make several sets of flags at once when one has the materials handy and the sewing machine set up.

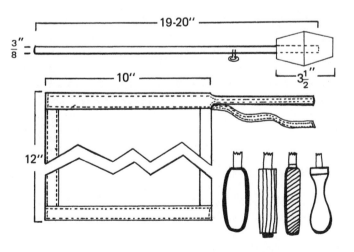

Figure 31: LINESMAN'S FLAG

Laws 1, 2, and 4 all deal with provisions which are supposedly met before the ball has even been put into play to start the game. It is wise for the referee to carry a short ruler and a tape measure in his kit-bag so that he can check cleat dimensions, touchline, goal line, and goal post widths, the circumference of the ball, and such sundries as the height of corner flags. Usually you will check these things with a calculated eye estimate, but it is well to be prepared in the event a coach, captain or league official asks for an accurate assessment. In the event you do not have with you such measuring equipment, you can make fairly accurate measurements with improvised tools.

The measurements in Law 4 pertain to minimum width (1/2-inch) and maximum length (3/4-inch) of studs and/or bars, allowance being made for multiple molded-sole cleats whose diameter may not exceed three-eighths of an inch. (Collegiate rules call for molded cleats to be no longer than 5/16-inch and not extremely conical in design.)

A penny will suffice to cover the measurements involving footwear. The diameter of a penny is three-quarters of an inch and studs and bars deeper than a penny are not in strict conformity to the laws. It is half an inch from the bottom of the penny to the top of the Lincoln Memorial replica on the verso of the penny; it is three-eighths of an inch from the bottom of the penny to the center of the memorial (the middle of the tiny figure of Lincoln); and it is five-sixteenths of an inch from the bottom of the penny to the floor level of the memorial, that is, where the top of the stairs meets the bottom of the columns. Furthermore, a penny is acceptable as an extra coin to have in your pocket for the toss required at various times during matches.

The quarter has a diameter of 15/16-inch and is useful to make a rough measurement of goal-line widths, etc. A 3 x 5 inch card provides a basis for some measurements, such as the five-inch maximum width of field markings.

Naturally one can suggest homemade devices such as a string or card with various measurements marked off along it, but then one might as well carry a plastic-coated cloth measuring tape. The beauty of the above-mentioned "tools" lies in the fact that they are improvised from things either automatically with you or readily available from a coach or spectator. One can take a personal inventory and see if other things he takes on the field with him are of a useful dimension, such as the length of his whistle thong or lanyard, length of detachable cuffs, and so forth. For my car key, I have a key chain with a small folding knife on it. I have marked this blade — useful in its own right for mending nets, trimming a protruding ball-nipple, and the like — as a stud gauge with the appropriate measurements of 3/8, 1/2, and 3/4 inches.

I sweat fairly profusely, especially on a humid summer day. At half time my nylon shirt has a zigzag of salt on the front and back that looks like an Alpine landscape. This is one reason why I prefer the polyester uniform which "breathes" and doesn't turn white with salt. The first time I refereed a vigorously contested junior game, I returned as a sodden mass the pack of players' passes which I had checked and retained in my shirt pocket for the duration of the game. Since that experience I always carry to each game two sandwich bags into which I insert the two stacks of passess. I can then return them to the coaches in the same condition they were in when I received them.

20

Pregame Formalities

Having considered at some length the referee's equipment, let us turn to his first duties upon arriving at the field. There are certain pregame formalities to see to and he should go about them efficiently but without undue fuss. The players will be watching him and, if they do not know him, trying to size him up. The way he speaks to them, the attention he gives to his task, and the like, will do much to tell them whether he "knows his business" or is unsure of himself.

The referee should arrive at his assigned field at least a half-hour before the scheduled kick-off, earlier if the league requirements so dictate. He will need to allow at least ten minutes prior to the start of play for such things as checking line-ups, players' passes (where required), and reviewing substitution rules and the like with the coaches and/or captains. He should, therefore, take care of other duties immediately upon arrival. A quick eye-check of the field lining to verify that all markings — including corner quadrants, restraining arcs near the penalty areas, the center circle, and the goal line — are present and the referee will then be ready to check more closely the crucial dimensions.

The area which is most frequently measured off improperly is also the most vital besides the goal line: namely the penalty area. If the areas are not properly measured, the referee should point this out to the home captain and, if it is impossible to rectify the error, inform both captains how he will operate in terms of the incorrect markings, i.e., use them "as is" or use his own judgment; and he should urge that it be corrected prior to the next game. If penalty spots have been marked, the referee should verify their accuracy and inform the captains that they are correct or — in the event that they are not and cannot be rectified — that he will pace off the distance should a penalty kick be awarded.

The referee should take note of any dangerous conditions or circumstances which need explanation before the kick-off. I once officiated an amateur game between 18-year-olds on a field which had two noteworthy hazards. There was a sharp metal rim to a cinder track which formed an arc well into one side of the field and there was a metal pipe sticking out of the ground about a yard outside the opposite touchline near midfield. The pipe was the same color as the cyclone fence five yards beyond it and was perfectly camouflaged. The captain, in pregame discussion, pointed it out to me and said that a player had once run right into it at full speed and been knocked unconscious. I had the home team drape a bright red jacket over the pipe and told the captains to alert their players to the potential hazard. I also informed them that a serious injury, such as a torn Achilles tendon, could result from the metal track-rim and that I would, therefore, stop play and have a drop ball away from the hazard if the players became embroiled in a contest for the ball at that point and it appeared that injury might result. I called for two such drop balls during the game and there were no complaints since policy had been established prior to the start of the game.

Similarly, one must establish a policy with regard to such things as overhanging branches and make certain that the captains are fully aware of how you intend to handle these irregularities. There is one high-school field where I officiate where a branch sticks at least four yards out into the field of play over one of the goals. I always inform the players how I shall handle a ball which hits the branch although the branch is some thirty or forty feet above the ground and the players have informed me that no one can remember it having been struck. One day a ball may very well strike that branch, fall to the

Another break through the defense. The goalkeeper is faked out of the play and the ball is slowly rolled toward a corner of the goal. (Doug Schwab)

ground in front of the goal, and be kicked into the net; and if that occurs when I am the official, I want to be certain that discussion occurred before the kick-off and not subsequent to the ball entering the net!

As we mentioned in Part One, it is very important to check carefully the goal nets and to have the home team repair any holes and attach the net more securely to the uprights, crossbar, and the ground behind the net if there is any possibility of a ball slipping through, either from the inside or the outside. Particular attention should be paid to the side nets at the foot of the uprights and to the upper corners where sometimes nets are casually hooked and stretched over the corner point. A good hard shot can go into the goal and out the side net or top or, conversely, it can strike the side net on the outside and go through it into the goal. I once had to deal with a hard shot by the right winger which I could have sworn struck the side net just behind the upright and went through it into the goal. I could see, however, from the defenders' dejection and the attackers' elation that it must have been a goal. I had made a careful check of the goal nets before the game and even half-hitched the cord to the nails in several places, so I unobtrusively ran past the goal, saw that the side net was still secure, and could give the goal with a clear conscience.

Had I not prechecked the nets and now found them loose, I should have been in a quandary as to whether to disallow a goal I had not clearly seen or to go with the circumstantial evidence of the behavior of the players from both sides. The referee should, in this context, recall that more sophisticated players sometimes will try to exploit the fact that they suspect the referee is not sure of a shot by instantly acting out the emotions natural to the decisions they would like to encourage. In other words, the defense would not look dejected about such a goal but grab the ball, clap hands, and run out to the six-yard line for the taking of a goal kick. Such behavior may be grounds for a caution.

If good markings are required to conform to the laws, the condition of the nets is most vital to the successful prosecution of one's duties. As I have already said, even if the referee must assist the managers in securing the nets and patching holes, it is time and effort well spent. It is of the utmost importance that the nets be staunch!

The meeting with the two captains at the center of the field can be an elaborate ceremony or little more than the taking of the toss, depending on the personality of the referee, the matters to be discussed (obstacles, tie-breaking kicks, etc.), and the type or level of game. In one of the first games I refereed, I was so determined to cover everything that I forgot to flip the coin. When I told the players to bring out their teams, one captain asked: "Aren't we going to have the toss?"

One should really not be garrulous nor inject more than is essential. However, if the referee feels that he may have some problems with a clash in team styles or senses that tempers may get a bit heated (you can tell from the immediate hostility of some coaches — even though they have never laid eyes on you and have no reason to be spiteful save through a generic dislike for referees — that the players have surely not been inculcated with respect for you), he may want to inform the captains that they have come to play soccer and that he, as referee, has come to decide infractions, determine intent, and decide when and if to apply the advantage clause. He can let them know that they should concentrate on their job and he will concentrate on his. If expressed courteously but firmly, a few words of this nature suffice, if not to guarantee a smooth match, at least to serve notice that he as referee does not intend to tolerate dissent, ungentlemanly conduct, and persistent infringement or any other kind of wanton behavior — no matter how subtle — that will bring the game into disrepute.

If the referee has been assigned neutral linesmen, he should be sure to go over all the technical aspects of game control, coverage, signaling, and so forth (dealt with elsewhere in this book), and he should instruct club linesmen as to their duties — reminding them that all of the ball must be over the entire line before they signal out-of-play. This should be done calmly and in an unofficious manner and not be left, therefore, till the last minute.

21

Signaling

There are certain procedural techniques not covered in the laws but which make up an important part of the referee's "image". The only gesture prescribed by law is the signal of the hand aloft for an indirect free kick. The referee is not forbidden to make additional signals and there is no earthly reason he shouldn't make them, as long as they are not confusing. The British, with the traditional restraint — what the French call *le flegme britannique* — for which they are famous, look askance at any signaling not absolutely necessary, although several of the F.A. referees have spoken out in favor of more communication with fans and players through hand and body signals. In a sense those people have a right to know what is going on — this is in keeping with modern disclosure in politics and the like — and communication will help prevent the referee's motives from being misunderstood as they so often are!

Some personal set of signals will ultimately be developed by every referee, but it is wise to standardize them according to region and country. His signals should, in any event, be clear, prompt, and crisp. He should be firm in rendering the signals, for the way he does them will reflect his state of mind. A wavering directional signal will bespeak an uncertainty in the mind of the referee as to which side committed the infraction. By the same token, the referee should avoid being theatrical or arrogant in his demeanor and gestures. I saw one game in France where the referee gave a play-on signal — arm outstretched with his palm upwards, his other palm on his breast — which would have been more appropriate for an opera singer in full aria or Romeo courting Juliet. Furthermore, he had instructed his linesmen to make a full twirl of the flag to attract his attention before indicating the direction. These linesmen looked more like toreadors whirling capes than linesmen!

Some referees are wont to hold up one finger to indicate a direct free kick and two fingers to indicate an indirect free kick. This is not proper, for the one finger aloft could be construed as a signal for indirect and would provide grounds for an appeal should films support the assertion that the referee then allowed a goal to stand which had gone untouched into the net. The players could argue, even well after the fact, that they had thought it was an indirect free kick since the referee held up his arm.

Some referees are low-key, others are shouters. I tend to talk a lot to the players and to call out infractions and instructions like "Play on" loud and clear. One must develop his own effective style that works best for him in the maintenance of game control and to permit the fair prosecution of the match. Both styles can be defended, but, for what it's worth, a friend of mine who played for the Philadelphia Flyers and other professional ice hockey teams and who had the reputation of being a "ref-hater", said that he always felt that the best referees were the talkers. He said the players respected a referee who would communicate with them, talk to them, function down in the trenches as it were. I do not believe that the referee should swear with the players, or touch them or get too familiar with them, but he should always let them know what he is doing and thinking in connection with the mechanics of the game. He can be a shouter as part of his technique without being emotional. If I yell "Play on!" I want not only the player in question to hear it but the goalkeepers and the benches as well! I personally recommend a combination of hand signals and word signals to be absolutely certain that the message has been received!

There are two types of signal: directional and informational. As we have said, the only signal prescribed by law is that for an indirect free kick. This is an informational signal. The rest of the signals are customary or part of the referee's personal communications system. As has been said, some countries frown on extraneous signaling whereas others feel that a good bit of "public address" is desirable. The American referee tends to be in the latter category, partly no doubt as a result of the very elaborate systems of signaling in other popular American sports like football, basketball, baseball, and hockey.

The soccer referee officiating according to FIFA laws is not required to give more than the rudimentary directional and informational signals to permit the game to proceed correctly — for example, he might indicate the direction by pointing, the place the free kick is to be taken from, and that it is direct by *not* putting his hand in the air — and is not required to satisfy the curiosity of the public with regard to which of the major or minor offenses he is calling. However, the player who courteously asks what the call is has a right, it seems to me, to an answer although the laws do not say that the referee must so answer. I believe that it is not only a good idea for the enjoyment of those playing and watching, if the referee gives additional signals for holding, obstruction, and the like, but also believe that such communication will help avoid unnecessary dissent.

Once, when I was running line near the coaches' bench, a defending player dove about two feet above the ground to head out the ball and the referee blew the whistle. The coach was very upset because he thought a penalty kick had been called for something he had not seen and by the time he understood that the call involved the diving head and would be punished by a less dangerous indirect free kick, he had already shouted some hysterical, abusive, and foul things. The referee is not expected to satisfy the idle curiosity of the coaches, nor is it his job to placate them when they get emotional, but at least five or six times a game he can avoid taking unnecessary artillery fire simply by consistently making it clear (by voice and/or hand signal) why he is stopping play.

The three things which he must basically indicate are the

place where the infraction occurred, the direction the kick should be taken, and the kind of free kick. On a typical direct free kick for pushing, the referee will blow his whistle, point clearly up or down field to indicate which team has been awarded the kick, and point to the spot for the restart. Some referees reverse the order, indicating the spot and then the direction or even indicate both simultaneously, using both arms. The referee may also show by a hand signal that it involves pushing (a pushing gesture with one or both hands) and yell "Pushing on White, Blue's kick, *direct*" or whatever.

I know from personal experience as a sometimes goalkeeper before becoming a referee, that goalkeepers do not know the laws any better than do the other players and will often call out to the referee for a clarification, even when he is holding his hand aloft! I make sure that I call out "direct" or "indirect", especially when the kick is being taken near the goal. I even address the goalkeeper loud and clear: "Direct kick, goalkeeper!" If a goal is to be scored, it should be through skill and not merely the result of confusion or poor communication. The more the referee can do to keep the players' attention on the game of soccer rather than on trying to figure out technicalities, the better the game will be for all concerned, including himself!

There are no standardized international signals for the various infractions, but in the United States one can use some of the signals dictated by the school and college rules and which are generally understood by the American public.

Caution should be exercised, however, as several of these signals might merely add to the confusion. The referee should, for example, be certain that his signal for jumping at an opponent is not easily confused with an indirect free kick signal. By the same token, the advantage signal prescribed by the college rules looks like the indirect free kick signal and the referee should rather use one of the international signals for this according to his own preference:

1) a rolling up and out of the hands as though emptying a bucket straight in front of the stomach; see Fig. 33, p. 242.

Figure 32: SOME REFEREE SIGNALS

2) an arm or both arms held out palm upward as though to invite the players to continue;

3) a waving of the two arms held outstretched. (See Fig. 34 on page 242.)

I personally favor the latter as being most self-explanatory, but I also yell out "Play on!" to avoid any confusion.

The offside signal borrowed from American football — hands striking hips, arms akimbo — is understood universally in

Figure 33: ADVANTAGE

Figure 34: PLAY ON

Figure 35: ALTERNATE OFFSIDE GESTURE

this country and should be used; but the referee may prefer to use another signal if one of the teams is from abroad. The usual signal in this instance is to hold one or both arms outstretched in front of oneself and, with the hands held down at right angles to the forearm, to draw an imaginary line back and forth, parallel to the ground and to the goal line. (Fig. 35).

Tripping may be indicated by a swipe of the foot or an undercutting gesture of the hand.

Holding may be indicated by grabbing one wrist with the other hand.

Handling of the ball may be indicated by tapping the arm or the hand with the other hand. The hands should be held high when making this signal as it will otherwise not be seen. One must be sure, at the same time, not to make the gesture in such a way that it looks like a time-out signal.

Obstruction may be indicated by tapping the chest with the palms as shown on the diagram, but this will not be understood by non-Americans. The signal for carrying by the goalkeeper beyond the four steps is the traveling signal from basketball and will be understood by most Americans, but others may confuse it with the signal European coaches sometimes use of twirling the fingers to signal a substitution to the referee. The referee should think through his "communications system" and keep in mind those he is communicating with. He should try to communicate but avoid being "showy", as people will then find him ludicrous and unprofessional.

End-line decisions must be made clearly and promptly to avoid discussion between opponents. For the goal kick, the referee shall point directly at the goal area; for a corner, out at the corner with the palm open and the arm held at a 45-degree angle in the air. Thus players and spectators will recognize the difference between these two calls regardless of the angle whence they view it.

Similarly, throw-in decisions should be shown clearly and promptly if there is a chance that players will disagree. If it is obvious who gets to throw the ball, the referee need make no signal, but he should be ready to intervene if the wrong team tries to take the throw. Some players automatically try to take the throw-in with the intention of influencing the referee's directional signal. Such players bear watching and possibly deserve cautioning if they persist in this practice.

It should be recalled that the referee is out on the field to referee a game and not to put on a mime show. If he injects himself into the play overly much, the players and fans will start riding him. He should not try to suppress his personality but find a way to meld his own character with the standardized gestures and any additional items he feels will help him officiate efficiently.

Some signals are more urgent than others. I personally feel that the advantage decision should be clearly communicated to

A fullback lunges heroically to clear, but is injured. With minutes to play in a 1-0 game the injury must be handled quickly, lest the crowd grow restive. (Will Everly)

all as it might otherwise be thought — albeit as a result of ignorance like as not — that the referee has not seen or understood the foul or, worse yet, seen it and not dared or cared to call it! I yell "Play on!" so loudly that once I had a nearby player complain that I made his ear drum ring.

There is one instance in which no signal is required and, in a sense, should not really be made. This is when there has been something which is not in violation of the laws but looks quite a bit like an infraction. Examples of this are unintentional handling of the ball or a player tripping himself over an opponent's foot which is making contact with the ball. One should not make a practice of calling "Play on!" for all of these instances as they are too frequent and will sabotage the effect of the genuine advantage calls by whose brilliance a referee shall ultimately distinguish himself.

Once or twice a game there will, however, be situations which it appears to the referee might cause bad blood between opponents despite the fact that no foul has occurred. In such cases — for example, rather hard contact on a high head or in simultaneous tackling for a loose ball — the referee should call out "Play on, no foul!" or something in that vein. He should develop a slightly different style for this so it will not be confused with his advantage call. Perhaps the one arm held out as though to invite play to continue might be reserved for this use.

No two referees act or signal alike. Some squat when they signal, some make perfunctory gestures, some make many, some make few. It reminds me of a little children's book my boys enjoyed when they were small and which stressed the fact that it takes all kinds to make the world go round. It began with a description of little boys:

> "Some are plump,
> Some are thin,
> And some are in-between."

One can learn from watching other referees, but to ape an effective one may be disastrous for one's own temperament.

The above-mentioned French referee — not Vautrot, who was exemplary, but the opera singer with toreador linesmen — taught me many things *not to do!* By the same token, I saw a First Division game in Helsinki where the referee was excellent and taught me one good technique. The laws state that when the referee indicates the indirect free kick by raising his arm he "shall keep his arm in that position until the kick has been taken." This particular referee, I noticed, held his arm aloft until *another player* touched the ball. This was a most sensible adaptation of the gesture since the referee will have the physical evidence of an invalid goal should the ball go straight into the net. I find that if you pull down the hand the moment the seond player touches the ball, the players and fans soon understand the rationale behind the gesture. This technique would be most useful in an instance where the ball rebounds from the upright and bounces across and hits the other upright before going in. All that action and time elapsed might lead players and possibly the referee to forget that the ball has not been touched by a second player. If his arm is still held aloft, however, the difficulty is obviated.

In the 1970 World Cup, yellow and red cards were introduced to indicate official cautions and ejections. This was done to avoid misunderstanding. The waving of the book at a player is not a caution! Most referees' associations have now adopted the card system and even the high-school and college rules have made them mandatory.

The technique of issuing the caution and ejection is important in the maintenance of game control, just as the very fact that he is taking this extreme action is done in part to "enforce the laws" and in part to keep the game under control. The referee should not get emotional about cautions and ejections. If he does, he has probably waited too long before taking action!

When administering a caution, the referee should hold the yellow card overhead for all to see and record in his book, on his scorecard, or on the back of the yellow card: (1) the player's full name, (2) the player's jersey number and team affiliation, and (3) the nature of the offense and at which time it occurred. He should then inform the player of the reason for the caution, referring to the appropriate category of persistent infringement, ungentlemanly conduct, or dissent. He may add the specific reason, but he should be certain that he refers to the category. In other words, the referee should not merely say, "I am cautioning you for raising your foot in front of the goalkeeper when he was clearing." The referee should rather instruct the player that he is being cautioned for ungentlemanly conduct for having attempted to prevent the goalkeeper from putting the ball into play. The guilty player should also be informed that repetition of the deed or any further misconduct will cause him to be sent off. All this must be done quickly but articulately in order that the game may be restarted swiftly in the interest of avoiding further problems as players stand idly around.

The same procedure is followed with the red card for ejections. Only here, after a player has been ejected, he may not be replaced, the team rather having to play with one less player for the remainder of the game.

In both cases, the referee should be alert to all the events going on and make a note of the time of the misconduct so that he may make an accurate, detailed, and fair postgame report. I heard of a game being replayed because the referee abandoned the game when both teams wanted to square off and fight. The spark that ignited this was apparently the ejection of a player when two opponents bumped heads going for a high ball. The contact apparently didn't annoy the players, but the fact that the player — and only one of them — was ejected made them upset. The referee must be certain that he is firm but fair, and he should not throw out an innocent opponent to make the first ejection easier.

Sometimes a player will complain that an opponent spat at him or hit him first. If the referee has seen that both players were guilty of violent or unseemly conduct he can eject them both, the one for fighting (violent conduct) or spitting (unseemly behavior), the other for retaliating (violent conduct). In these heated moments of great emotion, the referee must be sure to remain calm and to choose his words carefully. The way he handles the situation can sometimes – not always, of course – de-fuse the situation and restore game control. If the referee has not seen the alleged spitting that prompted the reprisal – and if his linesmen cannot give him a definitive statement about it should he be using neutral linesmen – he cannot punish the player in question for the alleged offense.

It is easy for a conniving player to accuse his opponent of something like spitting. Gamesmanship of this sort is difficult to control and seems to be appearing lower and lower in the age divisions. I had one game in the under-12 bracket in which with less than a minute to go, a player on the team which was ahead one goal handled the ball less than six inches outside the penalty area. I was right on the line and had a clear view of the infraction. I ran to the spot to place the ball and one of the little attackers pointed just inside the penalty area and said, "It happened right there, in the penalty area; it should be a penalty kick." I laughed and replied, "You're too young to be starting to pull tricks like that."

It is, of course, no laughing matter and can lead to rather far-reaching action. I once saw a player ejected for unseemly conduct which he had not committed. He had been cautioned and was in trouble, so his credibility was not enormous at that point. As everyone returned upfield after a shot missed the goal, this player and an opponent exchanged a few words loudly but not abusively. Just as the referee turned around to see what was going on, the opponent of the player in question fell down with an oath, his feet tangled together (he was a full three feet from the nearest player). It appeared as though this other man had tripped him and the referee ejected the supposed tripper. The referee must watch out for such devious actions and, if he is certain of its intentionality, discipline the perpetrator of this ungentlemanly or unseemly act.

In one of his excellent articles in **Soccer America**, Robert Evans tells of how Peter Johnson, a Canadian referee, handled a bit of histrionics designed to draw a penalty kick out of the referee during NASL action:

A forward, with the ball at his feet, strode into his opponents' area and was challenged by a defender. In the ensuing tackle, the forward went down dramatically and the defender came away with the ball. There was an appeal for a penalty, but the referee ignored it, waved play on and then spoke to the forward about faking fouls in an attempt to gain a penalty.

A few moments later, in a similar incident, the ball was taken from the same forward, and again he ended up flat on his face appealing for a penalty. This time Johnson ran over and cautioned the player for 'ungentlemanly conduct' for his unsuccessful attempt to fool the referee.[26]

The reasoning behind this action may not be apparent to everyone although it certainly should be. If a player, through trickery, gains an unfair advantage, his action is contrary to the spirit of the game. In this case it is obvious that the player automatically tries — upon being beaten fair and square — to combat his opponent's skill with skulduggery. As Evans concludes:

The players know that a referee will not award a penalty for a trifling or dubious foul; it has to be a 'good 'un' as we say in the trade. Knowing this, an unscrupulous player may dramatize an incident with a headlong plunge and a feigned injury, to ensure that the man in black notices. This particular referee *did* notice, and took appropriate action.

There are several confrontational situations in soccer which must be handled efficiently by the referee in order to avoid bad play between opponents. Two of these place no specific distance restriction on the players and one does but is often abused. I am speaking, of course, on the one hand, of the taking of throw-ins and drop balls; on the other, of the taking of free kicks.

The laws state that the throw-ins shall be taken at the point where the ball went out of touch. This means that the player throwing in must be within, say, a yard of the line. His opponent may stand at the line in the playing area. Some players will try to leap up to head the ball as it is thrown in. This is not directly against the laws and there is no reason why a player cannot try to head the ball one foot inside the line; however, should it be apparent to the referee that this player is merely trying to distract the player or impede his delivery, the referee should instruct him to desist and caution him if he continues. Leaping up and dancing around is specifically proscribed in Law 15, Decision 3: "If, when a throw-in is being taken, any of the opposing players dance about or gesticulate in a way calculated to distract or impede the thrower, it shall be deemed ungentlemanly conduct, for which the offender(s) shall be cautioned." Conversely, the thrower may not deliberately throw hard at a player standing near the line. If he thus strikes the player, the referee shall caution or eject the player depending on the degree of the offense (ungentlemanly in intent, possibly violent in effect).

The drop ball is usually made between two players, but more are permitted in the area. The referee should see to it that players are sufficiently away from the ball to allow it to hit the ground. The referee must not, however, throw the ball down at the ground in an effort to have it get into play unexpectedly — like a puck thrown down at a face-off in hockey. In reviewing the offside in a series on the laws, **Soccer Monthly** (February, 1975) says that a player is not offside if he "received the ball directly from a *bounce-up* by the referee." Now, there is no such thing authorized, and several of the official guides clearly remind us that the laws call for the ball to be dropped, not thrown down or bounced. This presents the referee with a problem, for a dropped ball falls slowly and the eager players are apt to kick the ball before it hits the ground. It is difficult to persuade them to step back, as I have already said, but there is another solution I learned from Mario Donnangelo at a high-school rules meeting. It works like a charm.

If the referee, when executing the drop ball, places the loose hand over the top of the ball and then pulls away the undermost hand, he will avoid telegraphing the drop. The players will be watching the upper hand and not anticipate the ball hitting the ground quite as early as they do when the ball is dropped with one hand. I find that this method is especially effective if the referee slowly and very deliberately places the hand on top of the ball while instructing the players not to play the ball till it has touched the ground. They are momentarily mesmerized by the gesture and, when you let the ball drop out from under the upper hand, they usually will not react before the ball has had time to reach the ground and thus be lawfully in play.

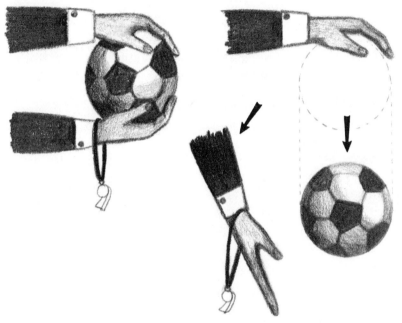

Figure 36: DROP BALL

When dropping the ball, the referee should always stand with his back to the touchline, away from the focus of likely action. Players should not be obliged to play around the referee after the drop ball. If he stands with his back toward the center of the field he will find that he is more likely to have the ball and the players bump into him.

As I have mentioned elsewhere in this study, the moment of the taking of free kicks is fraught with tension and potential dissent and violence. The laws state that the opponents shall remain ten yards away from the ball until it is kicked (or on their own goal line between the uprights if that is less than ten yards), but players are always trying to steal a yard or two, especially near their goal. The referee does not want to delay the game unduly, and if it is approximately ten yards, he should ignore pleas from the kicking team to measure off the distance. However, if it is manifestly less than ten yards, the offended team has a right to have the law enforced. Two yards less than the lawful distance on the part of the defensive wall can radically reduce the percentages of goal mouth open to the kicker. In an interesting article, Les Radunchev demonstrates the decreasing area to be protected on a straight shot by the goalkeeper.[27]

In taking a wall of five players to be about 2.10 meters wide, the available strikable area of the goal diminishes radically if a wall cheats by two meters on the prescribed 9.15 meter distance (= ten yards). In the following metric chart, DG= distance from ball to goal, DW=distance from the ball to the wall, DA=area of goal defended by the wall, and SA=the strikable area of the goal.

DG	DW	DA	SA
17	9.15	3.90	3.42
20	9.15	4.60	2.72
25	9.15	5.72	1.60
DG	DW	DA	SA
17	7	5.11	2.21
20	7	6.00	1.32
25	7	7.50	- - - -

It would appear, from this calculation, that cheating yields better results for the defense on a kick from some distance out, but there are other factors to consider: a shot from 25 yards out will be more easily curved up, over, and down into the goal than one close up, but the latter will require greater reactions on the part of the goalkeeper. Suffice it to say that each yard is statistically important down in the area of pay-dirt! The referee should see to it that the wall keeps its distance. If the offended team does not take a quick kick but asks that the distance be enforced, the referee should impose what is known as a ceremonial free kick. The quick kick option having not been exploited, the referee should delay play until everything is properly set up. He must avoid a farce or confrontation. He should do his utmost to avoid situations such as the following one:

> The whistle blew loudly for the infraction at the edge of the box, and the referee rushed over as the forwards cried out: 'Ten yards, ref!' The official stood on the ball and motioned to the wall of defenders. None showed any inclination to retire toward the goal, so the referee began pacing off ten yards, very efficiently and smartly, to ensure that Law 13 was complied with. 'One, two, three, four...,' he called out, striding away from the ball toward the defenders who stood watching with expressions of innocent inscrutability. '...Nine, ten!' he intoned, and the defenders smiled in unison, for the referee still had not reached the wall of supposedly encroaching players! In the meantime, as the man-in-black strode away in his earnest task of measurement, one of the forwards, taking advantage of the referee's back, gently rolled the ball forward a few feet!
>
> Feeling perhaps a little foolish when his tenth pace came down some two yards in front of the wall of smiling players, the referee did an about-face and returned to the ball, now of course a mere eight yards away. As he paced back, the defenders looked at each other. smiled again, and moved two or three paces toward the ball![28]

As we intimated in an earlier section of this book, there are several ways of avoiding this sort of Alphonse and Gaston procedure. One obvious lesson of the preceding account is that the referee should not turn his back on either the wall or the ball during the taking of free kicks. He can stand on the ball, as Evans goes on to suggest, waving the players back until he is satisfied that they are ten yards away from the ball; then step off the ball, signaling for the kick to be taken. He can, in this manner, prevent displacement of the ball while keeping the action before him. He also avoids striding into the group of more-than-likely-hostile players!

The referee must be firm when it comes to his evaluation of what is ten yards lest he find himself in the embarrassing situation of that official who came up short. If necessary, he can let the players know that he is quite aware of what "ten yards" looks like; after all, there are a number of areas which have trained his eye to judging distances between eight and twelve yards. There are ten-yard radiuses of the center circle and the restraining arcs; there are the twelve-yard distances from goal line to the penalty spot and from the goal area to the edge of the penalty area in three directions at each end of the field; and the goal mouth is eight yards wide.

Another procedure is for the referee to place the ball down and tell the attacking player to wait for the signal to restart play. Then he sprints to what he judges to be a line ten yards from the ball, glancing back if he feels the kicker might try some tricks. He shall run *not* into the wall, but to the side of it, facing both the wall and the kicker and indicate with outstretched arm the nearest point where the defenders may stand. He should not "pace off" the distance as this distraction of his attention may lead him into trouble. I pleasantly tell complaining players that I am quite satisfied that I can tell ten yards when I see it and that they should get on with the game. Under no circumstances should the referee walk or run right through the wall with his arms outstretched, pushing back the players. As I have said, one should not touch a player, especially at moments of tension and frustration!

If the wall simply will not obey the referee's instructions to move back to a given point, he must screw up his courage to the peak, for this can be the moment when to falter leads to the complete breakdown of authority and game control. The referee must be prepared to caution or even eject several players if it is obvious that the defending wall intends to make an issue of the matter. In a follow-up to the article just mentioned, Evans details procedures one can adopt in this instance, procedures which are both fair and effective. Having told the defending line to move back, the referee finds that they refuse to move. They are, in essence, "refusing to comply with the requirements of Law 13 and the referee considers this is misconduct."[29]

So what does he do? Having told the attackers to hold the kick, he goes over to the first player in the wall (Player A), shows him the yellow card and says that he is going to caution him. Before writing up the caution, he turns to the next player (Player B) and says that if B is still there when he is through cautioning A, he will caution him as well. If B is still there, he should show him the yellow card and inform Player C that when he is through with B he will caution him. He should also turn to A if that player has remained in his place and tell him that he will also consider that A is persisting in infringing after having been cautioned if A has not complied by the time he has booked B and he will have to send A off the field. As Evans concludes: "If necessary, the referee can repeat the process for the whole defensive wall, but based on the experience of others, you will never reach the third player, for the wall will retreat the necessary distance."

Furthermore, Evans reminds the referee that he cannot avoid this man-by-man procedure through the issuance of a "captain's" or "team caution": "In these free-kick situations, the referee cannot, absolutely cannot, caution a captain for the misconduct of his teammates. (...) Similarly there is no such thing as a 'team' caution under the international Laws of the Game."

If the kicking team claims that what the referee considers to be ten yards is, in fact, less, he can again inform them that it is ten yards in his opinion and that he is not about to tape-measure the distance, besides which he has left his micrometer calipers at home! One amusing story I heard from a referee I pass along for its humor value only, for I would not personally recommend the same procedure. The ball was placed on the restraining arc for a direct free kick and the referee indicated that the defense could set up by the penalty spot. When the defense complained that the referee was making them stay more than ten yards from the ball, this referee pointed out that the arc is ten yards from the penalty spot. The players insisted, however, that the referee pace off the ten yards for them. The referee shrugged his shoulders and paced off ten giant strides that brought him near the goal area, at least fifteen yards from the ball. He then turned to the defense and said, "All right, there's *my* ten yards if you prefer it to the field's ten yards! Play on!"

Everyone can see the yellow card and the red card, but there is much in the way of discipline and game control that goes on down on the field and which the spectator does not even notice. This type of discipline, which doesn't require that the referee become a public figure, is the hallmark of the best officials. Depending on the situation, the sensible and intelligent referee would try to make the immovable wall comply with a pertinent remark or even a joke. He might be able to say something like "Come on! I know what you're trying to do, and you know that I know; get back where you belong!" and achieve the same results as with a caution or two. He must constantly have his wits about him, seeking new and subtle ways to cajole the game along rather than bully it along! A quiet unemotional word or two will sometimes serve notice whereas a caution might do little good. A caution, it should be remembered, makes a player wary of committing further misconduct but it also tends to inhibit his play ever so slightly.

What may appear from up in the stands to be a serene game may actually be replete with tensions and byplay among players and between players and the referee. The latter should not permit dissent, but he should keep open verbal communication to a certain point as that may be a safety valve preventing physical violence. One often sees a marginal tackle after which the referee runs for a moment alongside the player who might have had bad intentions. He is telling the player in a quiet but firm manner to be careful lest he get himself in trouble. The referee is not humiliating the player and the player will generally respect this courtesy as will knowledgeable fans.

Remarks which are especially effective are those which reveal not anger or rancor on the part of the referee but rather the fact that he understands what is going on even as he informs the player or players that he isn't going to tolerate such action. The referee should not be interested in winning a popularity contest — good referees will not be immune to difficulty but will know how to cope with it — but should rather try to win the player over to the side of lawful play and good sportsmanship. Let me give an example of how one can turn events toward the brighter side.

In a game between 18-year-olds, the goalkeeper punted the ball into the behind of the opponent who was walking away but trying to remain directly in front of the keeper. The opponent was sort of impeding, but the goalkeeper had not made any effort to get around him. I called for dangerous play against the goalkeeper and an indirect free kick six yards out. The goalkeeper stood there sullenly and one of his teammates started yelling, "But the other guy was in his way!" I laughed and said, "I saw what both of them were doing and I also played goalkeeper for fifteen years, so I know *very well* what the goalkeeper was trying to do." The goalkeeper broke into a big sheepish grin and ran back to his goal line to get ready for the free kick.

Such remarks do not always work, and there are some players who take themselves far too seriously or are not bright enough to appreciate what the referee is trying to do; some simply will not be placated and usually end up cautioned or ejected, but three-fourths of the time the right word will smooth over things and set the scene for continued game control. The problem lies not so much in the fact that words will not do the trick, but in coming up with the *right* words and the right tone. I believe that this approach merits at least a try before moving to more drastic action, unless the misconduct is of a blatant nature that demands disciplinary action.

The notion of talking during the game brings us to another matter which presents certain problems to the referee, especially at the senior levels where players are less inhibited and more clever at breaching the laws. Just as there are players who make the defensive wall a problem area, there are others who flirt with dissent to see just how much they can get away with. They

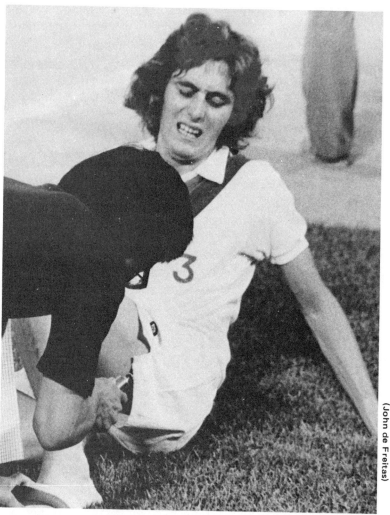

(John de Freitas)

call this "talking over the head" of the referee. It is difficult for the referee to know at what point he should make an issue out of such tactics and seldom does the quiet word help in these instances, the player rather tending to protest his innocence as part of his ploy.

This subtle form of dissent may be something like shaking the head (if confronted, the player will say that he had some mud in his ear) or calling out to a teammate things like, "Do you think that the referee saw that hand ball?" During a National Cup game, the captain of one team had been grumbling at calls and finally — when the referee blew the whistle for tripping and indicated a free kick against this player's team — he yelled out loudly, "All right men, whenever the whistle blows just drop back." It was obvious that he meant to suggest that all fouls called would be against his team, in short, that the referee was not impartial. If the referee had disciplined him, he certainly would have protested that he was simply exhorting his players to co-operate with the referee by dropping back the prescribed ten yards. The referee soon cautioned this player for ungentlemanly conduct for shouting "I got it!" with the intention of distracting an opponent! The player was silent thereafter.

Players find the most ingenious explanations for their "innocent" gestures. Burtenshaw reports the following contradictory explanations of the officials and the player in a cautionary case involving the Ipswich captain Mick Mills. Burtenshaw and his linesman reported that after Mills had fouled an opponent he gave him the "two-fingered up you" sign and "simulated the action of masturbating in the direction of the Coventry player he had fouled." Here is the explanation given by Mills to explain for arbitration his alleged V-sign and masturbatory gesture:

> A foul was awarded against me. The opposing player picked up the ball and threw it at me deliberately. His words to me at the time were 'here you are, you can have the ball.' I replied: 'I don't need it, we are 2-0 up.'
>
> At the same time I indicated the score to the other player with finger sign language, i.e. two fingers indicating two and my other hand indicating zero.
>
> No doubt Mr. Burtenshaw, who was some distance from the scene, presumed I was making a two-fingered-up-you sign at my opponent and also indicating another indecent gesture.
>
> I was really quite amazed when I had my name taken for the offense.[30]

22

FIFA Systems
of Game Coverage

I should like, now, to consider the basic techniques of game control from the point of view of positioning and field coverage. There are two systems used internationally and authorized by FIFA's laws and a third system used in some sections of the United States despite the fact that it is not sanctioned by FIFA. I shall discuss this third system, however, for it is also widely used in school and college soccer games throughout this country. There have been experiments with other techniques (such as three referees on the field with whistles, both linesmen on one side of the field, two referees assisted by two or four linesmen), but these are, to date, "maverick" systems and shall not detain us here.

The three systems widely used are (1) the one-man refereeing system, (2) the system using one referee and assigned neutral linesmen, and (3) the dual-referee system.

Most referees will not be assigned neutral linesmen for several years, so it is appropriate to first discuss the positioning involved in the one-man system. This system, in which the referee works the game alone with, at most, the assistance of club linesmen who call the ball in and out along the touchlines, is not the ideal way to cover a game; but economic realities find most clubs up to the very top amateur level unwilling to pay for neutral linesmen. In short, they are willing — although it does not sound that way to the referee when he is out there doing the job — to forego some areas of coverage in the interest of economizing. No matter how hard the referee runs, no matter how excellent his positioning, he will miss some infractions. He might have sprinted out to the side the better to cover the offside only to have a player in the middle of the field turn his back to him and handle the ball out of the referee's vision! And if he is not out on the wing, he will not be in the ideal position to call the offside infractions. Despite the shortcomings built into this one-man system, it is the one with which we must live in reality, so one must do the best he can with it.

Ideally the referee should run a field pattern somewhat like the basic diagonal he will eventually have to use when he is assigned neutral linesmen. He might as well get into good habits from the start. The basic diagonal would be for him to move roughly along a line between points A and B during the first half and along a line between points C and D in the second half. This way he covers the area occupied by each wing during at least half the game:

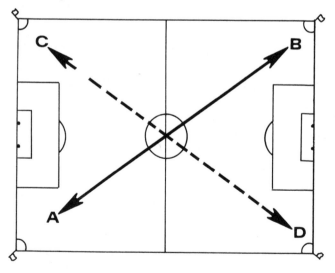

Figure 38: ONE-MAN DIAGONAL

The referee should obviously be flexible in applying this diagonal since he is not bound by the presence of neutral linesmen along the touchlines. Sloppy field conditions, sun in the eyes, a slanting rain, player friction at a certain spot, a desire to avoid a particular section of the gallery of spectators, and a number of other factors may cause him to maintain one diagonal throughout the game or even shift back and forth during the flow of play. He may, due to sun or wind, prefer to keep facing in one direction. I like, for example, to keep rain at my back rather than have it come into my face. The referee should avoid running straight up and down one side line, however, as some of them have a tendency to do. If they are abandoning the diagonal for some legitimate reason, they should still go out to the middle and then cut back over to the same side again, as with half an "X":

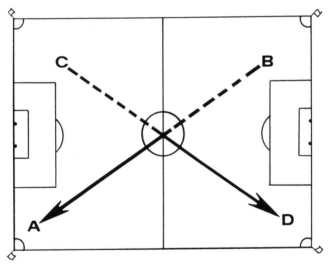

Figure 39: HALF-X COVERAGE

Thus, should there be a problem, the referee can continue over to C or B at a moment's notice.

The area to be covered by the referee on the one-man system is shaped like an old Phoenician ingot or a sheepskin and in this area he must move about to assure the best possible coverage of offside and fouls and misconduct. He will tend to move in a fat X area, not going to the midfield side line area or in front of the goal unless absolutely necessary, the former because he would be removed from the play area and the latter because he does not want to interfere with the play or have a goal deflected off his body:

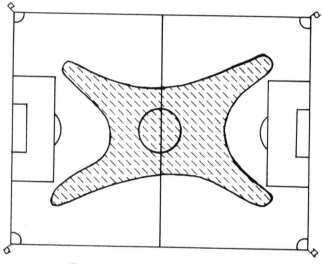

Figure 40: FAT-X COVERAGE

There are different theories as to how the single referee can best cover offside infringements. Harris & Harris, in their **Fair or Foul?** suggest that the referee run a more or less straight line between the penalty areas, up and down the middle of the field. Their logic is presumably that it is most difficult to judge offside at a 45 degree angle, and therefore the referee should view the line of play from behind. In addition, the referee does not have to run as far if he adopts their suggestion. It is true that offside is easier to judge from behind than from an angle, but the best place is obviously out to the side, where the neutral linesman would be. The position generally recommended is out on the wing, and there are some one-sided games in which the single referee can maintain this position successfully. Usually, however, he will find that it is impossible always to reach the ideal position and he should then instinctively opt for a position where he can next best judge the infringement, either at a 45 degree angle or behind the play at a 90 degree angle to the offside line. Just as they suggest in tennis that the player not get caught during a return of his shot inside that "no man's land" between the base line and the service line, there is as well a no man's land in soccer refereeing which should be avoided as an attack is developing. Thus, the referee should try to get to A, but if he sees that he is bound to be caught at C when the ball is played to the possible offside infringer, he might swerve over toward B in order to get a perpendicular vantage point of the offside line.

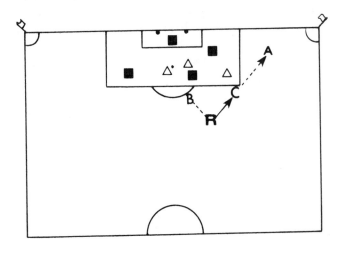

Figure 41

One of the most valuable visual aids, regardless of where the referee is positioned, is the marking of the field. If the offside activity is within a yard or two of the front of either the penalty area or the goal area, the referee can use the line as a point of reference. If the next to the last defender is standing inside the box (assuming, of course, that the lining has been checked and found to be true), an attacker standing on the line parallel to the goal line cannot be offside. If the referee is at C in our illustration and the front line of action is right around the penalty line, he can use that to assist him until he has an opportunity to reach A where he will be in a better position to judge offside by the time the action gets into the unlined area of the field.

The only time that a referee might want to commit himself to the straight line behind the play action will be if he has pulled a muscle or is in the third game of a triple-header in hot weather and simply cannot get out to the side in time to make the calls. This middle-of-the-field line of action requires less running and is something to remember in case of an emergency. It will, however, require no specific learning as the referee will find that as he gets tired or when he is hurt, he will instinctively go less and less out to the side in order to pace himself. If this is happening, he might as well recognize it and switch to the straight line lest he repeatedly find himself stranded at C with a poor angle of vision.

There are some matters of positioning during special situations which need mentioning. Most of them will be the same for refereeing with neutral linesmen and will be discussed next, but one or two things pertain specifically to the single-referee system.

During corner kicks, the referee will place himself on the goal line a few yards away from the upright *farthest* from the ball. He may choose to position himself out in the field if his view is obstructed, but he should stay clear of the action and be on the far side of the penalty area. The only time he might take a position on the near side of the goal would be in very young divisions where the corner kicks seldom reach much beyond the edge of the penalty area and the players bunch up and screen off the referee if he is on the far side of the field.

When throw-ins are being taken and he is in the area, he should place himself downfield from the thrower. He will learn that any yard he can save by foresight will leave him physically stronger as the game nears its end. It is impossible to give the same coverage alone as with three referees, but the new referee generally tries and pulls muscles or gets sore legs for a few months. He will soon learn tricks to pace himself, learning from

(Horst Müller)

experience which areas and moments are more urgently in need of his attention.

When first refereeing, I ran every play up the field and pulled up lame although I was in excellent shape. I soon learned from some old hands that you set up priorities and alternative ways of handling situations. In some games, especially juvenile games — there will be a vastly superior defender who can thwart nine out of ten offensive thrusts. Instead of trotting fifty yards ten times out of ten, the referee will hold back a bit, knowing that the ball would be sent booming right on back downfield to where he was a moment before, catching him out of position. The one time out of ten that his defender is beat, the referee will sprint with all his might and easily get in line with the play, having saved up his reserve energy just for this eventuality. Thus, rather than run 1,000 yards, most of them chasing the ball up and down the field for nought, the referee will *dash* fifty yards when he must. Most referees are better conditioned for the latter.

He will learn to watch for signs as to how the play will turn. Some referees watch the players warming up and store in their minds for later exploitation during the game insights into the players' skills and temperaments. Let me give an analogy of what I mean by signs. If you are driving a car and suspect that a parked car with a person behind the wheel might be ready to pull out, you can best foretell the move of the car by watching not the car itself, but the front outer wheel for telltale movements. Similarly, players telegraph their moves. If a defender stumbles, the referee knows that he should not wait but should get right down to cover the play as there is a good chance that the attack will break through or that the off-balance player will come back from a bad angle and foul his opponent.

The single referee will be entitled to the assistance of club linesmen if they are available. His positioning may vary slightly if he has club linesmen he finds to be reliable. Doubt about the competence of a club linesman is another reason which might dictate the switching of one's diagonal or its being abandoned altogether in favor of the half-X coverage.

The technique of game control when the referee has been assigned neutral, that is, certified linesmen is rather specifically counseled by the memorandum on co-operation found in the FIFA rule book. He shall run a diagonal in which his outermost limit finds him on the opposite side of the field from one of his linesmen. Statistically, the amount of running is less, unfortunately. Harris & Harris report that the following average mileage is recorded by referees and neutral linesmen during the ninety minutes of a typical game:

Single referee. . . . . 7 - 10 miles
Referee who has neutral linesmen. . . . . .6 - 9 miles
Linesman. . . . . .2 - 3 miles
Referee in dual system .5 - 7 miles[31]

I say "unfortunately" because it would be nice to believe that the referee takes advantage of his linesmen not to run less but to give the game that much better coverage. There will be times, in fact, that the referee will be obliged to run as though he were alone, as when he has reason to feel that a linesman is missing some offside calls. Be that as it may, the dynamics of the so-called diagonal three-man system provides for excellent game coverage if each man does his job as he should and if the team truly co-operates as a unit. The lines of action or dynamics of the three-man system are as follows:

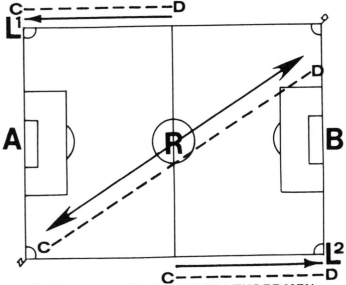

Figure 42:   DIAGONAL WITH THREE MEN
As play moves along between "A" and "B", so do the officials move along their respective "C-D" lines.

Linesmen L^1 and L^2 move toward the corners as play develops, even as the referee (R) moves along his diagonal. The linesman will place himself in a position whence he can judge offside unless circumstances or the referee's instructions supersede this position, as when the linesman moves down to cover the goal line.

The various positions to be assumed by these three men are covered in the rule book and some of the techniques more properly fall under the heading of linesmanship and will be dealt with separately. Essentially, the three men will place themselves as follows in the pertinent situations.

SITUATION	REFEREE	LINESMEN
KICK-OFF	Behind and to one side of center, on circle	Both of them at midfield on touchline, or downfield ready to assume offside duties
CORNER KICK	On goal line by far post or out near side of penalty box	Lead linesman at corner or on goal line near corner, trailing linesman near midfield stripe
GOAL KICK	Near midfield	Trailing linesman at 18-yard line and then to offside position, lead linesman downfield at offside position
FREE KICK AT MIDFIELD	Down along his diagonal at offside line	Trail linesman in line with spot of kick, lead linesman opposite referee on offside line
FREE KICK NEAR GOAL	On offside line	Lead linesman moves down to goal line, trail linesman back upfield
PENALTY KICK	Out at some point on a line extending from the corner of the goal area laterally out to the penalty area limit	Lead linesman on goal line at 18-yard line, trailer back near midfield stripe
THROW-IN	Referee leaves his diagonal and goes toward area of throw to watch for hand faults	Lead linesman goes down to where he can watch for foot faults as well as eventual offside, trailer remains back at his offside line

I should like to discuss several of these situations. It is obvious that the co-operation must run smoothly to be effective, and this is especially true of action near the goal. If one of the two co-operating officials assumes the other's task momentarily, he should make sure that the other has resumed the task before abandoning it. For example, when a free kick is being taken near the goal, the referee will generally assume the function of offside judge and wave his linesman down to the goal line at the corner flag to act as goal judge should there be a direct hard shot. When the action swings back upfield, the linesman should run swiftly back to cover the offside line, thus freeing the referee to move upfield with the play. A smooth transition here is important. The same transition occurs in the situations placing the linesman on the goal line (corner kick, penalty kick) and he should cut across the corner of the field if necessary to regain his offside position. If he can do so backpedaling, so much the better.

In waving the linesman down to the goal line, the referee should have a signal that is not easily confused with a signal for the taking of the kick. Some referees wave the linesman down the line with a flat, palm-downward karate-type gesture parallel to the ground. This is quite different from the usual waving gesture and therefore recommended.

There are several suggested positionings for the referee and linesmen during the taking of corner kicks, usually calling for the referee to stand either out at the corner of the penalty area or on the goal line by the post on his side of the diagonal of coverage, and the linesman to stand out by the flag or on the goal line a bit in from there, sometimes as far in as by the eighteen-yard line. See Fig. 43, page 272.

Whichever positions he chooses for his linesman and himself, the FIFA memorandum expects them to adopt the same ones for either corner: "Positions of officials the same no matter at which corner-area the kick is taken." It seems to me, however, that the dynamics of officiating differs according to the side from which the kick is taken.

In his unique and brilliant **Manual for Linesmen**, Robert

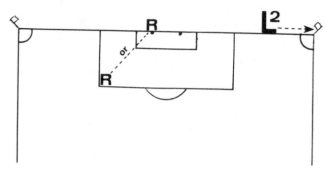

Figure 43

Evans positions both officials on the goal line and suggests that the official "furthest from the ball will signal whether the ball has crossed the goal line after the kick, the other will pay little attention to the kicker, but will look INTO the field to watch for illegal play. . . . Should the ball remain close to the goal, one official will stay on the goal line to act as goal judge, and the other, usually the linesman, will move out, taking the responsibility for 'Offside'."[32]

The implication is that for an important instant the referee will concentrate on being the goal judge instead of looking for infractions in the critical penalty area. I believe that no referee will wittingly do this, preferring to have his well-positioned linesman act at all times as principal goal judge until the ball moves upfield or the linesman has clearly regained his touchline position. The only time, indeed, that the referee's goal line position is patently superior to the eighteen-yard position is when the kick is from the opposite corner and the linesman would have difficulty judging whether a kick goes out over the goal line as it sails directly over his head. Otherwise, the positioning of both officials on the goal line makes it difficult for either (especially the linesman who hasn't the liberty to run straight out into the middle of the field as has the referee) to judge offside infractions immediately following the kick, both being in front of the line of play.

For example, if Player B heads the corner kick back to Player A, neither official has had sufficient time to regain an ideal position to judge if the latter is offside at his position "A2".

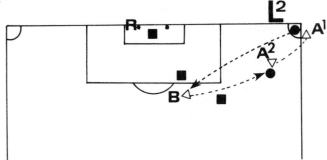

Figure 44: IS "A" OFFSIDE AT "A²"?

Thus, if the corner kick is taken from the linesman's corner, the referee might still do better to position himself out by the eighteen-yard line (letting his linesman try to call out balls over his head), per the memorandum's alternate suggestion, or, better yet, about three yards into the field on the goal-area line, where he can hustle over to the goal line to judge out-balls or into the field to judge offside until the linesman gets back to the touchline. The linesman will then continue to watch the goal line and assist in surveillance of activity in the penalty area.

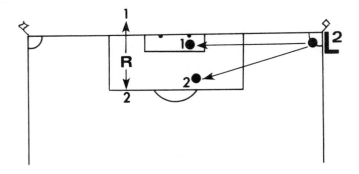

Figure 45: FLEXIBILITY

The referee can place himself away from the goal line when the kick is taken on his own side of the field as the goal line would be observed by his linesman. He would do well to stay at a point where he can assume an eventual offside call without interfering with play. He can opt for the eighteen-yard line or closer to the goal-line position dependent on the deployment of the players. In addition, according to this deployment and the nature of the kick (a short pass to a teammate or a long high cross to the goal area), he will drift one way or another in order not to interfere with play, but still to maintain a good angle from which to judge goals, offside, and infractions in front of the goal.

In short, the referee may well find that he prefers *not* to position himself in the same place, as FIFA dictates, "no matter at which corner-area the kick is taken," but to have distinct policies for near kicks and far kicks, adjusting his policies in turn according to the strength of the kicker, the skill level of the teams, wind, and other conditions.

In 1974, FIFA slightly amended the instructions to officials, instructing the referee to place his linesman out by the corner flag rather than on the goal line by the eighteen-yard line as had previously been the policy. There are some merits to this position, although referees have been slow to pick it up.

Although the linesman will be in a poorer position to serve as goal judge out by the corner, he will have a better overall view of the field from that position and can assist both on goal calls and such difficult offside situations as that illustrated above (Fig. 44), in which the corner kick is kicked or headed right back to the kicker. However, the 1974-75 memorandum continued to state that the position of the officials should be the same, regardless of the side whence the kick approaches, denying the referee the flexibility I have suggested might assure better game coverage in light of such variables as player movement, defensive tactics, the age of the players, the weather, and field conditions.

Even maintaining the basic positioning prescribed by the memorandum, it seems to me that during a kick from the

(Doug Schwab)

referee's side of the field, the referee might wish to place himself out at the corner of the penalty box and have his linesman stand on the goal line between the flag and the eighteen-yard line; whereas during a kick from the linesman's side, the referee might wish to stand by the goal post and have his linesman remain out by the flag. Such positioning would take into account the difference in dynamics on the two sides of the field and yet assure good coverage of the goal line, possible offside infractions, and the critical area in front of the goal mouth. Finally, such an approach to the matter is not a radical departure from the FIFA memorandum.

Despite the fact that the new FIFA advice is to place the linesman "near the corner flag or on the goal line near the corner flag," many referees will no doubt interpret very liberally the word "near" in the second part of the phrase and continue to place their linesmen down at the juncture of the goal line and the penalty area.

At *no time* during the game should the offside line be neglected. There are moments in which it is more likely to be neglected and both the referee and linesman must watch out for these moments. One is that which we have already mentioned in connection with corner kicks in which the ball is sent back to the kicker who finds himself in an offside position. It must be clear who is to assume the responsibility for this call, presumably he who is farthest from the kicker, be that official the referee or linesman. These are items to be considered in pregame discussions among experienced officials who would aspire to total game coverage. Another moment which can catch the officials napping or out of step is that which occasionally develops through a momentary misunderstanding regarding the referee's call.

For example, I was caught out of position as linesman on one or two occasions when I thought a throw-in was to be taken and was watching for foot faults not too far from the place where the ball had gone out. Unbeknownst to me, the referee had actually called for a free kick right at the touchline where he had detected an infraction just before the ball went out. Suddenly the player placed the ball on the ground and took a quick kick, booming the ball up to his forward. I was caught hopelessly out of position and when I turned to look into the field, I could not tell if the man had been onside or offside at the moment of the kick although he was by now two yards offside and prancing toward the goal with the ball.

In one instance I guessed to the best of my ability, but in the other, true co-operation took place and the referee called the offside, bailing me out. Just as I tried to be there when he needed me, the one time I really needed him, he was there — and it was a good feeling! I had been lulled into a false sense of security by the knowledge that there is no offside on a throw-in (irrelevant knowledge in this case) and that I would be able to proceed in positioning myself after the ball had been put into play. The lesson of this is that one should, even on throw-ins — in sum, at *all* times — have someone responsible covering the offside line.

There are numerous other matters of interest with regard to co-operation, but I shall take them up when discussing the art of running line and the essential instructions to be given linesmen before a game. Before leaving the three-man system for the moment, I should mention that the diagonal is not to be rigidly followed and that the referee will move out off the hypothetical line to maintain a position whence he can observe the action and control the players. He may want to maintain the same diagonal throughout the game as recommended by FIFA, or switch at half time, as recommended by the NASL. Some referees are most comfortable running to one side or the other, but if there is no strong preference nor circumstances such as weather or field conditions or a troublesome player to keep under surveillance, the referee should switch his linesmen across the field at half time.

The reason for doing this rather than having them switch ends is obvious. The switch of diagonal will cause the referee to cover every section of the field during the game, but to move the linesmen down the line instead of across the end of the field would cause the linesman to cope with the same offensive line during the entire game. It is more fair to the linesmen and to the teams to cross the linesmen over. In this way each linesman will have to deal with each team's offense one half. If the linesmen are of differing ability or philosophy (as to what constitutes being "out of the play", for instance), one of the teams may very well be unfairly penalized in a subtle way by having to suffer a particular linesman through the entire game.

Furthermore, if the teams are mismatched, one linesman may have to do all the work for the entire game as the ball will remain at his end of the field. Thus, if the referee switches diagonals, he should cross over his linesmen; if he retains the same diagonal in the second half, he should leave the linesmen where they were.

The only time the referee might reasonably see fit to switch the linesmen's *ends* of the field would be if he has reason to trust one of the linesmen more than the other and feels he needs him down where most of the action is during the whole game. This could be because one has a good bit more experience or because the referee has worked with the one before and co-operates well with him but knows nothing about the other person.

My friend Jim Ross once refereed a National Amateur Cup game to which I was assigned as linesman. Due to a mix-up, the other linesman never showed, and Ross had the man who had done the preliminary game stay on to run line. He knew nothing about this other referee although he was surely competent, but he and I had worked together in amateur and school games and we had always dovetailed beautifully in responsibility and coverage. In this instance, he had me run the line at the end of the stronger attack (Philadelphia Inter, the defending Amateur champions who ultimately repeated again that year) and, having seen that our communications system was working as well as ever, he had me cover Inter the second half. Normally he would have switched the two linesmen but he wanted to go with a known quantity in this rather tight game.

Running line is a very special part of officiating. It has its own techniques which must be learned and the job provides its own special joys to the linesman who has done his work well. One could referee fifteen years and he would have to start learning all over again if he then started to run line. Most assignors nowadays see the wisdom of exposing young and new referees to lining on fairly important games so that they can develop a sense of the style of play at the top as well as prepare for co-operation from the other side when they are assigned linesmen. Some referees who did not have early training on the line find it difficult either to subordinate themselves to another official as one must when running line or to give the linesmen they, themselves, are assigned the respect and responsibility they are entitled to.

23

Running Line

There are a number of fundamental signals which make up the language of co-operation essential to game control. We have already discussed the technique of positioning in the diagonal system, but there is also the work with the flag and the body which is almost more important though not described in the memorandum. The NASL has put out a mimeographed memorandum on running line which is useful, but the linesman must be flexible and use the set of signals and positionings (which are also sometimes signals in themselves) which the referee instructs him to use in their pregame discussion.

Signals consist of (1) flag and hand signals indicating direction and nature of offense, (2) positioning as a communication system, and (3) "silent signals" when to flag would be undesirable.

The linesman should raise the flag to indicate such things as the moment the ball goes out of play, the occurrence of an infraction which the referee appears not to have seen, or a desire to discuss something with the referee. If he raises the flag during play he must recognize that the referee is bound to stop play. The primary functions of the linesman call for him to flag for out-of-touch balls, end-line free kicks, and for offside infringements. It must be stressed, however, that these flag signals are not official recognition of the matters signaled, but rather an opinion expressed by the linesman. The opinion only becomes officially recognized when the referee acknowledges it by blowing his whistle. If overruled by the referee, the linesman should pull down his flag and continue to fulfill his duties. The referee will have informed the linesmen before the game what signal he will use to wave off an opinion from them.

The linesman will not only signal the moment the ball has gone out of play over the touchline, but also immediately point his flag at a 45-degree angle in the direction the throw-in is to be taken.

Figure 46: LINESMAN INDICATES DIRECTION OF THROW-IN

If it involves an end-line decision, for a corner kick he shall point his flag at the corner quadrant and then proceed to the place where the referee has told him to be during the taking of the kick. If it is a goal kick, he should move back toward the eighteen-yard line. He should not sprint, however, but move casually, lest the referee think that he is sprinting back to midfield. This would be confusing were a shot to just miss the post and the referee thought it had gone in the goal and out the side net. The latter should be able to tell at a glance the difference between the linesman's return to the eighteen-yard line and his postgoal sprint.

If there is a goal and the linesman thinks it is valid, he should indeed sprint back to the midfield line to signal that opinion to the referee. If he feels, for whatever cause, that a goal should not be allowed, the linesman should go to the corner and stand there at attention until the referee comes to talk to him or waves him back upfield. The referee should, properly, check with the linesman under these circumstances as the matter may not be the one the referee assumes it to be.

The linesman should be the primary judge of offside except when the referee replaces him in this function to send him down to the goal line. Offside should be handled by the linesman the same way he would if he were refereeing the game himself. That is, he should only raise his flag for an *infringement*, not simply every time a player is in an offside position! To indicate offside, the linesman should raise his flag straight overhead and point out into the field with the free hand. He should hold this position until the ball is set up for the free kick. If the referee fails to see the signal, the linesman should pull down his flag after two or three seconds and if a goal results directly after this infraction, the linesman would freeze at attention rather than run back to the midfield stripe. Obviously if a good bit of back and forth play has evolved after the missed infringement, the linesman should not bring it up if a goal is scored.

The linesman must be prepared to signal for an infraction of any sort if he feels the referee did not *see* it and if he feels that the referee would *want* him to signal for it. He will have some notion of how "tight" the referee is calling the game within the first five or ten minutes and he should act according to the referee's policy. The most unusual infringement I have called as a linesman was when I noticed that there was an invalid game in progress with only *one* team on the field! Perhaps I should explain. One team was playing with only eight players and after the opponent was awarded a penalty kick two players of the shorthanded team left the field in disgust without anyone noticing. After the restart I suddenly noticed the two players sitting on a bench behind me, taking off their shoes. I asked them what they were doing and they replied that they were leaving. I realized that there could only be six players on that team on the field. I counted to make sure and then raised my flag aloft to everyone's astonishment. As soon as the referee realized what had happened and all efforts to get those players to return had failed, he declared the game over.

An area where a linesman's call can cause some consternation is in the penalty box. If the linesman is going to signal for an infraction which would result in a penalty kick, he must be absolutely *certain* (1) that the referee did not see the infraction and (2) that the infringement was clearly deliberate. As one colleague put it, the linesman must be 200% sure before he calls the penalty kick. When signaling for infractions outside the penalty area, the linesman should raise the flag and then point in the direction the kick will be taken, signaling with the free hand what sort of infringement occurred (grasping the other wrist for holding, tapping it for handling, etc.), and then raise his free hand in the air if it involves an indirect free kick offense.

The referee may very well wave off the call if he has judged the infringement unintentional or has decided to invoke the advantage clause. In this case, the linesman should graciously withdraw his signal and not shake his head or make any other sign of disapproval or contempt. His job is not to enforce the laws, it is to *assist the referee* in his enforcement of the laws. The linesman can assist a marginally competent referee more by co-operating with him than by constantly opposing him or upstaging him. He should take pride in the fact that he can help a referee through a rough game rather than show him up.

The serious linesman should make a thorough and thoughtful study of the **Manual for Linesmen** by Robert Evans, as well as the pertinent pages in Denis Howell's **Soccer Refereeing**. There are fascinating bits of advice in both texts which will help the linesman whether he be a novice or an old veteran along the lines. The out-of-touch and end-line calls are not much more than is required of a club linesman, and a referee on top of the play will only need assistance in calling fouls or making goal decisions once every few games.

The most important task, then, of the linesman is to cover offside. To do this he must always keep on an exact line perpendicular to the sideline which runs through the player he is concentrating on. As Evans points out, there are three different approaches to this "offside line". The linesman can keep abreast of the next to the last player (of either side), the next to the last defender, or the farthest forward attacker. It is customary in my region to line up with the next to the last player. This is the easiest way to cover the greatest number of potential situations. There is only one time that it is weak. There might be three people offside, and if you line up with the forwardmost attacker or the next to the last player, you will not be able to judge with accuracy the two other players who are offside. In this one instance it would have been better to have lined up with the next to the last defender.

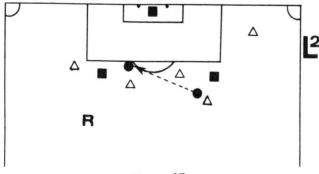

Figure 47

This advice of staying in line with the next to the last player is contrary to that counseled by Evans, but I personally think it is the best, especially if one is not highly experienced. As he points out, however, as one gains experience, he will watch out for situations in which the system is inadequate for coverage and will move to compensate for its deficiencies.

For example, in the situation where a player is way offside on the right wing and the action is moving out to the left where a player may or may not be offside, the linesman should temporarily abandon his position and move in line with the particular play back upfield. The inexperienced linesman should not do this, however, but rather leave that special case to the referee or try to make the call from the bad angle he has on the play if the referee is behind the infringement and unable to judge it.

In the diagram, L^2 leaves his position in line with A and goes to where he can cover B, knowing still from his new position that any pass up to A will obviously be an offside infringement. Unless he has run line on several dozen games, however, the linesman is not likely to be comfortable enough with his basic duties to start thinking along these more sophisticated lines (no pun meant). If he tries to do too much too early, he will start missing the easy calls, as I found out when experimenting with my rubber band color coding!

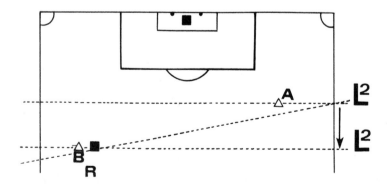

Figure 48: IMPORTANCE OF ANGLE OF VISION

From his original position B appears to be offside, but from the second position L^2 can see that B is onside by a narrow margin and may receive a pass that would leave A out of the play. There are different ways of holding the flag when not actually signaling. It should never be furled. It should either be left to hang loose (as was done in the World Cup games) or the end should be held stretched taut with the thumb and released when the signal is made. Waving and showiness is to be avoided. There are advantages to the loose and the stretched-taut techniques. The flagstaff can be used as a pointer (as when pointing at the corner quadrant for a corner kick) without it being construed as a flag signal. On the other hand, the loose flag will flutter just a bit when the linesman runs with it held at his side, and it can serve as a constant peripheral-vision reminder to the referee just where to look when he glances up in anticipation of an offside call.

The linesman may be called on to take over for an injured or incapacitated referee, so he should always keep correct time and a complete record of the game. The referee will often instruct the senior linesman to keep time with all time added for delays, as though he were in the middle, and the second linesman to keep running time without any deductions or time added. The linesmen should communicate *their* last five minutes of time in each period with outspread fingers held down against the black leg of their shorts. When their time is up, they should place the hand across the chest or make some similar pre-arranged signal which the referee should acknowledge, after which they need no longer signal for time.

The linesman should never signal with the flag to indicate time is through. I remember refereeing a youth game between a local all-star team and a team from Quebec. Both linesmen were inexperienced. I instructed the senior linesman to keep time and put his hand across his chest when his time was up. Play was moving downfield late in the second half when suddenly this fellow raised his flag. I whistled and asked him what the call was. He replied that it was time for the game to end! I cursed privately to myself and dropped the ball to restart play so that I might add the two minutes for time lost due to injuries and balls kicked down a steep hill.

I said earlier that the linesman should indicate direction of the kick when signaling an infraction outside the penalty area. Within the penalty area he should be extremely cautious although not to signal for a clear deliberate infraction may be a greater disservice to the referee than to flag for the foul. If one must flag for a penalty kick infraction, he should raise the flag straight up and neither point for the direction nor at the penalty spot. The referee can then override the linesman with less reaction. The referee may even have seen an offsetting infraction and end up giving the free kick to the defense and for the linesman to have pointed at the penalty spot would be to give the referee unnecessary flak.

If there is some activity in the penalty box which leads the referee to suspect there might be some unlawful activity calling for a penalty kick, or if he sees an apparent infraction but wants

(Newspix)

an instant second opinion from his linesman, the referee should look out questioningly at the linesman. The latter will respond with a "silent signal," that is by body language not requiring that the flag be raised nor attracting unnecessary attention to the incident. In response to this request for an opinion, the linesman will either snap to attention with his flag held straight down the side of his leg (signifying that he feels a penalty kick should indeed be awarded), or he will stand "at ease" with the flag held behind his back (signifying that he feels there was no punishable offense warranting the granting of a penalty kick).

Let us take a series of actions demonstrating co-operation between the referee and his linesman. There is a fierce attack being mounted by the "Blue" team against a beleaguered "Red" side. The ball goes down toward the end line and two adversaries fight for possession on the line. The referee sees that the linesman is at the corner and making no signal, so the ball is still in play. The "Blue" player manages to center the ball and it is headed awkwardly by a "Blue" teammate back to the first player. The referee sees the linesman's flag go up and his hand pointing to the spot where offside occurred.

So far, so good. The free kick is taken and soon "Blue" is back on the attack. There is a skirmish in front of the goal and the ball rolls lazily over the goal line when it is kicked clear by a "Red" defender coming from out of nowhere. The referee glances over and sees that the linesman is keeping his flag down and shaking his head slightly as though to say, "No goal, not all the way over." The referee shouts "Play on!"

Undaunted, "Blue" returns downfield with the ball and there is a bullet-like cross into the goal area. A "Blue" player leaps up and apparently heads the ball into the corner of the goal. The referee, before awarding what he assumes to be a goal, looks quickly over to see if his linesman is running back to the midfield stripe. The linesman is standing there at attention. There is also a lot of shouting going on from the stands. The referee runs over quickly to his linesman who informs him that the player used his fist up near his ear to "punch" the ball into the goal. The referee indicates that the goal shall not stand and cautions the player for ungentlemanly conduct. "Red" is awarded a direct free kick because the "Blue" player had handled the ball.

Soon "Blue" is back down near the goal and an attacker dribbles with great trickiness into the penalty area. He goes down, but the referee is not certain as to what happened because he was screened at the moment the opponents had tangled. He looks over questioningly at his linesman who stands relaxed with his hands behind his back. Good, thinks the referee, I almost blew that one, and he thanks his lucky stars that he has an excellent linesman that day.

If nothing else, this little dramatization illustrates the importance of the goal line in running line. Every ball, no matter how innocuous it may appear, should be followed down to the goal line. The one time in a great many that the decision falls entirely to the linesman, he *must* be there! And he cannot predict when that one time will come. I ran line ten games in a row without having to make a decision which a club linesman could not have made from mid-field. But in the eleventh game I had three crucial calls at the end line and was glad that I had followed the advice of my instructors and tracked each and every ball down to the goal line.

The goalkeeper in the game in question had a habit of not catching a routine shot on his chest but of deflecting it out to either side to fool the offense and to remove the action from in front of the net. This day he twice deflected shots poorly and had to scamper and dive to save his ball from going over the end line for a corner kick. Both times the ball stayed in by 1/100 of an inch and I was there on the line to make the call. In the third instance, the forward got free and advanced on the other goalkeeper. The goalkeeper leaped at the ball, but this player coolly dribbled around the prostrate keeper and flicked the ball into the goal. It seemed that a goal was inevitable, but the ball was traveling slowly and a defender miraculously appeared to slam the ball hard out of the goal.

The referee looked over at me. The decision was obviously mine to make one way or the other. In my opinion (which the referee had sought) the ball still had a minute part of its bulge not yet over the line and I shook my head and made no signal. The game went on and some fans behind the goal complained (when don't they?), but the fellow who had kicked the ball showed no sign of disapproval. The call was a very tough one and there was only one person in the proper position and with the vested authority to make the decision, and that was me. The game was not a very good soccer game — one of those one-sided affairs without particularly good action — but it was one of the most exciting ones for me as a linesman because it contained situations in which I was constantly involved and in intimate communication with the referee. Since that day I have always enjoyed assignments to run the line.

The picture I have portrayed is that of a good reliable linesman. The assistance works both ways, however, and the linesman is only as strong as his support from the man in the middle! If the referee feels gratified to know that the man on the line is trustworthy and in the right position where needed, the linesman is also most grateful for the support of the referee. He takes a good bit of abuse from the side line and must turn a deaf ear, but there are times when his limited authority is put to the test, such as when spectators will not comply when asked by the linesman to step behind spectator-restraining cordons. Some referees do not want to become involved in such feuds, but the linesman is powerless to pursue the matter without the referee's backing. Usually such moves or instructions on the part of the linesman are designed to assist the referee and he should expect the latter to support him in return. I have run line for some referees whose fundamental ability may not have been as great as that of some others, but I shall always be grateful in retrospect for their having stopped the game to come over to find out what was wrong and then informed the dissident fans that if they did not move back the game would not continue. It seems a little less lonely along the hostile side line after such a show of support and solidarity.

The Dual System of Game Coverage

Although the dual system of refereeing is not authorized by a narrow interpretation of the FIFA rules which state that "A Referee shall be appointed to officiate in each game," there are areas in this country where the referees cover amateur games in pairs, either despite FIFA's rules or because they are not affiliated with FIFA. In addition, most school games are covered by the dual system. Thus, for the sake of completeness, I shall comment briefly on the technique of refereeing with two men on the field.

There is a little booklet issued by NISOA some years ago outlining the principles of the dual system, but it is not without its flaws.* There are essentially three principles to state:

1) Both referees have equal authority anywhere on the field.

2) The referees shall run diagonal halves of the field.

3) The lead man shall generally blow the whistle for restarting play.

Let us consider these three areas one at a time.

Referees have equal authority. The idea behind the dual system is that two referees can see more than one, and therefore the fouls which go undetected in a single-man game will more likely be spotted when there are two men. Despite the fact that

---

*Reprinted in **1974 Official Manual of the NISOA**.

they have equal authority, some sort of staking out of territory is inevitable. The degree of encroachment into one another's territory will depend variously on such things as great mutual trust or great mistrust.

For example, I called from the other side of the field an infraction which occurred not ten feet from Jim Ross, one of our finest referees. He took no umbrage at this but was genuinely grateful. There was mutual trust. He had been watching a head ball driven at the goal and was concerned primarily with making the goal-line call. That is as it should be. I was free of such worries and could help him with the other things he had to neglect momentarily due to the natural priorities. The player who had headed the ball had, in his leaping follow-through, elbowed a defender in the neck.

It works both ways, for in another game where I was burdened with the wind and a team which was repeatedly offside, Ross came way down into my half of the field although there were many counterattacks which meant he had to work extra hard. As he explained at half time, he had noticed that I was having to spend most of my time and effort on judging offside, so he had dropped down to help me with the other infractions.

There is sometimes the opposite of this. I appeared for one game to find a worried co-referee waiting for me. He said, "I was up here last week and called hands and then gave an indirect kick. I thought they would hang me. I can use all the help I can get today." He was literally trembling. I ran my legs off that day and twice cautioned players who attempted to impede the goalkeeper in my co-referee's end of the field. He called one or two infractions and I must have called twenty-five. As we left the field after the game, several people turned to him in all sincerity and said, "Very good game, ref!" He looked very happy and I only hoped that I had served in some way to help him get through his difficulty.

Generally one will practice the same restraint with regard to calling fouls at the feet of one's colleague as the linesman would about calling fouls in the penalty box. Some contend that this restraint, which is naturally mutual, leaves a large area between the two referees relatively untended! Generally one will work things out with those partners he can work with and do the best he can with those with whom he finds it difficult to work. Basically, he should leave most calls to the person covering the half of the field, only intervening to help his colleague or nail an infraction he knows the other man did not see or possibly to redress a flagrant sin of omission.

For example, one would normally not call offside in the sector covered by his co-referee. I have done so two or three times. In most instances the colleague was grateful because the offside was obvious but they had either frozen or been caught looking elsewhere. In one instance the referee was upset that I had made the call in his area — and he has remained upset over the years! — although the quick bounce back was a classic case of offside and I called it myself because he did not, I assume either because he missed it or thought the ball had come off a nearby defender. He has never forgiven me, but I was in no way trying to upstage him and his rancor is misplaced, I feel. He should rather be upset by the referee who through laziness or timidity does not assist the co-referee to the best of his ability.

The NISOA booklet calls for the referees to run identical wings at opposite ends of the field. See Fig. 49, p. 294.

The referees will move to and fro so as to "box in" the play at all times, especially down in the critical penalty area. When free kicks are being taken, the trailing official will move right down close to the play to help out. The best technique for thus boxing in the play is to run an "L" shape down the sideline and in toward the goal. See Fig. 50, p. 294.

The NISOA booklet says that the lead official shall whistle for the restart of play save on kick-off and goal kicks which shall be blown by the trailing official. I have found, however, that most officials prefer to use common sense, having the referee in proximity to the kicker call the restart after having seen that his colleague is ready, unless the restart is fairly near the goal in which case the lead referee will blow the whistle — it being he, in all likelihood, who whistled for the foul! Strict

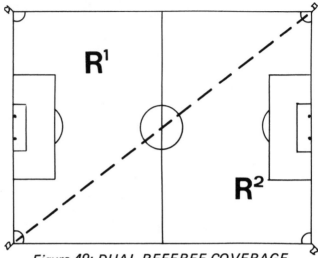

Figure 49: DUAL REFEREE COVERAGE

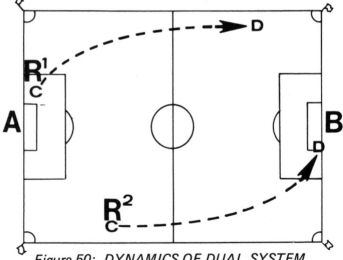

Figure 50: DYNAMICS OF DUAL SYSTEM
(As play moves between "A" and "B", so do referees
tend to move along their "C-D" lines.)

adherence to the principle of the lead whistle will create an annoying distraction to players, coaches, and fans alike.

Let me give an example. In an NCAA postseason tournament game, the referees observed to the letter the lead-whistle policy. At least five times in the game, which I watched from the stands, there was an infringement in the defensive section of the field and when the lead official who was a full sixty yards away blew for the restart, everyone, including the kicker, looked downfield to see what was bothering that official. It appeared that he wanted to draw everyone's attention to some irregularity on the field of play. He was merely signaling for the kick to be taken. Each time the trailer had to whistle as well before the kicker understood that he was supposed to go ahead and play ball. This little misunderstanding occurred virtually every time there was an offside as well as when several fouls were committed by the offense deep in the attack zone. The referees did a very good job during this game and it was only their apparent wish to adhere to prescribed policy that caused these blemishes in their performance.

I believe that the lead man should call all corners, penalty kicks, and free kicks inside his own half of the field and perhaps even some twenty yards into the other side of the field, but farther back than that — as on the typical offside call — the restart should be signaled by the trailing official. It is even better sometimes to have two whistles than to have the unfortunate situation I described above.

At half time the officials should cross over to the other side of the field, the same principle of coverage and fairness we discussed in the three-man system applying in this case.

There has been much controversy over which system is better for game control. The dual-referee advocates maintain that two men with full authority near the action assure better control and spot more infractions, citing the linesmen's reluctance to intervene to call fouls. The three-man advocates cite the virtues of having six eyes rather than four and the fact that one single authority permits the avoidance of spotty coverage in certain sectors of the field that can happen in the dual coverage.

I am afraid that both systems are just as good as the men who use them. If a referee cannot make proper use of his linesmen, or if the linesmen are inadequate, the system fails. Likewise, the dual-system will not work if one or both referees are weak or they are incompatible. In other words, when it *works*, either system works *well*. It only fails when it is not done at all. In short, properly administered, both systems are good. I personally feel that the method which has the edge in game coverage (not necessarily in game control) is the system using a referee and neutral linesmen.

Assuming that the job is done as well as it can be by both types of referee team, I think that the one having three men will see more fouls, have a clearer view of goal-line action, and so forth. If you argue about where it can go wrong, either system seems poor, but if you assume that all things are going right, both are good, especially the three-man system. I suspect that more and more colleges and eventually the schools will move toward the three-man system as they see it in action on films and in watching ASL and NASL action, unless they try to combine the best of both systems by using linesmen with whistles as has been done experimentally with some apparent success.

25

Physical Fitness and Game Control

One of the major factors in game control is physical fitness. A referee who is having obvious difficulty getting into position to call the game will not only fail to inspire respect in the players and coaches, but will also become vulnerable to a special kind of dissent. Once when I was still playing, we had a referee who was terribly out of shape and was consistently forty yards behind the play. On a crucial game-winning shot — or should I say game-losing from our viewpoint — the referee failed to call offside whereas the attacker who received the ball and put it in the net was at least three yards offside. I pointed to the man and yelled, "He was offside," but did not pursue the matter as I was never one of those players who argues with the officials. A fellow defender, however, was beside himself with rage and immediately vectored in on the one thing that was obviously lacking in the official: physical fitness.

The official's judgment in points of fact shall be final with regard to the outcome of the game (meaning that the man who scored was *not* offside for all practical effects if that is the way the referee maintains that he saw it), but it was a visible fact that he had been in a very poor position to judge this *fact*. My teammate berated the official and said, "I don't care what call you make, but you could at least get your heavy ass up here where the play is." It is a sign of the validity of his remark that the referee did not caution or eject him but merely appeared confused and on the defensive.

As the saying goes, "Presence lends conviction."* One will sometimes be caught out of the ideal position no matter what shape he is in, but a certain effort should be made to keep in top form as the better one's conditioning, the better coverage he can give with a commensurate improvement in game control.

Many referees have difficulty maintaining their top form. They are no longer adolescents, they have jobs that take up much of their time, they have families which not only means that they eat regularly but often too much for their energy needs. There are seasonal hazards, as well, the summer layoff and the winter snow-outs being the prime villains. I can usually cope readily with the summer as there are other sports and outdoor training is pleasant. It is the one or two months of winter semi-idleness coupled with the annual round of festive dining at Christmas which is my nemesis.

When I referee I never eat lunch — so I run and miss a meal. If I am rained-out, I do not do the game and I eat lunch. It is easy to gain a couple of pounds a week during such periods and also to lose the edge of conditioning one has achieved during the heavy fall season. Lest one think that size is the equivalent of conditioning, let me say that there are thin referees who are weak or out of shape. The important thing is to be the right weight for the strength of one's legs and lungs and heart!

There are many different training systems for physical conditioning, but I believe that a realistic one stresses the moves useful to officiating. Stamina is good to have and can be built up by such things as running or jogging five or ten miles a week, but the crux of the program should be short dashes and the various moves essential to game control, such as backpedaling, or used constantly in running line, such as taking sideways hops along the line.

The program I am outlining here is simply a sample one

*I should perhaps mention that referees should not be so zealous about being on top of the play that they interfere with the game. Most calls can be better made from fifteen or twenty yards than from six feet!

and each individual must vary it according to where he lives, his proximity to an athletic field, whether or not he has access to a health club, the climate in his region, and his own life style and work schedule. During the busy season when a referee may be officiating three or four times a week, little or no extra conditioning is needed, but he should still maintain his morning set-up exercises. The need for conditioning exercises is obviously greatest after a long layoff due to weather, business, illness, or a seasonal break in game scheduling. It is especially important to work out after a layoff in cold weather. The combination of coldness and stiff or untuned muscles can cause serious muscle or tendon pulls.

There are three areas of conditioning: (1) daily routine exercises, (2) endurance training, and (3) special drills.

1) *Daily routine.* It is a good idea to have some exercise every day. They say that a workout that is less than twenty minutes long is not effective, but many people do not have the time or place to go through a half-hour drill after which there must be showering and so forth. I have found that the Canadian RAF exercise book provides a magnificent routine. It is especially suited to referees because it scientifically takes into account age, realistic achievement levels, and such things as short or long layoffs for illness or other reasons. It is called the **Royal Canadian Air Force Exercise Plans for Physical Fitness** and is readily available in bookstores. This program, which consists of an 11-minute daily plan for men and a 12-minute daily plan for women, will, if followed in every particular instruction, provide for a conditioning program that is gradual, painless, and effective. Since progress is carefully programmed, there is little or no risk of pulling muscles or getting sore and one does not work up an inordinate sweat in the allotted time.

2) *Endurance building.* Endurance training is useful not only for breathing and for muscle tone, but it actually is vital in a medical sense according to some specialists. In an article entitled, "Hidden Factors in Soccer Fitness," Ellington Darden and David Ponsonby point out the unseen areas of neurological efficiency, cardiovascular condition, muscular strength, and

(Horst Müller)

glycogen storage capacity, all of which can be developed through endurance or stamina training.[33]

True, the physical demands made of the referee are usually not quite the same as those made of the player. The referee "works" just as hard, if not harder, than the player and covers more total mileage than most players, but he does not have to extend himself in the same way as the player who must in a brief spurt of activity not only display conditioning but also engage in strenuous muscular exertion by kicking, tackling, leaping, heading, and so forth.

Nevertheless, some building up of endurance is a good thing for the referee. There are times, such as in very hot weather, or when Cup games go into extra periods, that the referee may very well need the "hidden" energy reserve suggested by the development of those above-mentioned factors. I personally have an aversion to lap-running (Dettmar Cramer has been quoted as saying "If you run a lot of laps, you become a good lap-runner") so I build up endurance through riding a stationary bicycle 10-15 miles a week or scrimmaging with other people who have the same idea. Sometimes I work out with my son, combining my fitness program with teaching him fundamentals of the game.

I also take periodical saunas. This is not merely for the relaxing virtues of this Finnish panacea, it also builds up tolerance for heat. I found that after I started taking regular saunas, I did not get nearly as drained physically when officiating in above-ninety temperatures. Perhaps if Davies had been accustomed to a similar regimen, he would not have found the heat so debilitating during the NASL Final in Miami.

3) *Special drills.* Perhaps I should distinguish stamina into two kinds, the steady endurance kind we have just dealt with and the kind that permits the referee to continue sporadic activity as long as he is required to without getting winded or

becoming lame. The **F.A.** **Guide for Referees and Linesmen** maintains:

> Above all else a referee needs stamina as a runner. If you can run over a distance of 4 to 5 miles without serious puffing, you should be in good trim to referee a fast game. Long steady jogging, however, is not the kind of running called for in a match. Like the players, sometimes you have to sprint, and next you will jog, walk, or even stand for a moment or two while waiting for a restart.34

The **Guide** goes on to suggest that the referee, therefore, work at training through "interval running" with sequential periods of walking, jogging, and sprinting over short distances. They then provide a training program and suggest that it be done once or twice a week. Here is the sample program they suggest:

1. Warming Up.
   (a)   Jog lightly for 200 yards.
   (b)   Knee-raising for about 30 seconds.
   (c)   Jog 200 yards.
2. General Exercises (10 minutes).
   (a)   Skipping or skip-jumping.
   (b)   Stand with feet astride. Trunk-bending from side to side, trunk-twisting, and trunk-circling. Repeat each exercise 10-15 times.
   (c)   Back-lying. Trunk-raising and lowering to touch knees. Legs-raising and lowering. Repeat both exercises 10-15 times.
   (d)   10 'burphee' jumps (stand, jump to crouch on count one, jump legs backward to front support position on count 2, jump legs back to crouch position on count 3, jump to standing position on count 4).
3. Stamina Running (20 minutes).
   (a)   Ten 'wind' sprints (each wind sprint consists of a walk for 25 yards, jog 25 yards, and sprint 25 yards). Rest, then repeat.
   (b)   Jog 50 yards and sprint 25 yards. Repeat 10 times.

A variation of this routine can be worked out to incorporate such items as running sideways and backwards. The important thing is to develop the legs and the wind. An alternate routine can be devised with the use of four small flags on 18 x 3/8 inch dowels, easily made in ten or fifteen minutes. Here is a sample program which the individual can augment or vary according to his own predilections.

1. Jog two laps with periods of sprints and walks.

2. Place the four flags in a square about 25 yards to a side. One flag will be the starting point. Make two circuits of the flags going clockwise, always keeping the body facing the same direction. In other words, run forward, sideways to the right, backwards, and sideways to the left back to the starting flag. After two circuits, reverse the direction and do two circuits counterclockwise.

3. Jog three laps without sprints or walks.

4. Place the four flags in a row ten yards apart. Run to the first flag and back, then to the second flag and back, then to the third flag and back, and finally to the fourth flag and back. When you can run it quickly without pain, add a fifth flag.

5. Run two laps, dashing 100 yards on two of the straightaways.

The F.A. plan or this other plan must be worked up to slowly. One should try to complete the drill, but resting appropriately between exercises and not overly pressing himself until the movements become easier through training. A combination of gradually decreased time per exercise and the addition of laps or flags should be made if one is already on Chart 3 of the Canadian Air Force book.

The individual can vary the tedium of these drills by inventing new ones, such as slalom running through the flags, running straight at the line of flags and skipping over the flagstaffs. He should try to devise exercises related to potential match movements. For example, the skipping over the flags is related to the occasional necessity of jumping over a ball so as not to interfere with play.

NOTES

[1]Ted Copeland, "Checklist for Referees," **Soccer World**, 1:5 (December 1974), 23.

[2]**Ibid**

[3]**Can-So-Ref!**, 2:3 (November 1974), 6.

[4]Robert Evans, **Manual for Linesmen** ([Dallas]: North Texas Soccer Referees Association, 1973), p. 1.

[5]Denis Howell, **Soccer Refereeing** (London: Pelham Books, 1968), p. 71.

[6]Paul E. Harris, Jr. and Larry R. Harris, **Fair or Foul?** (Torrance, CA: AYSO, 1973), p. 106.

[7]**Can-So-Ref!**, 1:4 (November 1973), 5; article is reprinted in **Soccer America** issue of May 7, 1974.

[8]Patrick J. Smith, "Casebook," in **1974 Official Manual of the NISOA**, p. 25.

[9]Howell, p. 85.

[10]**Soccer Monthly**, 1:10 (April 1975), 8-9.

[11]Joseph Mercier, **Le Football** (Paris: Presses Universitaires de France, 1966), p. 24.

[12]Diogenes Cordero, "Important Decisions," **Soccer America**, September 3, 1974, p. 12.

[13]Norman Burtenshaw, **Whose Side Are You On, Ref?** (London: Arthur Baker, Ltd., 1973), p. 177. This advice is pursuant with the 1969 FIFA memorandum on the Laws and the Spirit of the Game.

[14]Diego De Leo, **Regole del Calcio**, 8e ed. (Modena: Panini, 1971), pp. 136-37.

[15]Ted Smits, **Soccer for the American Boy** (Englewood Cliffs, NJ: Prentice-Hall, 1970), p. 57.

[16]Howell, p. 131.

[17]De Leo, pp. 230-32.

[18]**The F.A. Guide to the Laws of the Game** (London: Heinemann, 1969), pp. 102-3.

[19]**Association Football — Know the Game** (London: Education Products, Ltd. & The Football Association, 1970), p. 16.

[20]Howell, p. 131.

[21]Association Football – Know the Game p. 17.

[22]Jack Hyde, " 'I've Decided' a Key Part," Soccer America October 29, 1974, p. 7.

[23]Robert Evans, "Guidance for Referees," Soccer America August 13, 1974, p. R1.

[24]Ken Mullen, "Sounds of the Whistle," Soccer America, January 7, 1975, p. 16.

[25]Burtenshaw, p. 149.

[26]Robert Evans, "Guidance for Referees," Soccer America, August 7, 1973, p. 15.

[27]Les Radunchev, "Two Meters: A Little or a Lot?" Soccer World 2:1 (February 1975), 10.

[28]Robert Evans, "The 10-Yard Free Kick Fiasco," Soccer America, September 18, 1973, p. 12.

[29]Robert Evans, "The Wall That Will Not Move," Soccer America December 18, 1973, p. 28.

[30]Burtenshaw, p. 134. Preceding quotation is from same page.

[31]Harris and Harris, Fair or Foul?, p. 4.

[32]Evans, Manual for Linesmen, p. 22.

[33]Darden and Ponsonby, "Hidden Factors in Soccer Fitness," Soccer World, 2:1 (February 1975), 16-17.

[34]F.A. Guide for Referees and Linesmen (London: The Football Association, 1968), pp. 55-56.

Appendices

Laws of the Game	Decisions of the International Board

LAW I

(1) **Dimensions.** The field of play shall be rectangular, its length being not more than 130 yards nor less than 100 yards and its breadth not more than 100 yards nor less than 50 yards. (In International Matches the length shall be not more than 120 yards nor less than 110 yards and the breadth not more than 80 yards nor less than 70 yards.) The length shall in all cases exceed the breadth.

(2) **Marking.** The field of play shall be marked with distinctive lines, not more than 5 inches in width, not by a V-shaped rut, in accordance with the plan, the longer boundary lines being called the touch-lines and the shorter the goal-lines. A flag on a post not less than 5 ft. high and having a non-pointed top, shall be placed at each corner; a similar flag-post may be placed opposite the halfway line on each side of the field of play, not less than 1 yard outside the touch-line. A halfway-line shall be marked out across the field of play. The centre of the field of play shall be indicated by a suitable mark and a circle with a 10 yards radius shall be marked round it.

(3) **The Goal-Area.** At each end of the field of play two lines shall be drawn at right-angles to the goal-line, 6 yards from each goal-post. These shall extend into the field of play for a distance of 6 yards and shall be joined by a line drawn parallel with the goal-line. Each of the spaces enclosed by these lines and the goal-line shall be called a goal-area.

(4) **The Penalty-Area.** At each end of the field of play two lines shall be drawn at right-angles to the goal-line, 18 yards from each goal-post. These shall extend into the field of play for a distance of 18 yards and shall be joined by a line drawn parallel with the goal-line. Each of the spaces enclosed by these lines and the goal-line shall be called a penalty-area. A suitable mark shall be made within each penalty-area, 12 yards from the mid-point of the goal-line, measured along an undrawn line at right-angles thereto. These shall be the penalty-kick marks. From each penalty-kick mark an arc of a circle, having a radius of 10 yards, shall be drawn outside the penalty-area.

(1) In International matches the dimensions of the field of play shall be: maximum 110 x 75 metres; minimum 100 x 64 metres.
(2) National Associations must adhere strictly to these dimensions. Each National Association organising an International Match must advise the visiting Association, before the match, of the place and the dimensions of the field of play.
(3) The Board has approved this table of measurements for the Laws of the Game:

130 yards	. . . .	120 Metres
120 yards	. . . .	110
110 yards	. . . .	100
100 yards	. . . .	90
80 yards	. . . .	75
70 yards	. . . .	64
50 yards	. . . .	45
18 yards	. . . .	16.50
12 yards	. . . .	11
10 yards	. . . .	9.15
8 yards	. . . .	7.32
6 yards	. . . .	5.50
1 yard	. . . .	1
8 feet	. . . .	2.44
5 feet	. . . .	1.50
28 inches	. . . .	0.71
27 inches	. . . .	0.68
9 inches	. . . .	0.22
5 inches	. . . .	0.12
3/4 inch	. . . .	0.019
1/2 inch	. . . .	0.0127
3/8 inch	. . . .	0.010
14 ounces	. . . .	396 grams
16 ounces	. . . .	453 grams
15 lb./sq.in.	. . . . .	1 kg/cm^2

(4) The goal-line shall be marked the same width as the depth of the goal-posts and the cross-bar, so that the goal-line and goal-posts will conform to the same interior and exterior edges.
(5) The 6 yards (for the outline of the goal-area) and the 18 yards (for the outline of the penalty-area) which have to be measured along the goal-line, must start from the inner sides of the goal-posts.
(6) The space within the inside areas of the field of play includes the width of the lines marking these areas.
(7) All Associations shall provide standard equipment, particularly in International Matches, when the Laws of the Game must be complied with in every respect and especially with regard to the size of the ball and other equipment which must conform to the regu-

Laws of the Game

LAW 1 *(continued)*

(5) **The Corner-Area.** From each corner-flag post a quarter circle, having a radius of 1 yard, shall be drawn inside the field of play.

(6) **The Goals.** The goals shall be placed on the centre of each goal-line and shall consist of two upright posts, equidistant from the corner-flags and 8 yards apart (inside measurement), joined by a horizontal cross-bar the lower edge of which shall be 8 ft. from the ground. The width and depth of the goal-posts and the width and depth of the cross-bars shall not exceed 5 inches (12 cm). The goal-posts and the cross-bars shall have the same width.

Nets may be attached to the posts, cross-bars and ground behind the goals. They should be appropriately supported and be so placed as to allow the goal-keeper ample room.

Decisions of the International Board

lations. All cases of failure to provide standard equipment must be reported to F.I.F.A.

(8) In a match played under the Rules of a Competition if the cross-bar becomes displaced or broken play shall be stopped and the match abandoned unless the cross-bar has been repaired and replaced in position or a new one provided without such being a danger to the players. A rope is not considered to be a satisfactory substitute for a cross-bar.

In a Friendly Match, by mutual consent, play may be resumed without the cross-bar provided it has been removed and no longer constitutes a danger to the players. In these circumstances, a rope may be used as a substitute for a cross-bar. If a rope is not used and the ball crosses the goal-line at a point which in the opinion of the Referee is below where the cross-bar should have been he shall award a goal.

The game shall be restarted by the Referee dropping the ball at the place where it was when play was stopped.

(9) National Associations may specify such maximum and minimum dimensions for the cross-bars and goal-posts, within the limits laid down in Law I, as they consider appropriate.

(10) Goal-posts and cross-bars must be made of wood, metal or other approved material as decided from time to time by the International F.A. Board. They may be square, rectangular, round, half-round or elliptical in shape Goal-posts and cross-bars made of other materials and in other shapes are not permitted.

(11) 'Curtain-raisers' to International matches should only be played following agreement on the day of the match, and taking into account the condition of the field of play, between representatives of the two Associations and the Referee (of the International Match).

(12) National Associations, particularly in International Matches, should
— restrict the number of photographers around the field of play,
— have a line ("photographers' line") marked behind the goal-lines at least two metres from the corner flag going through a point situated at least 3.5 metres behind the intersection of the goal-line with the line marking the goal area to a point

---

Footnote:

Goal nets. The use of nets made of hemp, jute or nylon is permitted. The nylon strings may, however, not be thinner than those made of hemp or jute.

Laws of the Game	*Decisions of the International Board*

situated at least six metres behind the goal-posts,
- prohibit photographers from passing over these lines,
- forbid the use of artificial lighting in the form of "flashlights".

LAW II. – THE BALL

The ball shall be spherical; the outer casing shall be of leather or other approved materials. No material shall be used in its construction which might prove dangerous to the players.

The circumference of the ball shall not be more than 28 in. and not less than 27 in. The weight of the ball at the start of the game shall not be more than 16 oz. nor less than 14 oz. The pressure shall be equal to 0.6-0.7 atmosphere, which equals 9.0-10.5 lb./sq.in. (= 600-700 gr/cm^2) at sea level. The ball shall not be changed during the game unless authorised by the Referee.

(1) The ball used in any match shall be considered the property of the Association or Club on whose ground the match is played, and at the close of play it must be returned to the Referee.

(2) The International Board, from time to time, shall decide what constitutes approved materials. Any approved material shall be certified as such by the International Board.

(3) The Board has approved these equivalents of the weights specified in the Law. 14 to 16 ounces = 396 to 453 grammes.

(4) If the ball bursts or becomes deflated during the course of a match, the game shall be stopped and restarted by dropping the new ball at the place where the first ball became defective.

(5) If this happens during a stoppage of the game (place-kick, goal-kick, corner-kick, free-kick, penalty-kick or throw-in) the game shall be restarted accordingly.

LAW III. – NUMBER OF PLAYERS

(1) A match shall be played by two teams, each consisting of not more than eleven players, one of whom shall be the goalkeeper.

(2) Substitutes may be used in any match played under the rules of a competition, subject to the following conditions:

(a) that the authority of the international association(s) or national association(s) concerned, has been obtained,

(b) that, subject to the restriction contained in the following paragraph (c) the rules of a competition shall state how many, if any, substitutes may be used, and

(c) that a team shall not be permitted to use more that two substitutes in any match.

(3) Substitutes may be used in any other match, provided that the two teams concerned reach agreement on a maximum number, not exceeding five, and that the terms of such agreement are intimated to the Referee, before the match. If the Referee is not informed, or if the teams fail to reach agreement, no more than two substitutes shall be permitted.

(4) Any of the other players may change places with the goalkeeper, provided that the Referee is informed before the change is made, and provided also, that the change is made during a stoppage in the game.

(5) When a goalkeeper or any other player is to be replaced by a substitute, the following conditions shall be observed:

(a) the Referee shall be informed of the proposed substitution, before it is made,

(b) the substitute shall not enter the field of play until the player he is replacing has left, and then only after having received a signal from the Referee,

(c) he shall enter the field during a stoppage in the game, and at the half-way line.

Punishment:

(a) Play shall not be stopped for an infringement of paragraph 4. The players concerned shall be cautioned immediately the ball goes out of play.

(b) For any other infringement of this law, the player concerned shall be cautioned, and if the game is stopped by the Referee, to administer the caution, it shall be re-started by an indirect free-kick, to be taken by a player of the opposing team, from the place where the ball was, when play was stopped.

(1) The minimum number of players in a team is left to the discretion of National Associations.

(2) The Board is of the opinion that a match should not be considered valid if there are fewer than seven players in either of the teams.

(3) A competition may require that the referee shall be informed, before the start of the match, of the names of not more than five players, from whom the substitutes (if any) must be chosen.

(4) A player who has been ordered off before play begins may only be replaced by one of the named substitutes. The kick-off must not be delayed to allow the substitute to join his team.

A player who has been ordered off after play has started may not be replaced.

A named substitute who has been ordered off, either before or after play has started, may not be replaced (this decision only relates to players who are ordered off under Law XII. It does not apply to players who have infringed Law IV.)

(5) A player who has been replaced shall not take any further part in the game.

(6) A substitute shall be deemed to be a player and shall be subject to the authority and jurisdiction of the Referee whether called upon to play or not. For any offence committed on the field of play a substitute shall be subject to the same punishment as any other player whether called upon or not.

Laws of the Game	Decisions of the International Board

LAW IV. – PLAYERS' EQUIPMENT

(1) A player shall not wear anything which is dangerous to another player.

(2) Footwear (boots or shoes) must conform to the following standard:

(a) Bars shall be made of leather or rubber and shall be transverse and flat, not less than half an inch in width and shall extend the total width of the sole and be rounded at the corners.

(b) Studs which are independently mounted on the sole and are replaceable shall be made of leather, rubber, aluminium, plastic or similar material and shall be solid. With the exception of that part of the stud forming the base, which shall not protrude from the sole more than one quarter of an inch, studs shall be round in plan and not less than half an inch in diameter. Where studs are tapered, the minimum diameter of any section of the stud must not be less than half an inch. Where metal seating for the screw type is used, this seating must be embedded in the sole of the footwear and any atachment screw shall be part of the stud. Other than the metal seating for the screw type of stud, no metal plates even though covered with leather or rubber shall be worn, neither studs which are threaded to allow them to be screwed on to a base screw that is fixed by nails or otherwise to the soles of footwear, nor studs which, apart from the base, have any form of protruding edge rim or relief marking or ornament, should be allowed.

(c) Studs which are moulded as an integral part of the sole and are not replaceable shall be made of rubber, plastic, polyurethene or similar soft materials. Provided that there are no fewer than ten studs on the sole, they shall have a minimum diameter of three eights of an inch (10 mm.). Additional supporting material to stabilise studs of soft materials, and ridges which shall not protrude more than 5 mm. from the sole and moulded to strengthen it, shall be permitted provided that they are in no way dangerous to other players. In all other respects they shall conform to the general requirements of this Law.

(d) Combined bars and studs may be worn, provided the whole conforms to the general requirements of this Law. Neither bars nor studs on the soles shall project more

(1) The usual equipment of a player is a jersey or shirt, shorts, stockings and footwear. In a match played under the rules of a competition, players need not wear boots or shoes, but shall wear jersey or shirt, shorts, or track suit or similar trousers, and stockings.

(2) The Law does not insist that boots or shoes must be worn. However, in competition matches Referees should not allow one or a few players to play without footwear when all the other players are so equipped.

(3) In International Matches, International Competitions, International Club Competitions and friendly matches between clubs of different National Associations, the Referee, prior to the start of the game, shall inspect the players' footwear, and prevent any player whose footwear does not conform to the requirements of this Law from playing until such time as it does comply.

The rules of any competition may include a similar provision.

(4) If the Referee finds that a player is wearing articles not permitted by the Laws and which may constitute a danger to other players, he shall order him to take them off. If he fails to carry out the Referee's instruction, the player shall not take part in the match.

(5) A player who has been prevented from taking part in the game or a player who has been sent off the field for infringing Law IV must report to the Referee during a stoppage of the game and may not enter or re-enter the field of play unless and until the Referee has satisfied himself that the player is no longer infringing Law IV.

(6) A player who has been prevented from taking part in a game or who has been sent off because of an infringement of Law IV, and who enters or re-enters the field of play to join or re-join his team, in breach of the conditions of Law XII, shall be cautioned. If the Referee stops the game to administer the caution, the game shall be restarted by an indirect free-kick, taken by a player of the opposing side, from the place where the offending player was when the Referee stopped the game.

Laws of the Game	*Decisions of the International Board*

LAW IV *(continued)*

than three-quarters of an inch. If nails are used they shall be driven in flush with the surface.

(3) The goalkeeper shall wear colours which distinguish him from the other players and from the referee.

Punishment: For any infringement of this Law, the player at fault shall be sent off the field of play to adjust his equipment and he shall not return without first reporting to the Referee, who shall satisfy himself that the player's equipment is in order; the player shall only re-enter the game at a moment when the ball has ceased to be in play.

Laws of the Game	*Decisions of the International Board*

LAW V. – REFEREES

A Referee shall be appointed to officiate in each game. His authority and the exercise of the powers granted to him by the Laws of the Game commence as soon as he enters the field of play.

His power of penalising shall extend to offences committed when play has been temporarily suspended, or when the ball is out of play. His decision on points of fact connected with the play shall be final, so far as the result of the game is concerned. He shall:

(a) Enforce the Laws.

(b) Refrain from penalising in cases where he is satisfied that, by doing so, he would be giving an advantage to the offending team.

(c) Keep a record of the game; act as timekeeper and allow the full or agreed time, adding thereto all time lost through accident or other cause.

(d) Have discretionary power to stop the game for any infringement of the Laws and to suspend or terminate the game whenever, by reason of the elements, interference by spectators, or other cause, he deems such stoppage necessary. In such a case he shall submit a detailed report to the competent authority, within the stipulated time, and in accordance with the provisions set up by the National Association under whose jurisdiction the match was played. Reports will be deemed to be made when received in the ordinary course of post.

(e) From the time he enters the field of play, caution any player guilty of misconduct or ungentlemanly behaviour and, if he persists, suspend him from further participation in the game. In such cases the Referee shall send the name of the offender to the competent authority, within the stipulated time, and in accordance with the provisions set up by the National Association under whose jurisdiction the match was played. Reports will be deemed to be made when received in the ordinary course of post.

(f) Allow no person other than the players and linesmen to enter the field of play without his permission.

(g) Stop the game if, in his opinion, a player has been seriously injured; have the player removed as soon as possible from the

(1) Referees in International Matches shall wear a blazer or blouse the colour of which is distinct from the colours worn by the contesting teams.

(2) Referees for International Matches will be selected from a neutral country unless the countries concerned agree to appoint their own officials.

(3) The Referee must be chosen from the official list of International Referees. This need not apply to Amateur and Youth International Matches.

(4) The Referee shall report to the appropriate authority misconduct or any misdemeanour on the part of spectators, officials, players, named substitutes or other persons which take place either on the field of play or in its vicinity at any time prior to, during, or after the match in question so that appropriate action can be taken by the Authority concerned.

(5) Linesmen are assistants of the Referee. In no case shall the Referee consider the intervention of a Linesman if he himself has seen the incident and from his position on the field, is better able to judge. With this reserve, and the Linesman neutral, the Referee can consider the intervention and if the information of the Linesman applies to that phase of the game immediately before the scoring of a goal, the Referee may act thereon and cancel the goal.

(6) The Referee, however, can only reverse his first decision so long as the game has not been restarted.

(7) If the Referee has decided to apply the advantage clause and to let the game proceed, he cannot revoke his decision if the presumed advantage has not been realised, even though he has not, by any gesture, indicated his decision. This does not exempt the offending player from being dealt with by the Referee.

(8) The Laws of the Game are intended to provide that games should be played with as little interference as possible, and in this view it is the duty of Referees to penalise only deliberate breaches of the Law. Constant whistling for trifling and doubtful breaches produces bad feeling and loss of temper on the part of the players and spoils the pleasure of spectators.

(9) By para. (d) of Law V the Referee is

Laws of the Game	*Decisions of the International Board*

LAW V *(continued)*

field of play, and immediately resume the game. If a player is slightly injured, the game shall not be stopped until the ball has ceased to be in play. A player who is able to go to the touch or goal-line for attention of any kind, shall not be treated on the field of play.

(h) Send off the field of play, any player who, in his opinion, is guilty of violent conduct, serious foul play, or the use of foul or abusive language.

(i) Signal for recommencement of the game after all stoppages.

(j) Decide that the ball provided for a match meets with the requirements of Law II.

empowered to terminate a match in the event of grave disorder, but he has no power or right to decide, in such event, that either team is disqualified and thereby the loser of the match. He must send a detailed report to the proper authority who alone has power to deal further with this matter.

(10) If a player commits two infringements of a different nature at the same time, the Referee shall punish the more serious offence.

(11) It is the duty of the Referee to act upon the information of neutral Linesmen with regard to incidents that do not come under the personal notice of the Referee.

(12) The Referee shall not allow any person to enter the field until play has stopped, and only then, if he has given him a signal to do so, nor shall he allow coaching from the boundary lines.

Laws of the Game	Decisions of the International Board

LAW VI. – LINESMEN

Two Linesmen shall be appointed, whose duty (subject to the decision of the Referee) shall be to indicate when the ball is out of play and which side is entitled to the corner-kick, goal-kick or throw-in. They shall also assist the Referee to control the game in accordance with the Laws. In the event of undue interference or improper conduct by a Linesman, the Referee shall dispense with his services and arrange for a substitute to be appointed. (The matter shall be reported by the Referee to the competent authority.) The Linesmen should be equipped with flags by the Club on whose ground the match is played.

(1) Linesmen, where neutral, shall draw the Referee's attention to any breach of the Laws of the Game of which they become aware if they consider that the Referee may not have seen it, but the Referee shall always be the judge of the decision to be taken.

(2) National Associations are advised to appoint official Referees of neutral nationality to act as Linesmen in International Matches.

(3) In International Matches Linesmen's flags shall be of a vivid colour, bright reds and yellows. Such flags are recommended for use in all other matches.

(4) A Linesman may be subject to disciplinary action only upon a report of the Referee for unjustified interference or insufficient assistance.

LAW VII. – DURATION OF THE GAME

The duration of the game shall be two equal periods of 45 minutes, unless otherwise mutually agreed upon, subject to the following: (a) Allowance shall be made in either period for all time lost through accident or other cause, the amount of which shall be a matter for the discretion of the Referee; (b) Time shall be extended to permit a penalty-kick being taken at or after the expiration of the normal period in either half.

At half-time the interval shall not exceed five minutes except by consent of the Referee.

(1) If a match has been stopped by the Referee, before the completion of the time specified in the rules, for any reason stated in Law V it must be replayed in full unless the rules of the competition concerned provide for the result of the match at the time of such stoppage to stand.

(2) Players have a right to an interval at half-time.

LAW VIII. – THE START OF PLAY

(a) **At the beginning of the game,** choice of ends and the kick-off shall be decided by the toss of a coin. The team winning the toss shall have the option of choice of ends or the kick-off. The Referee having given a signal, the game shall be started by a player taking a place-kick (i.e., a kick at the ball while it is stationary on the ground in the centre of the field of play) into his opponents' half of the field of play. Every player shall be in his own half of the field and every player of the team opposing that of the kicker shall remain not less than 10 yards from the ball until it is kicked-off; it shall not be deemed in play until it has travelled the distance of its own circumference. The kicker shall not play the ball a second time until it has been touched or played by another player.

(b) **After a goal has scored,** the game shall be restarted in like manner by a player of the team losing the goal.

(c) **After half-time;** when restarting after half-time, ends shall be changed and the kick-off shall be taken by a player of the opposite team to that of the player who started the game.

Punishment. For any infringement of this Law, the kick-off shall be retaken, except in the case of the kicker playing the ball again before it has been touched or played by another player; for this offence, an indirect free-kick shall be taken by a player of the opposing team from the place where the infringement occurred. A goal shall not be scored direct from a kick-off.

(d) **After any other temporary suspension;** when restarting the game after a temporary suspension of play from any cause not mentioned elsewhere in these Laws, provided that immediately prior to the suspension the ball has not passed over the touch or goal-lines, the Referee shall drop the ball at the place where it was when play was suspended and it shall be deemed in play when it has touched the ground; if, however, it goes over the touch or goal-lines after it has been dropped by the Referee, but before it is touched by a player, the Referee shall again drop it. A player shall not play the ball until it has touched the ground. If this section of the Law is not complied with the Referee shall again drop the ball.

(1) If, when the Referee drops the ball, a player infringes any of the Laws before the ball has touched the ground, the player concerned shall be cautioned or sent off the field according to the seriousness of the offence, but a free-kick cannot be awarded to the opposing team because the ball was not in play at the time of the offence. The ball shall therefore be again dropped by the Referee.

(2) Kicking-off by persons other than the players competing in a match is prohibited.

Laws of the Game	*Decisions of the International Board*

LAW IX. – BALL IN AND OUT OF PLAY

The ball is out of play:

(a) When it has wholly crossed the goal-line or touch-line, whether on the ground or in the air.

(b) When the game has been stopped by the Referee.

The ball is in play at all other times from the start of the match to the finish including:

(a) If it rebounds from a goal-post, cross-bar or corner-flag post into the field of play.

(b) If it rebounds off either the Referee or Linesmen when they are in the field of play.

(c) In the event of a supposed infringement of the Laws, until a decision is given.

(1) The lines belong to the areas of which they are the boundaries. In consequence, the touch-lines and the goal-lines belong to the field of play.

Laws of the Game

LAW X. – METHOD OF SCORING

Except as otherwise provided by these Laws, a goal is scored when the whole of the ball has passed over the goal-line, between the goal-posts and under the cross-bar, provided it has not been thrown, carried or intentionally propelled by hand or arm, by a player of the attacking side, except in the case of a goalkeeper, who is within his own penalty-area.

The team scoring the greater number of goals during a game shall be the winner; if no goals, or an equal number of goals are scored, the game shall be termed a "draw".

Decisions of the International Board

(1) Law X defines the only method according to which a match is won or drawn; no variation whatsoever can be authorised.

(2) A goal cannot in any case be allowed if the ball has been prevented by some outside agent from passing over the goal-line. If this happens in the normal course of play, other than at the taking of a penalty-kick: the game must be stopped and restarted by the Referee dropping the ball at the place where the ball came into contact with the interference.

(3) If, when the ball is going into goal, a spectator enters the field before it passes wholly over the goal-line, and tries to prevent a score, a goal shall be allowed if the ball goes into goal unless the spectator has made contact with the ball or has interfered with play, in which case the Referee shall stop the game and restart it by dropping the ball at the place where the contact or interference occurred.

Laws of the Game	*Decisions of the International Board*

LAW XI. – OFF-SIDE

A player is off-side if he is nearer his opponents' goal-line than the ball **at the moment the ball is played unless:**

(a) He is in his own half of the field of play.

(b) There are two of his opponents nearer to their own goal-line than he is.

(c) The ball last touched an opponent or was last played by him.

(d) He receives the ball direct from a goal-kick, a corner-kick, a throw-in, or when it was dropped by the Referee.

Punishment. For an infringement of this Law, an indirect free-kick shall be taken by a player of the opposing team from the place where the infringement occurred.

A player in an off-side position shall not be penalised unless, in the opinion of the Referee, he is interfering with the play or with an opponent, or is seeking to gain an advantage by being in an offside position.

(1) Off-side shall not be judged at the moment the player in question receives the ball, but at the moment when the ball is passed to him by one of his own side. A player who is not in an off-side position when one of his colleagues passes the ball to him or takes a free-kick, does not therefore become off-side if he goes forward during the flight of the ball.

Laws of the Game	*Decisions of the International Board*

LAW XII. — FOULS AND MISCONDUCT

A player who intentionally commits any of the following nine offences:

(a) Kicks or attempts to kick an opponent;

(b) Trips an opponent, i.e., throwing or attempting to throw him by the use of the legs or by stooping in front of or behind him;

(c) Jumps at an opponent;

(d) Charges an opponent in a violent or dangerous manner;

(e) Charges an opponent from behind unless the latter be obstructing;

(f) Strikes or attempts to strike an opponent;

(g) Holds an opponent;

(h) Pushes an opponent;

(i) Handles the ball, i.e., carries, strikes or propels the ball with his hand or arm. (This does not apply to the goalkeeper within his own penalty-area);

shall be penalised by the award of a **direct free-kick** to be taken by the opposing side from the place where the offence occurred.

Should a player of the defending side intentionally commit one of the above nine offences within the penalty-area he shall be penalised by a **penalty-kick**.

A penalty-kick can be awarded irrespective of the position of the ball, if in play, at the time an offence within the penalty-area is committed.

A player committing any of the five following offences:

1. Playing in a manner considered by the Referee to be dangerous, e.g., attempting to kick the ball while held by the goalkeeper;

2. Charging fairly, i.e., with the shoulder, when the ball is not within playing distance of the players concerned and they are definitely not trying to play it;

3. When not playing the ball, intentionally obstructing an opponent, i.e., running between the opponent and the ball, or interposing the body so as to form an obstacle to an opponent;

4. Charging the goalkeeper except when he
   (a) is holding the ball;
   (b) is obstructing an opponent;

(1) If the goalkeeper either intentionally strikes an opponent by throwing the ball vigorously at him or pushes him with the ball while holding it, the Referee shall award a penalty-kick, if the offence took place within the penalty-area.

(2) If a player deliberately turns his back to an opponent when he is about to be tackled, he may be charged but not in a dangerous manner.

(3) In case of body-contact in the goal-area between an attacking player and the opposing goalkeeper not in possession of the ball, the Referee, as sole judge of intention, shall stop the game if, in his opinion, the action of the attacking player was intentional, and award an indirect free-kick.

(4) If a player leans on the shoulders of another player of his own team in order to head the ball, the Referee shall stop the game, caution the player for ungentlemanly conduct and award an indirect free-kick to the opposing side.

(5) A player's obligation when joining or rejoining his team after the start of the match to 'report to the Referee' must be interpreted as meaning 'to draw the attention of the Referee from the touch-line'. The signal from the Referee shall be made by a definite gesture which makes the player understand the he may come into the field of play; it is not necessary for the Referee to wait until the game is stopped (this does not apply in respect of an infringement of Law IV), but the Referee is the sole judge of the moment in which he gives his signal of acknowledgement.

(6) The letter and spirit of Law XII do not oblige the Referee to stop a game to administer a caution. He may, if he chooses, apply the advantage. If he does apply the advantage, he shall caution the player when play stops.

(7) If a player covers up the ball without touching it in an endeavour not to have it played by an opponent, he obstructs but does not infringe Law XII para. 3 because he is already in possession of the ball and covers it for tactical reasons whilst the ball remains within playing distance. In fact, he is actually playing the ball and does not commit an infringement; in this case, the

Laws of the Game	*Decisions of the International Board*

LAW XII *(continued)*

(c) has passed outside his goal-area;

5. When playing as goalkeeper,

   (a) takes more than 4 steps whilst holding, bouncing or throwing the ball in the air and catching it again without releasing it so that it is played by another player, or

   (b) indulges in tactics which, in the opinion of the Referee, are designed merely to hold up the game and thus waste time and so give an unfair advantage to his own team

shall be penalised by the award of an **indirect free-kick** to be taken by the opposing side from the place where the infringement occurred.

A player shall be **cautioned** if:

(j) he enters or re-enters the field of play to join or rejoin his team after the game has commenced, or leaves the field of play during the progress of the game (except through accident) without, in either case, first having received a signal from the Referee showing him that he may do so. If the Referee stops the game to administer the caution the game shall be restarted by an indirect free-kick taken by a player of the opposing team from the place where the ball was when the referee stopped the game. If, however, the offending player has committed a more serious offence he shall be penalised according to that section of the law he infringed;

(k) he persistently infringes the Laws of the Game;

(l) he shows by word or action, dissent from any decision given by the Referee;

(m) he is guilty of ungentlemanly conduct.

For any of these last three offences, in addition to the caution, an **indirect free-kick** shall also be awarded to the opposing side from the place where the offence occurred unless a more serious infringement of the Laws of the Game was committed.

A player shall be **sent off** the field of play, if:

(n) in the opinion of the Referee he is guilty of violent conduct or serious foul play;

(o) he uses foul or abusive language

(p) he persists in misconduct after having received a caution.

player may be charged because he is in fact playing the ball.

(8) If a player intentionally stretches his arms to obstruct an opponent and steps from one side to the other, moving his arms up and down to delay his opponent, forcing him to change course, but does not make "bodily contact" the Referee shall caution the player for ungentlemanly conduct and award an indirect free-kick.

(9) If a player intentionally obstructs the opposing goalkeeper, in an attempt to prevent him from putting the ball into play in accordance with Law XII, 5(a), the referee shall award an indirect free-kick.

(10) If after a Referee has awarded a free-kick a player protests violently by using abusive or foul language and is sent off the field, the free-kick should not be taken until the player has left the field.

(11) Any player, whether he is within or outside the field of play, whose conduct is ungentlemanly or violent, whether or not it is directed towards an opponent, a colleague, the Referee, a linesman or other person, or who uses foul or abusive language, is guilty of an offence, and shall be dealt with according to the nature of the offence committed.

(12) If, in the opinion of the Referee a goalkeeper intentionally lies on the ball longer than is necessary, he shall be penalised for ungentlemanly conduct and

(a) be cautioned and an indirect free-kick awarded to the opposing team;

(b) in case of repetition of the offence, be sent off the field.

(13) The offence of spitting at opponents, officials or other persons, or similar unseemly behaviour shall be considered as violent conduct within the meaning of section (n) of Law XII.

(14) If, when a Referee is about to caution a player, and before he has done so, the player commits another offence which merits a caution, the player shall be sent off the field of play.

Laws of the Game	*Decisions of the International Board*
LAW XII *(continued)* If play be stopped by reason of a player being ordered from the field for an offence without a separate breach of the Law having been committed, the game shall be resumed by an **indirect free-kick** awarded to the opposing side from the place where the infringement occurred.	

Laws of the Game	*Decisions of the International Board*

LAW XIII. – FREE-KICK

Free-kicks shall be classified under two headings: "Direct" (from which a goal can be scored direct against the offending side), and "Indirect" (from which a goal cannot be scored unless the ball has been played or touched by a player other than the kicker before passing through the goal).

When a player is taking a direct or an indirect free-kick inside his own penalty-area, all of the opposing players shall remain outside the area, and shall be at least ten yards from the ball whilst the kick is being taken. The ball shall be in play immediately it has travelled the distance of its own circumference and is beyond the penalty-area. The goalkeeper shall not receive the ball into his hands, in order that he may thereafter kick it into play. If the ball is not kicked direct into play, beyond the penalty-area, the kick shall be retaken.

When a player is taking a direct or an indirect free-kick outside his own penalty-area, all of the opposing players shall be at least ten yards from the ball, until it is in play, unless they are standing on their own goal-line, between the goal-posts. The ball shall be in play when it has travelled the distance of its own circumference.

If a player of the opposing side encroaches into the penalty-area, or within ten yards of the ball, as the case may be, before a free-kick is taken, the Referee shall delay the taking of the kick, until the Law is complied with.

The ball must be stationary when a free-kick is taken, and the kicker shall not play the ball a second time, until it has been touched or played by another player.

Punishment. If the kicker, after taking the free-kick, plays the ball a second time before it has been touched or played by another player an indirect free-kick shall be taken by a player of the opposing team from the spot where the infringement occurred.

(1) In order to distinguish between a direct and an indirect free-kick, the Referee, when he awards an indirect free-kick, shall indicate accordingly by raising an arm above his head. He shall keep his arm in that position until the kick has been taken.

(2) Players who do not retire to the proper distance when a free-kick is taken must be cautioned and on any repetition be ordered off. It is particularly requested of Referees that attempts to delay the taking of a free-kick by encroaching should be treated as serious misconduct.

(3) If, when a free-kick is being taken, any of the players dance about or gesticulate in a way calculated to distract their opponents, it shall be deemed ungentlemanly conduct for which the offender(s) shall be cautioned.

Laws of the Game	*Decisions of the International Board*

LAW XIV. – PENALTY-KICK

A penalty-kick shall be taken from the penalty-mark and, when it is being taken, all players with the exception of the player taking the kick, and the opposing goalkeeper, shall be within the field of play but outside the penalty-area, and at least 10 yards from the penalty-mark. The opposing goalkeeper must stand (without moving his feet) on his own goal-line, between the goalposts, until the ball is kicked. The player taking the kick must kick the ball forward; he shall not play the ball a second time until it has been touched or played by another player. The ball shall be deemed in play directly it is kicked, i.e., when it has travelled the distance of its circumference, and a goal may be scored direct from such a penalty-kick. If the ball touches the goalkeeper before passing between the posts, when a penalty-kick is being taken at or after the expiration of half-time or full-time, it does not nullify a goal. If necessary, time of play shall be extended at half-time or full-time to allow a penalty-kick to be taken.

Punishment:

For any infringement of this Law:

(a) by the defending team, the kick shall be retaken if a goal has not resulted.

(b) by the attacking team other than by the player taking the kick, if a goal is scored it shall be disallowed and the kick retaken.

(c) by the player taking the penalty-kick, committed after the ball is in play, a player of the opposing team shall take an indirect free-kick from the spot where the infringement occurred.

(1) When the Referee has awarded a penalty-kick, he shall not signal for it to be taken, until the players have taken up position in accordance with the Law.

(2) (a) If, after the kick has been taken, the ball is stopped in its course towards goal, by an outside agent, the kick shall be retaken.

(b) If, after the kick has been taken, the ball rebounds into play, from the goalkeeper, the cross-bar or a goal-post, and is then stopped in its course by an outside agent, the Referee shall stop play and restart it by dropping the ball at the place where it came into contact with the outside agent.

(3) (a) If, after having given the signal for a penalty-kick, the Referee sees that the goalkeeper is not in his right place on the goal-line, he shall, nevertheless, allow the kick to proceed. It shall be retaken, if a goal is not scored.

(b) If, after the Referee has given the signal for a penalty-kick to be taken, and before the ball has been kicked, the goalkeeper moves his feet, the Referee shall, nevertheless, allow the kick to proceed. It shall be retaken, if a goal is not scored.

(c) If, after the Referee has given the signal for a penalty-kick to be taken, and before the ball is in play, a player of the defending team encroaches into the penalty-area, or within ten yards of the penalty-mark, the Referee shall, nevertheless, allow the kick to proceed. It shall be retaken, if a goal is not scored.

The player concerned shall be cautioned.

(4) (a) If, when a penalty-kick is being taken, the player taking the kick is guilty of ungentlemanly conduct, the kick, if already taken, shall be retaken, if a goal is scored.

The player concerned shall be cautioned.

(b) If, after the referee has given the signal for a penalty-kick to be taken, and before the ball is in play, a colleague of the player taking the kick encroaches into the penalty-area or within ten yards of the penalty-mark, the Referee shall, nevertheless, allow the kick to proceed. If a goal is scored, it shall be disallowed, and the kick retaken.

The player concerned shall be cautioned.

(c) If, in the circumstances described in the foregoing paragraph, the ball rebounds into play from the goalkeeper, the cross-bar or a goal-post, the Referee shall stop

Laws of the Game	*Decisions of the International Board*
	the game, caution the player and award an indirect free-kick to the opposing team from the place where the infringement occurred.

(5) (a) If, after the referee has given the signal for a penalty-kick to be taken, and before the ball is in play, the goalkeeper moves from his position on the goal-line, or moves his feet, and a colleague of the kicker encroaches into the penalty-area or within 10 yards of the penalty-mark, the kick, if taken, shall be retaken.

The colleague of the kicker shall be cautioned.

(b) If, after the Referee has given the signal for a penalty-kick to be taken, and before the ball is in play, a player of each team encroaches into the penalty-area, or within 10 yards of the penalty-mark, the kick, if taken, shall be retaken.

The players concerned shall be cautioned.

(6) When a match is extended, at half-time or full-time, to allow a penalty-kick to be taken or retaken, the extension shall last until the moment that the penalty-kick has been completed, i.e. until the Referee has decided whether or not a goal is scored.

A goal is scored when the ball passes wholly over the goal-line.

(a) direct from the penalty-kick,

(b) having rebounded from either goal-post or the cross-bar, or

(c) having touched or been played by the goalkeeper.

The game shall terminate immediately the Referee has made his decision.

(7) When a penalty-kick is being taken in extended time:

(a) the provisions of all of the foregoing paragraphs, except paragraphs (2) (b) and (4) (c) shall apply in the usual way, and

(b) in the circumstances described in paragraphs (2) (b) and (4) (c) the game shall terminate immediately the ball rebounds from the goalkeeper, the cross-bar or the goal-post.

Laws of the Game	*Decisions of the International Board*

LAW XV. – THROW-IN

When the whole of the ball passes over a touch-line, either on the ground or in the air, it shall be thrown in from the point where it crossed the line, in any direction, by a player of the team opposite to that of the player who last touched it. The thrower at the moment of delivering the ball must face the field of play and part of each foot shall be either on the touch-line or on the ground outside the touch-line. The thrower shall use both hands and shall deliver the ball from behind and over his head. The ball shall be in play immediately it enters the field of play, but the thrower shall not again play the ball until it has been touched or played by another player. A goal shall not be scored direct from a throw-in.

Punishment:

(a) If the ball is improperly thrown in the throw-in shall be taken by a player of the opposing team.

(b) If the thrower plays the ball a second time before it has been touched or played by another player, an indirect free-kick shall be taken by a player of the opposing team from the place where the infringement occurred.

(1) If a player taking a throw-in, plays the ball a second time by handling it within the field of play before it has been touched or played by another player, the Referee shall award a direct free-kick.

(2) A player taking a throw-in must face the field of play with some part of his body.

(3) If, when a throw-in is being taken, any of the opposing players dance about or gesticulate in a way calculated to distract or impede the thrower, it shall be deemed ungentlemanly conduct, for which the offender(s) shall be cautioned.

Laws of the Game	*Decisions of the International Board*

LAW XVI. – GOAL-KICK

When the whole of the ball passes over the goal-line excluding that portion between the goal-posts, either in the air or on the ground, having last been played by one of the attacking team, it shall be kicked direct into play beyond the penalty-area from a point within that half of the goal-area nearest to where it crossed the line, by a player of the defending team. A goalkeeper shall not receive the ball into his hands from a goal-kick in order that he may thereafter kick it into play. If the ball is not kicked beyond the penalty-area, i.e., direct into play, the kick shall be retaken. The kicker shall not play the ball a second time until it has touched – or been played by – another player. A goal shall not be scored direct from such a kick. Players of the team opposing that of the player taking the goal-kick shall remain outside the penalty-area whilst the kick is being taken.

Punishment: If a player taking a goal-kick plays the ball a second time after it has passed beyond the penalty-area, but before it has touched or been played by another player, an indirect free-kick shall be awarded to the opposing team, to be taken from the place where the infringement occurred.

(1) When a goal-kick has been taken and the player who has kicked the ball touches it again before it has left the penalty-area, the kick has not been taken in accordance with the Law and must be retaken.

Laws of the Game	*Decisions of the International Board*

LAW XVII. – CORNER-KICK

When the whole of the ball passes over the goal-line, excluding that portion between the goal-posts, either in the air or on the ground, having last been played by one of the defending team, a member of the attacking team shall take a corner-kick, i.e., the whole of the ball shall be placed within the quarter circle at the nearest corner-flag-post, which must not be moved, and it shall be kicked from that position. A goal may be scored direct from such a kick. Players of the team opposing that of the player taking the corner-kick shall not approach within 10 yards of the ball until it is in play, i.e., it has travelled the distance of its own circumference, nor shall the kicker play the ball a second time until it has been touched or played by another player.

Punishment:

(a) If the player who takes the kick plays the ball a second time before it has been touched or played by another player, the Referee shall award an indirect free-kick to the opposing team, to be taken from the place where the infringement occurred.

(b) For any other infringement the kick shall be retaken.

Diagram 1.—OFF-SIDE

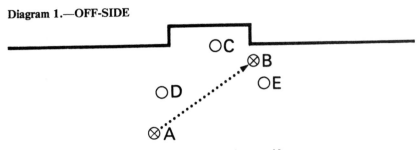

Clear pass to one of same side

    A has run the ball up, and having **D** in front passes to **B**. **B** is off-side because he is in front of **A** and there are not two opponents between him and the goal-line when the ball is passed by **A**.

    If **B** waits for **E** to fall back before he shoots, this will not put him on-side, because it does not alter his position with relation to **A** at the moment the ball was passed by **A**.

Diagram 2.—NOT OFF-SIDE

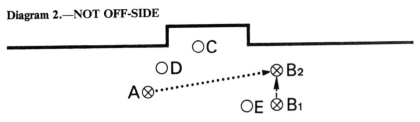

Clear pass to one of same side *(continued)*

    A has run the ball up, and having **D** in front passes across the field. **B** runs from position 1 to position 2. **B** is not off-side because at the moment the ball was passed by **A** he was not in front of the ball, and had two opponents between him and the goal-line.

Diagram 3.—OFF-SIDE

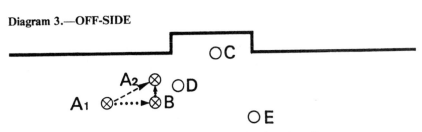

Clear pass to one of same side *(continued)*

    A and **B** make a passing run up the wing. **A** passes the ball to **B** who cannot shoot because he has **D** in front. **A** then runs from position 1 to position 2 where he receives the ball from **B**. **A** is off-side because he is in front of the ball and he had not two opponents between him and the goal-line when the ball was played by **B**.

Diagram 4.—OFF-SIDE

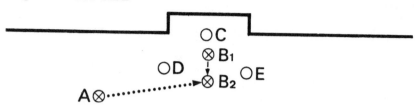

Running back for the ball

A centres the ball. **B** runs back from position **1** to position **2**, and then dribbles between **D** and **E** and scores. **B** is off-side because he is in front of the ball and he had not two opponents between him and the goal-line at the moment the ball was played by **A**.

Diagram 5.—OFF-SIDE

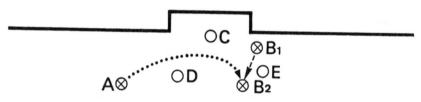

Running back for ball *(continued)*

A makes a high shot at goal, and the wind and screw carry the ball back. **B** runs from position **1** to position **2** and scores. **B** is off-side because he is in front of the ball and he had not two opponents between him and the goal-line at the moment the ball was played by **A**.

Diagram 6.—OFF-SIDE

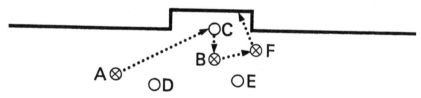

Shot at goal returned by goalkeeper **C**

A shoots at goal. The ball is played by **C** and **B** obtains possession, but slips and passes the ball to **F** who scores. **F** is off-side because he is in front of **B**, and when the ball was passed by **B** he had not two opponents between him and the goal-line.

Diagram 7.—NOT OFF-SIDE

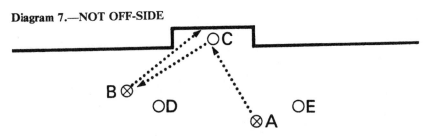

Shot at goal returned by goalkeeper *(continued)*

A shoots at goal. The ball is played out by **C** but **B** obtains possession and scores. **B** was in front of the ball and did not have two opponents between him and the goal-line when the ball was played by **A**, but he is not off-side because the ball has been last played by an opponent, **C**.

Diagram 8.—OFF-SIDE

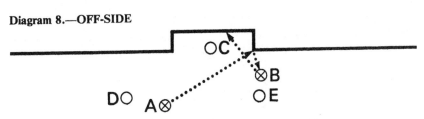

Ball rebounding from goal-posts or cross-bar

A shoots for goal and the ball rebounds from the goal-post into play. **B** secures the ball and scores. **B** is off-side because the ball is last played by **A**, a player of his own side, and when **A** played it **B** was in front of the ball and did not have two opponents between him and the goal-line.

Diagram 9.—OFF-SIDE

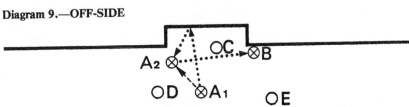

Ball rebounding from goal-posts or cross-bar *(continued)*

A shoots for goal and the ball rebounds from the cross-bar into play. **A** follows up from position 1 to position 2, and then passes to **B** who has run up on the other side. **B** is off-side because the ball is last played by **A**, a player of his own side, and when **A** played it **B** was in front of the ball and did not have two opponents between him and the goal-line. If **A** had scored himself at the second attempt, instead of passing to **B**, it would have been a goal.

Diagram 10.—NOT OFF-SIDE

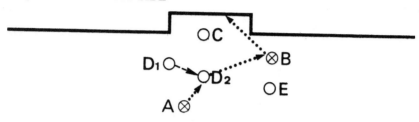

Ball touching an opponent

A shoots at goal. **D** runs from position **1** to position **2** to intercept the ball, but it glances off his foot to **B** who scores. **B** is not off-side because, although he is in front of the ball and has not two opponents between him and the goal-line the ball was last played by an opponent, **D**.

Diagram 11.—OFF-SIDE

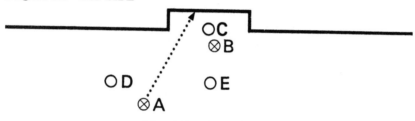

Obstructing the goalkeeper

A shoots for goal and scores. **B**, however, obstructs **C** so that he cannot get at the ball. The goal must be disallowed, because **B** is in an off-side position and may not touch the ball himself, nor in any way whatever interfere with an opponent.

Diagram 12.—OFF-SIDE

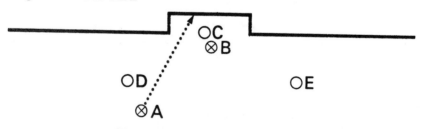

Obstructing the goalkeeper *(continued)*

A shoots for goal. **B** runs in while the ball is in transit and prevents **C** playing it properly. **B** is off-side because he is in front of **A** and has not two opponents between him and the goal-line when **A** plays the ball. When in this position **B** may not touch the ball himself, nor in any way whatever interfere with an opponent.

Diagram 13.—OFF-SIDE

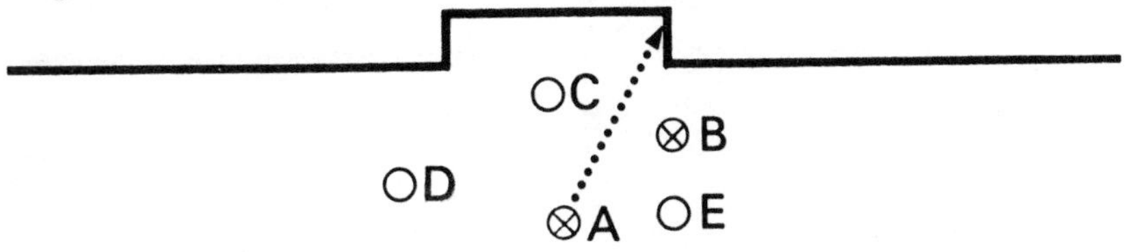

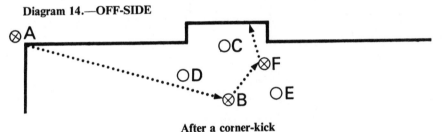

Obstructing an opponent other than the goalkeeper

A shoots for goal. **B** prevents **E** running in to intercept the ball. **B** is off-side because he is in front of **A** and has not two opponents between him and the goal-line when **A** plays the ball. When in this position **B** may not touch the ball himself, nor in any way whatever interfere with an opponent.

Diagram 14.—OFF-SIDE

After a corner-kick

A takes a corner-kick and the ball goes to **B**. **B** shoots for goal and as the ball is passing through, **F** touches it. **F** is off-side because after the corner-kick has been taken the ball is last played by **B**, a player of his own side, and when **B** played it **F** was in front of the ball and had not two opponents between him and the goal-line.

Diagram 15.—NOT OFF-SIDE

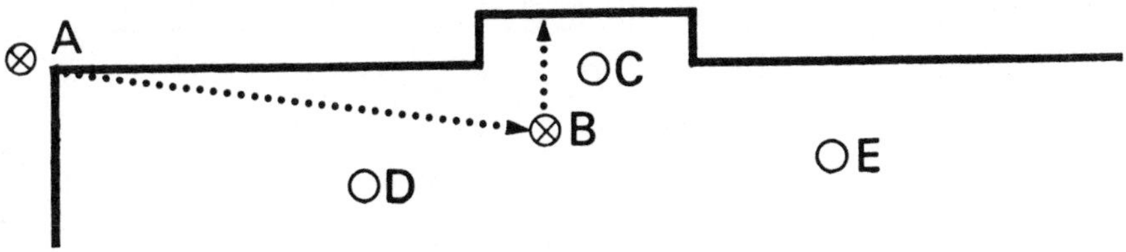

After a corner-kick (continued)

A takes a corner-kick and the ball goes to **B**, who puts it through goal. **B** has only one opponent between him and the goal-line, but he is not off-side because a player cannot be off-side from a corner-kick.

Diagram 16.—NOT OFF-SIDE

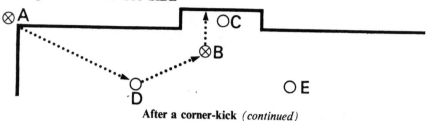

After a corner-kick *(continued)*

A takes a corner-kick and the ball glances off **D** and goes to **B**, who puts it through goal. **B** is not off-side because the ball was last played by an opponent, **D**.

Diagram 17.—OFF-SIDE

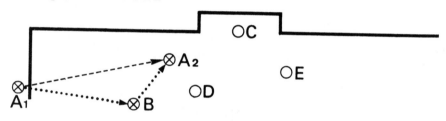

After a throw-in from the touch-line

A throws to **B** and then runs from touch-line to position **A2**. **B** passes the ball to **A** in position 2. **A** is off-side because he is in front of the ball and has not two opponents between him and the goal-line when the ball is passed forward to him by **B**.

Diagram 18.—NOT OFF-SIDE

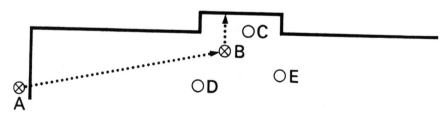

After a throw-in from the touch-line *(continued)*

A throws the ball to **B**. Although **B** is in front of the ball and has not two opponents between him and the goal line, he is not off-side because a player cannot be off-side from a throw-in.

Diagram 19.—OFF-SIDE

Diagram 20.—NOT OFF-SIDE

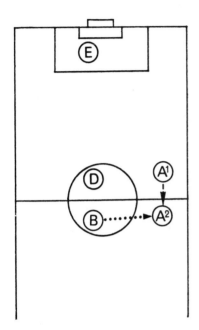

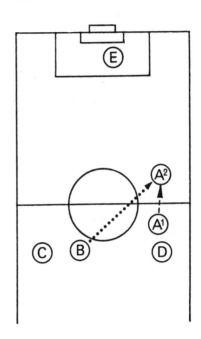

A player cannot put himself on-side by running back into his own half of the field of play

If **A** is in his opponents' half of the field of play, and is off-side in position when **B** last played the ball, he cannot put himself on-side by moving back into his own half of the field of play.

A player within his own half of the field of play is not off-side when he enters his opponents' half of the field of play

If **A** is in his own half of the field of play he is on-side, although he is in front of the ball and there are not two opponents nearer their own goal-line when **B** last played the ball. **A** is therefore not off-side when he enters his opponents' half of the field of play.

APPENDIX II: HIGH SCHOOL AND COLLEGE RULE VARIATIONS

I have purposely hewed close to the FIFA line throughout this book. I have done so for several reasons. First, the international FIFA rules govern the playing of soccer by millions of people around the world and constitute the basic laws whence any conceivable variance is made. Thus, a rule variance in NCAA competition is a departure from FIFA and it is not FIFA which has departed from the norm. In other words, referees should master the universal laws of the game and then include in their individual repertory such rule variations as they personally require on a state, regional, or national basis. Second, the rule variations which are not merely local or regional adjustments are few and have tended over the years to diminish as the school and college rules slowly but inexorably move toward conformity with the international laws of the game.

The adoption of halves rather than quarters, the use of running time rather than stopping the clock on every substitution, and the requirement that yellow and red misconduct signal cards be used by the officials are but several of the numerous recent emendations bringing the NCAA (college and some schools) and the Federation (high school) rule books nearer to the FIFA laws of the game. There remain in these other variations of the rules a good many departures from FIFA policy, however, such as the enumeration of the specific times during which substitutions may be made, the embroidering of the nine major offenses with such redundancies as "using the knee on an opponent" (already adequately covered by "kicking"), and the directive to officials that players intentionally charging into the goalkeeper shall be removed without prior caution (which the NCAA rules label "warning").

I shall not enumerate all the current variations in the laws adopted by high-school and college coaches. Those interested should read the annual NCAA **Soccer Guide**, available in major sports stores, and the National Federation **Soccer Rule Book**, available through one's State Interscholastic Athletic Association. The differences are also listed in **Fair or Foul?** by Harris and Harris. I wish only to give a sense of the differences and to mention those major distinctions where it would be most unfortunate if the referee remained impervious to the variation. I shall not concern myself with such pusillanimous differences as that describing lawful moulded-sole cleats, nor need I mention that nets are mandatory in school and college rules, whereas they are suggested in FIFA rules. In both cases, nets are usually required by the leagues, and if they are lacking, one is still bound to officiate the game, school or amateur. And such details as who does the timekeeping and scorekeeping and the placement of benches on the side line need not detain us here, being of import only to officials who will in any event read the complete official text of the rules in question.

The major distinctions are that school and college games are almost always refereed by two men on the field in the dual system of game control. Some games are refereed by one man, but the three-man system is not endorsed at the moment. These officials also *must* use a more thorough set of infraction signals than FIFA referees. Otherwise, if a USSF/FIFA referee stepped in and officiated a game he would generally be in conformity with the NCAA and Federation rules *in practice and ultimate effect.* There are only several important variances where he would be at odds with those rules, and it is perhaps appropriate to summarize them here.

NCAA:

A game may not start if a team has fewer than eleven players.* There may be a maximum of sixteen dressed participants in a given match who may be substituted and resubstituted any number of times. A player ejected for any cause other than an equipment violation may not take part in

---

*This, at least, is the interpretation I received from NISOA interpreter Ray Kraft regarding the intention of the 1975 word change from "played" to "started" in the phrase "The game shall be started by two teams of not more than eleven players each, one of whom shall be the goalkeeper." I presume that the wording will be changed yet again since this phrase is unfortunate in that it appears rather to permit the use of more than eleven players or the absence of a goalkeeper once the game has gotten under way, which everyone knows could not have been intended.

the remainder of the game but may be replaced by another player. The only time that an ejected player may not be replaced by a substitute is if the offending player has assaulted a referee.

There are some instances — such as when a disgruntled coach will not heed the referee's instructions to leave the field — when the referee can declare a forfeit, a power he is specifically denied under FIFA laws.

There may never be a drop ball in the penalty area; it shall be executed rather at the nearest spot on the field outside the penalty area. In FIFA rules, if a ball becomes defective, there is a drop ball at the point where the ball became defective; in NCAA rules it is dropped at the spot where last played.

Ball boys shall keep providing new balls as the one on the field goes out of play, there being three balls available during any contest. Now that college players play ninety minutes without waiting for the game ball to be brought back from out of play, there is often more running and actual playing time in college games than in amateur and professional games.

Federation:

In these rules a game may not be started with fewer than eleven players either; however, the Federation rules are in some ways nearer to FIFA's than are the NCAA's, disallowing a substitute, for example, for a player ejected from the game for any cause (save equipment adjustment). But these rules do contain some baffling and illogical rulings of considerable latent impact on the outcome of a game.

Most drastic, no doubt, is the proviso that, if in the referee's opinion a defender's intentional handling of the ball prevented a goal, he shall award a goal rather than the customary penalty kick! This is contrary to Law 10 and many referees take a very narrow view of eventualities — after all, if the player hadn't handled it, the ball might have hit a tuft of grass and been deflected or it might have been struck by a unique lightning bolt — and proceed to award a penalty kick.

The Federation laws call for a team in possession when the

whistle is blown for an injury, or similar cause where no infraction has occurred, to retain possession for the restart by taking an indirect free kick (rather than submitting to a drop ball). Most referees try to wait until the player in possession passes the ball and then blow the whistle when the ball is in neutral ground so that they can award a drop ball pursuant with FIFA policy as well as conform to these Federation rules.

The clauses which I term "illogical" are minor compared to some of the other variations, such as that already mentioned in which a goal may be awarded at the referee's discretion, but they are somehow irksome and utterly inadmissible within the framework of our old friend: the all-important "Law 18" of common sense!

I am referring to the several variances in which the Federation requires the referee to award a free kick for an infraction which has occurred while the ball is out of play. If the player kicking off does not put the ball into play in a proper fashion (for example, touching the ball a second time before it has traveled its circumference or kicking off backwards into his own half of the field), he is admonished and then, if he does it again, an indirect free kick is awarded the opponent. Playing two dropped balls in a row before the ball has touched the ground leads to the same punishment. Now, these two situations are not likely to occur frequently or with great consequence since they take place at midfield and outside the penalty area respectively, but they are most incongruous in the eyes of the dedicated referee who has been told repeatedly that he can use common sense to apply the laws to unforeseen incidents. With these rules it would be quite possible to find a player who miscues twice on the kick-off being punished with an indirect free kick given to the opponent . . . before the start of play, with zero time having elapsed on the game clock!

APPENDIX III: BIBLIOGRAPHY

THE SOCCER REFEREE'S SHORT REFERENCE SHELF

Books:

Association Football – Know the Game. London: Education Products, Ltd. & The Football Association, 1970. A slim illustrated primer of the basics of the Laws of the Game. Accurate in what it does cover.

Burtenshaw, Norman. **Whose Side Are You On, Ref?** London: Arthur Baker, Ltd., 1973. Candid and entertaining account of Burtenshaw's career with numerous game situations. Full of psychological insights into the referee-player relationship. Good pointers on game control. Appendix reprints the famous 1971 Football League memorandum calling for a crackdown on dissent and so-called professional fouls as well as a description of the point-system for misconduct adopted in England.

De Leo, Diego. **Regole del Calcio.** 8e ed. Modena: Edizioni Panini, 1971. De Leo's work has appeared in many various editions in Italian, Spanish, and English. The English edition (**Soccer – Laws of the Game**) is out of print and a new edition is in preparation. Many question-and-answer cases of interest to the referee. Some of the answers are unorthodox or based on Italian FIGC decisions and are taken with a grain of salt by most referees.

––––––. **Soccer – Laws of the Game.** Mexico, D.F.: "Olimpico," 1968. Out of print; see previous item.

Evans, Robert. **Manual for Linesmen.** [Dallas]: North Texas Soccer Referees Association, 1973. Excellent unique booklet on this neglected subject. Evans discusses the standard functions of the linesman, his co-operation with the referee, and techniques and crucial rules. He reviews the various positions to assure good game coverage and he provides much practical advice to the linesman eager to improve his performance.

F.A. Guide for Referees and Linesmen. London: The Football Association, 1968. Practical tips on refereeing and running line. Sections on physical fitness training methods, sample written tests, training syllabi, and the like. It provides more food for thought than it does real answers.

The F.A. Guide to the Laws of the Game. London: Heinemann, 1969. Once the unusual layout of this book is mastered, it turns out to be a good easy-paced text for self-instruction or for review of the laws.

[F.I.F.A.]. **Laws of the Game and Universal Guide for Referees.** Zurich. Annual editions in English, French, German, and Spanish. The basic authoritative text of the laws governing amateur and professional soccer throughout the world.

Handbook. Zurich: F.I.F.A., Annual. Of interest to those curious to know the workings of FIFA. Contains Constitution, Statutes, and By-Laws of FIFA and the relationship of national affiliates to FIFA, addresses of these affiliates and names and addresses of FIFA referees throughout the world.

Harris, Paul E., Jr. and Larry R. Harris. **Fair or Foul? The Complete Guide to Soccer Officiating in America.** Torrance, CA: AYSO, 1973. Revised edition, 1975. An admirable attempt to collect and collate the various sets of FIFA, NCAA, Federation, and AYSO rules. Advice to referees, question-and-answer tests, and so forth.

Howell, Denis. **Soccer Refereeing.** London: Pelham Books, 1968. Top referee's reflections on his career and on the game of soccer from the referee's point of view. Readable and articulate. Many valuable comments on game control, offside, co-operation between referee and linesmen, and so forth.

Lover, Stanley. **Association Football Laws Illustrated.** London: Pelham Books, 1971. Nicely illustrated manual which covers the basic interpretations of most of the important clauses of the laws.

Mullen, Ken. **A Case in Mind.** [2500 Lucy Lane, Walnut Creek,

CA 94595]. [1974] Fifty unusual real-life game situations to puzzle the referee; the answers drawn from the laws and from official rulings by top-level arbitration boards. Enjoyable and informative supplementary reading for referees new and old.

Referees' Chart and Players' Guide to the Laws of Association Football. London and Sydney: Pan Books, Annual edition revised every July. The authorized British edition of the basic FIFA **Laws of the Game.** Reprints the rules, Board Decisions, illustrations of diagonal system of control, etc. Contains additional advice to referees, players, managers.

Referees' Instructors Handbook. Zurich: F.I.F.A., 1973. A good book for those who teach other referees. Has syllabi, training approaches, suggestions for audio-visual methods of presenting material, and so on.

Smith, Patrick J. "Casebook," in **1974 Official Manual of the NISOA** (n.p.: NISOA, 1974), pp. 23-32. Available to NISOA members. For his situations and recommended procedures, such as the application of the advantage clause and the like, Smith relies heavily on Denis Howell and others. Some very good advice, much of it based more on the FIFA laws than on the NISOA rule book!

Journals:

Can-So-Ref! Quarterly. One year, $3.00. 6 Bridgetown Drive, Etobicoke, Ontario M9C 2P4, Canada. Bulletin of the Ontario Soccer Referees' Association. Each number has one or two brief articles on mechanics and rules interpretation which will interest the non-Canadian referee.

FIFA News. One year, 40 Sw.F. FIFA, Hitzigweg 11, 8032 Zurich, Switzerland. Technical articles of interest to referees and notification of rules changes and interpretations.

SOCCER America. Weekly. Half-year, $6.00; One year, $10.00. P.O. Box 9393, Berkeley, CA 94709. Frequent features on officiating by Ken Mullen, Robert Evans, and others.

Soccer Monthly. One year, $7.50. 7320 Sereno Court, No. 205, Tampa, FL 33614 or through USSF, Empire State Building, 350 Fifth Ave., New York, NY 10001. Regular features on officiating accompanied by good illustrations.

Soccer World. Monthly. One year $8.00; two years, $15.50. P.O. Box 366, Mountain View, CA 94040. Occasional articles on refereeing and items on physical fitness of interest to referees as well as players.

Notes